A BENEFIT FOR

HERO INITIATIVE
HELPING COMIC CREATORS IN NEED

IDW

Ted Adams
CEO & Publisher

Greg Goldstein
President & COO

Robbie Robbins
EVP/Sr. Graphic Artist

Chris Ryall
Chief Creative Officer/Editor-in-Chief

Matthew Ruzicka
CPA, Chief Financial Officer

Dirk Wood
VP of Marketing

Lorelei Bunjes
VP of Digital Services

Jeff Webber
VP of Licensing, Digital and Subsidiary Rights

Jerry Bennington
VP of New Product Development

FOR THE HERO INITIATIVE

EXECUTIVE COMMITTEE
Jim McLauchlin, President
Steve Borock
Mike Malve
Brian Pulido
Joe Quesada
Mark Waid
Beth Widera

DISBURSEMENT COMMITTEE
George Pérez, Chairman
Howard Chaykin
Charlie Novinskie
Dennis O'Neil
John Romita Sr.
Walter Simonson
Roy Thomas
Jim Valentino

DEVELOPMENT DIRECTOR
Christina Joyce

Special thanks to Ted Adams, David Althoff, Nick Barrucci, Jimmy Betancourt, Dan Buckley, Thomas Cho and Trivision Company, Inc., Bobby Curnow, Greg Goldstein, Joan Hilty of Nickelodeon, Christopher Ivy, Dennis Mallonee, Mike Pasciullo, John "JG" Roshell, Chris Ryall, Richard Starkings of Comicraft, Scott Tipton, Joss Whedon, and to all the creators, retailers and friends who helped so much in making this book come together.

IDW

COVER ART
J. SCOTT CAMPBELL
AND EDGAR DELGADO

COLLECTION DESIGN
JEFF POWELL

ASSISTANT EDITOR
MICHAEL BENEDETTO

ASSOCIATE EDITOR
JIM McLAUCHLIN

EDITOR
SCOTT DUNBIER

PUBLISHER
TED ADAMS

www.idwpublishing.com
www.heroinitiative.org

Facebook: facebook.com/idwpublishing
Twitter: @idwpublishing
YouTube: youtube.com/idwpublishing
Tumblr: tumblr.idwpublishing.com
Instagram: instagram.com/idwpublishing

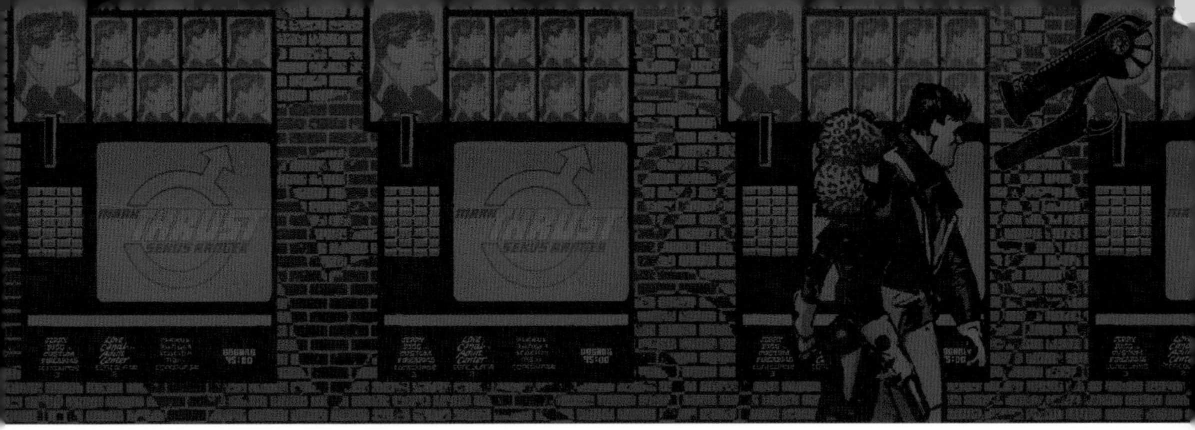

HERO COMICS

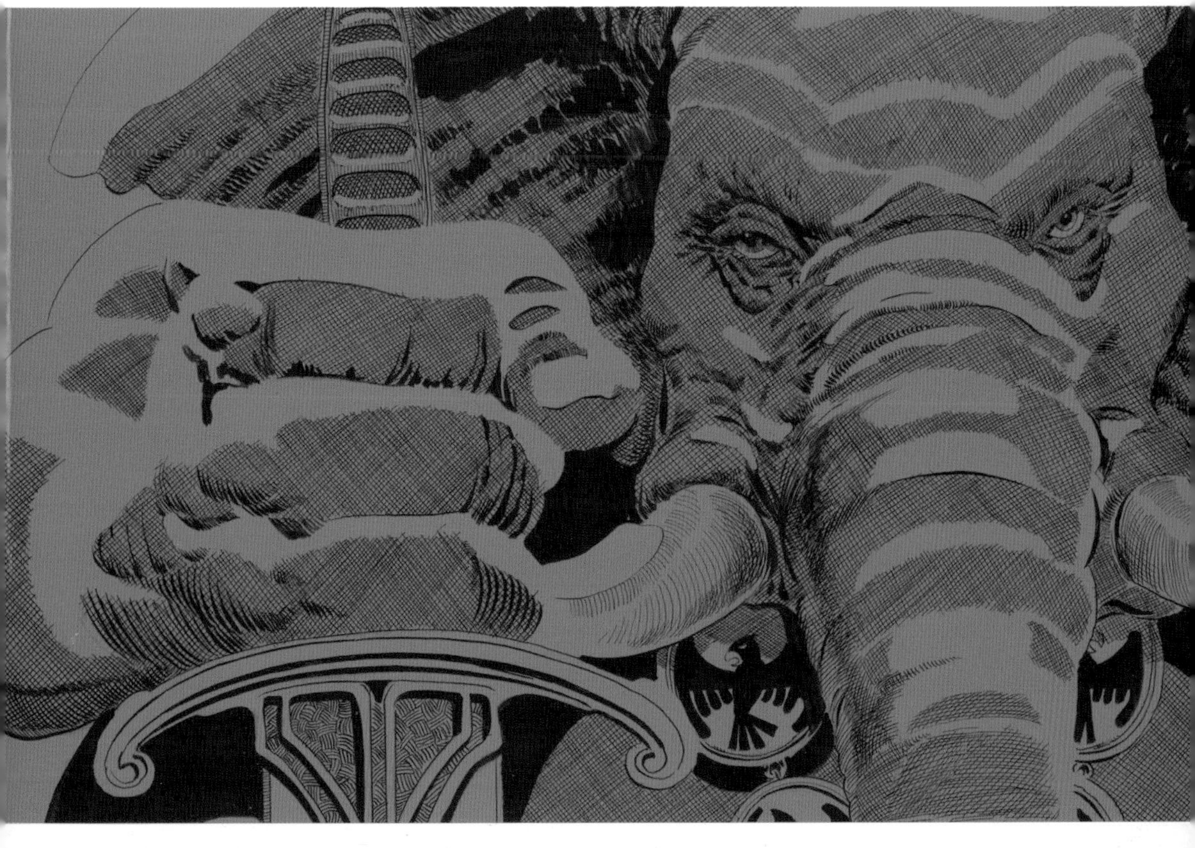

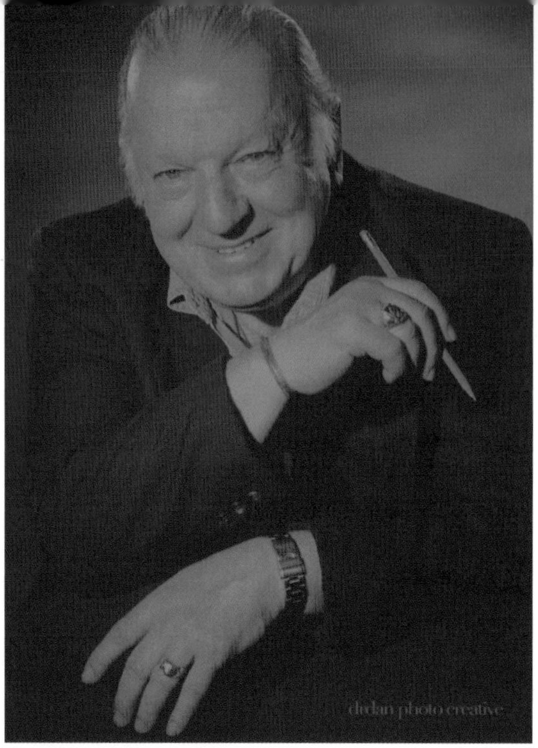
photo creative

MY HEROES

Aging comes with a whole passel of problems we never think about when we're young. You get your first letter from AARP which is, apparently, the modern equivalent of Pandora's Box, because the moment you open it the wheels fall off. Along with the plastic coin purse that allows you to count out exact change in pennies and dimes up to $17 and the little contraption you install in your car that permanently switches on the left-turn signal and sets the cruise control to 11 miles per hour *under* the posted limit, you get a whole bunch of aches and pains, bifocals, and a doctor whose services you may not have required for more than 20 years. Now you can't seem to stay out of his office for more than a few weeks at a time.

Compound this with the fact that comic artists and writers work in a business that has no unions, no guilds, no retirement programs, and no health care. The usual retirement plan is to simply work until we die. We are on our own.

Well, not entirely.

Somewhere around the end of July 2014, I found a small bug bite on my right calf. On July 31, I developed flu-like symptoms and achy joints. That night I fell asleep while reading and awoke at about 4 a.m. with a fever. Alarmingly, my right eye would not track and my first thought was STROKE. Fortunately, I quickly put myself through the stroke evaluation and passed on all counts, so I was confident it was NOT a stroke even before I arrived at Summit Pacific Medical Center, where I was admitted on August 1.

After CAT scans, MRIs, X-rays, ultrasounds and a spinal tap (nowhere near as much fun as the movie!) ruled out stroke, aneurysm, tumors, diabetes, meningitis, MERSA, Lyme disease, and necrotizing fasciitis, we were left with what pretty much everyone suspected from the start: cellulitis. By August 3rd, my vision had returned to 100% normal, my general condition was improving and my doctors expected me to be discharged shortly. Then the wheels fell off.

It seems cellulitis is a nasty bug that, even when you kill it off with antibiotics, produces toxins that destroy other tissue. As days went by, most of my right calf became an infected mass and my whole right leg swelled to twice normal size. After eleven days of around-the-clock IV antibiotics, it became evident that something wasn't working.

I was transferred to the Infectious Disease Center at Providence St. Peter's Hospital in Olympia, Wash., where they went to work on me, changed a couple of things in my treatment and, after two days, told me they were looking at sending me home on the August 16th. That was the best news I had had in all of August. Once they started me on physical therapy to get my muscles moving again, I improved rapidly and was discharged on August 16th.

Nearly three weeks later, my leg looked like the aftermath of a motorcycle accident (complete with fire), but at least it was still attached. But I missed an entire month's work and was forced to cancel three personal appearances, which put me in a serious financial bind.

It was my art rep Scott Kress (of CatskillComics.com) who reminded me of the Hero Initiative, mentioning that they had helped another of his clients over a rough patch. I've always supported The Hero Initiative whenever and wherever I've had the chance, but never expected to benefit from the program. One email got an immediate response and immediate assurance that I was in the right hands. Within a few days, my situation was resolved, quickly, professionally and, I must say, with dignity.

That last part is more important than you might think. It's very difficult to ask for help, even when you need it, even from folks whose whole purpose is to do just that. But the Hero Initiative takes the sting out of it with a caring, professional attitude that lets you know they do this because they really do care.

Since I first wrote of my experiences, the finger of fate proved every bit as fickle as we were warned as kids. A year after my first encounter with cellulitis, the bug was back and I was back in the hospital, this time for a somewhat shorter stay but with all the same problems of loss of income and overwhelming bills. Once again, The Hero Initiative stepped in to pull my fat out of the fire.

So, next time you're at a comic convention and you spot a green and white Hero Initiative donation jar on someone's table, remember the guys who brought years of entertainment and joy to generations of comic readers and remember the Heroes who are still fighting the good fight.

I.O.U.

Mike Grell

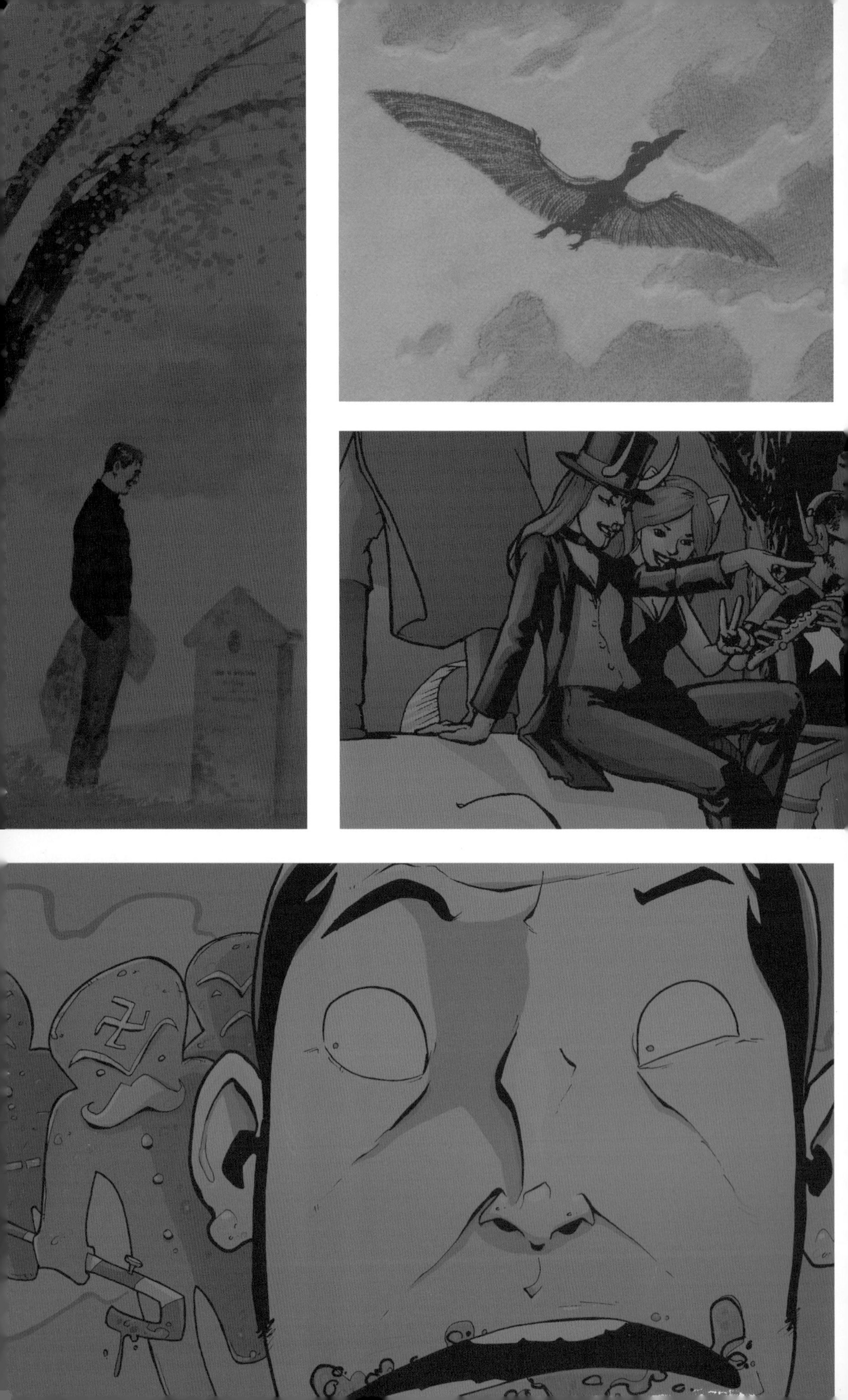

PART ONE STORIES

ALL LETTERING BY **COMICRAFT**
UNLESS OTHERWISE NOTED.

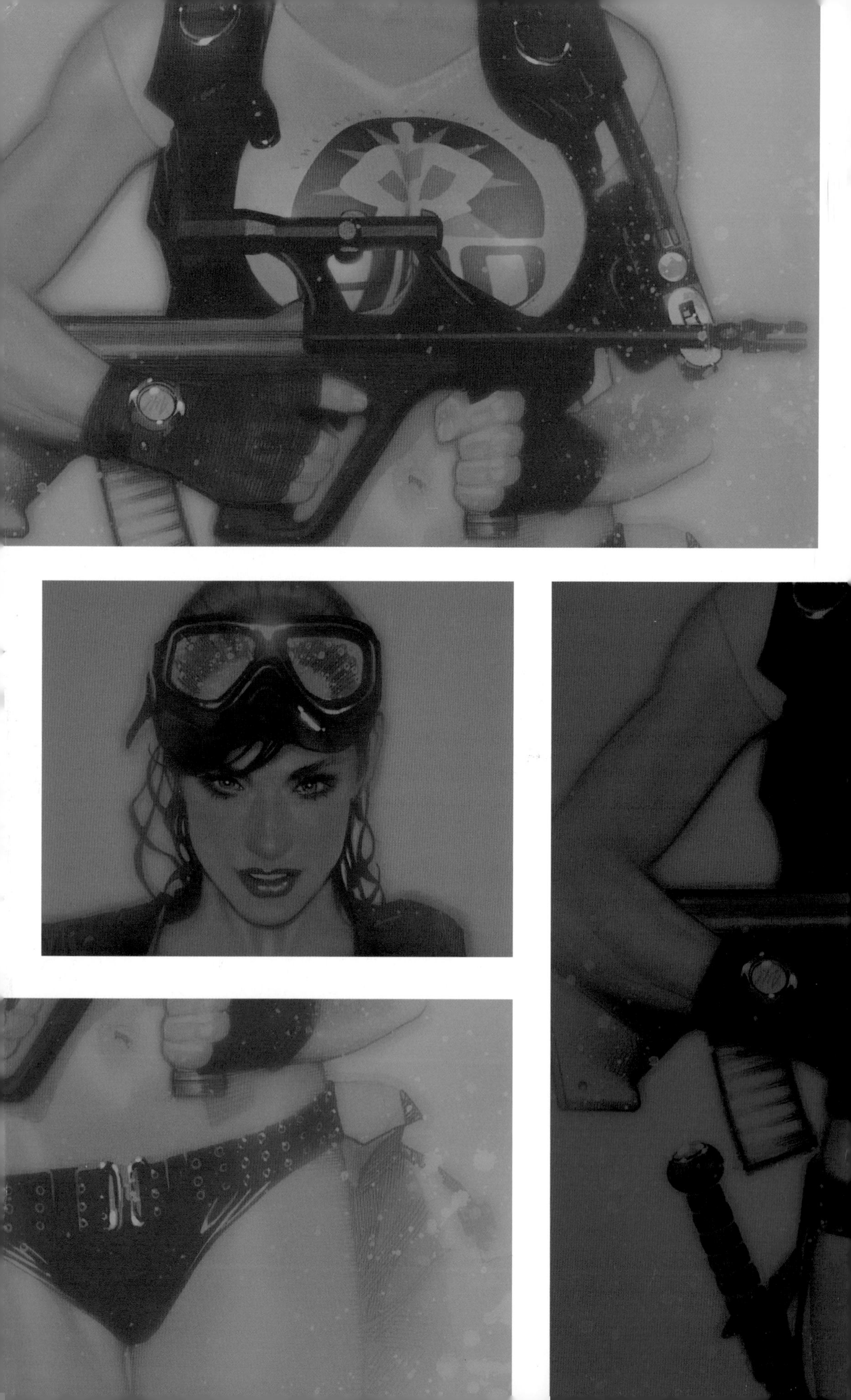

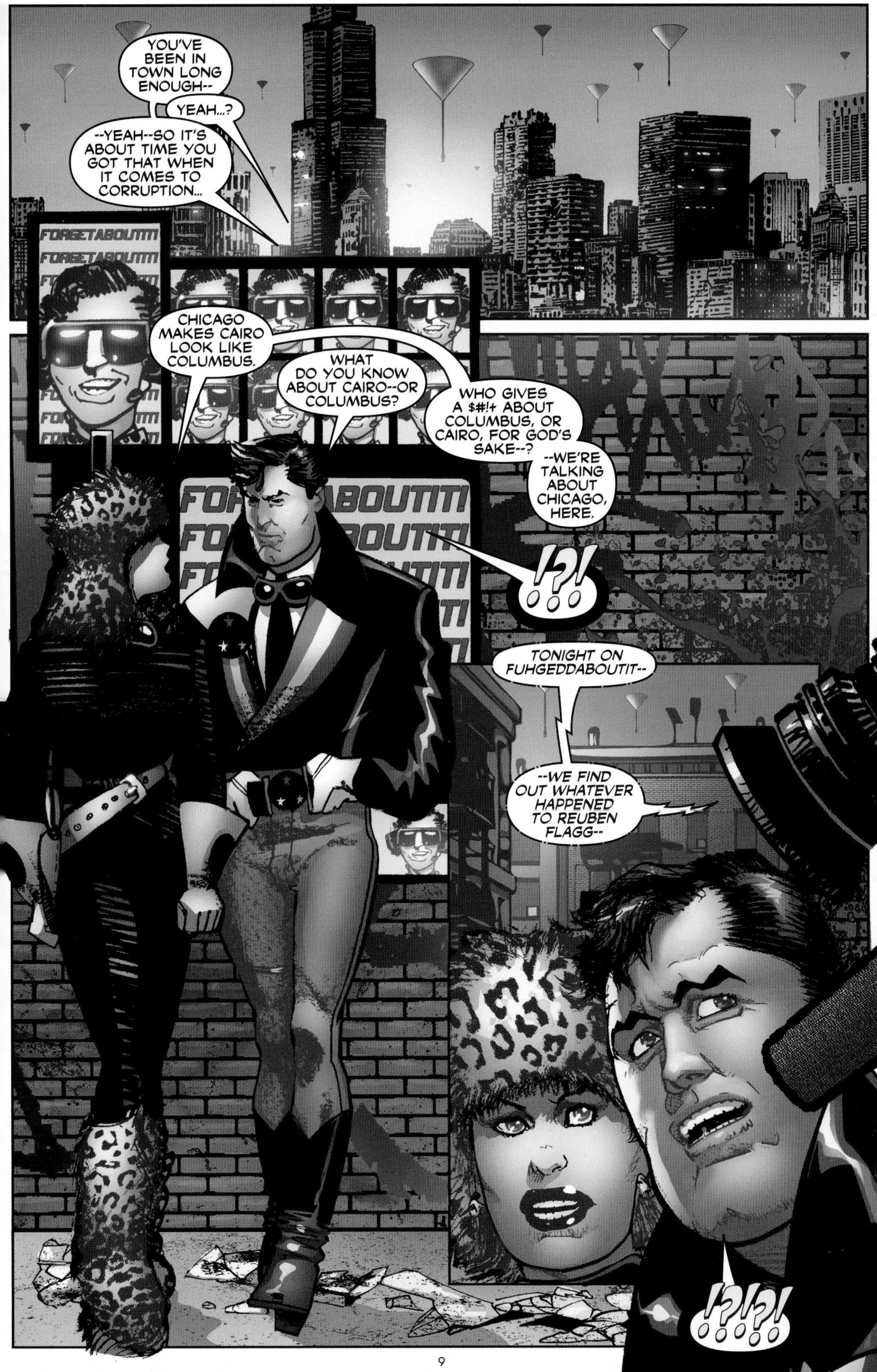
YOU'VE BEEN IN TOWN LONG ENOUGH--
YEAH...?
--YEAH--SO IT'S ABOUT TIME YOU GOT THAT WHEN IT COMES TO CORRUPTION...
FORGETABOUTIT!
CHICAGO MAKES CAIRO LOOK LIKE COLUMBUS.
WHAT DO YOU KNOW ABOUT CAIRO--OR COLUMBUS?
WHO GIVES A $#!+ ABOUT COLUMBUS, OR CAIRO, FOR GOD'S SAKE--?
--WE'RE TALKING ABOUT CHICAGO, HERE.
!?!
TONIGHT ON FUHGEDDABOUTIT--
--WE FIND OUT WHATEVER HAPPENED TO REUBEN FLAGG--
!?!?!

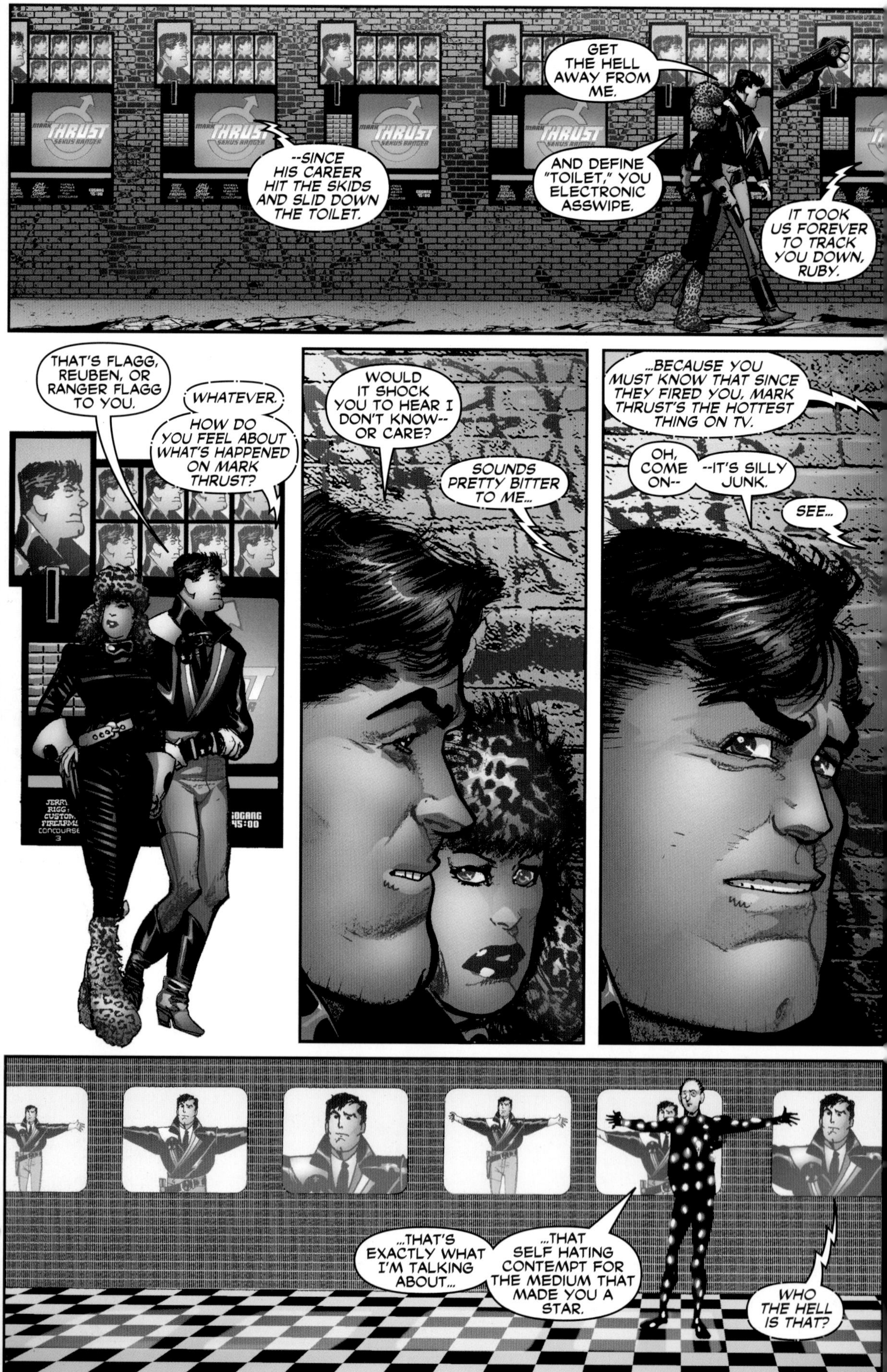
MARK THRUST SEXUS RANGER
--SINCE HIS CAREER HIT THE SKIDS AND SLID DOWN THE TOILET.
GET THE HELL AWAY FROM ME.
AND DEFINE "TOILET," YOU ELECTRONIC ASSWIPE.
IT TOOK US FOREVER TO TRACK YOU DOWN, RUBY.
THAT'S FLAGG, REUBEN, OR RANGER FLAGG TO YOU.
WHATEVER.
HOW DO YOU FEEL ABOUT WHAT'S HAPPENED ON MARK THRUST?
JERRY RIGG'S CUSTOM FIREARMS CONCOURSE 3
GOGANG 45:00
WOULD IT SHOCK YOU TO HEAR I DON'T KNOW-- OR CARE?
SOUNDS PRETTY BITTER TO ME...
...BECAUSE YOU MUST KNOW THAT SINCE THEY FIRED YOU, MARK THRUST'S THE HOTTEST THING ON TV.
OH, COME ON--
--IT'S SILLY JUNK.
SEE...
...THAT'S EXACTLY WHAT I'M TALKING ABOUT...
...THAT SELF HATING CONTEMPT FOR THE MEDIUM THAT MADE YOU A STAR.
WHO THE HELL IS THAT?

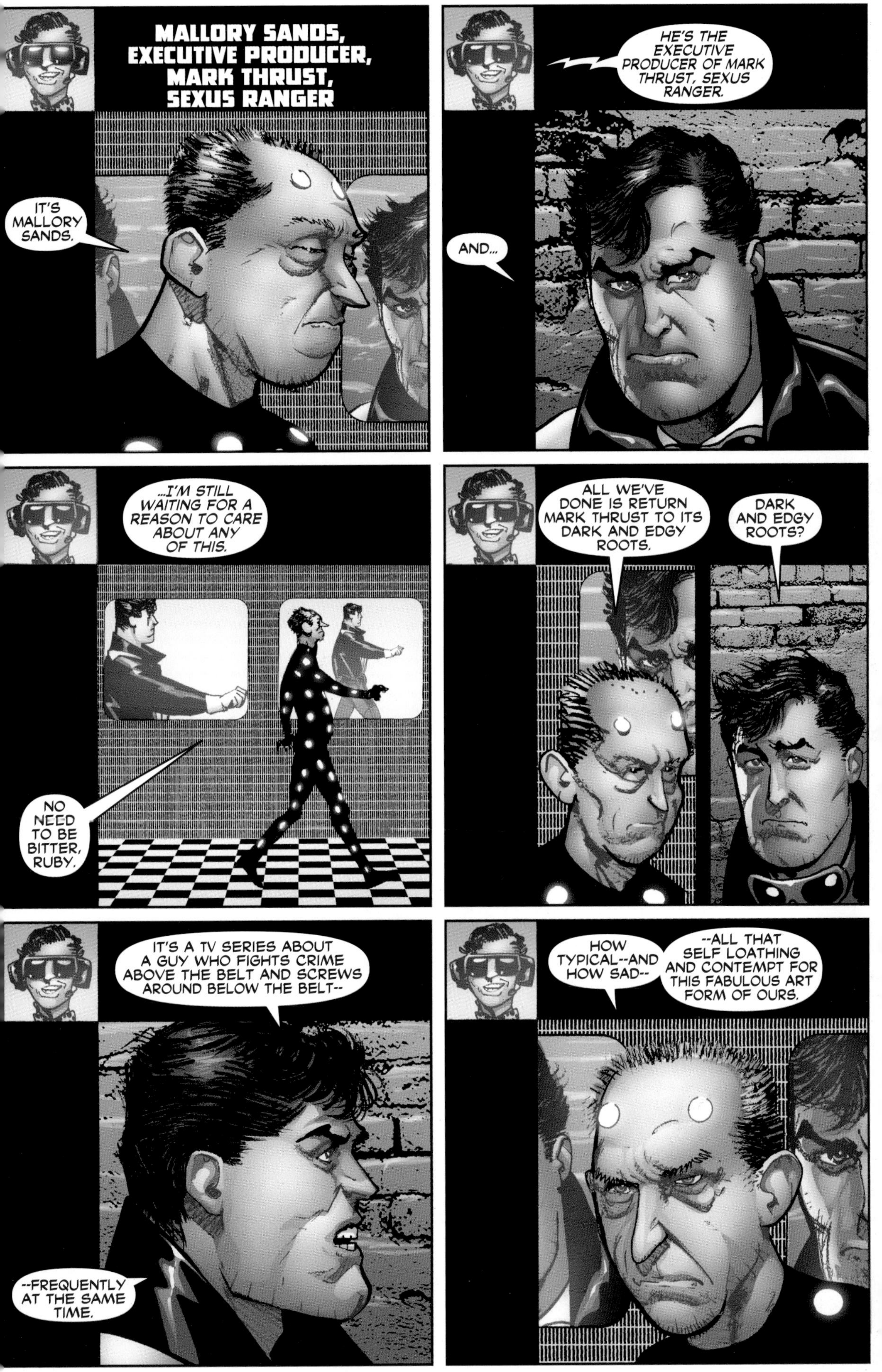
MALLORY SANDS, EXECUTIVE PRODUCER, MARK THRUST, SEXUS RANGER
IT'S MALLORY SANDS.
HE'S THE EXECUTIVE PRODUCER OF MARK THRUST, SEXUS RANGER.
AND...
...I'M STILL WAITING FOR A REASON TO CARE ABOUT ANY OF THIS.
NO NEED TO BE BITTER, RUBY.
ALL WE'VE DONE IS RETURN MARK THRUST TO ITS DARK AND EDGY ROOTS.
DARK AND EDGY ROOTS?
IT'S A TV SERIES ABOUT A GUY WHO FIGHTS CRIME ABOVE THE BELT AND SCREWS AROUND BELOW THE BELT--
--FREQUENTLY AT THE SAME TIME.
HOW TYPICAL--AND HOW SAD--
--ALL THAT SELF LOATHING AND CONTEMPT FOR THIS FABULOUS ART FORM OF OURS.

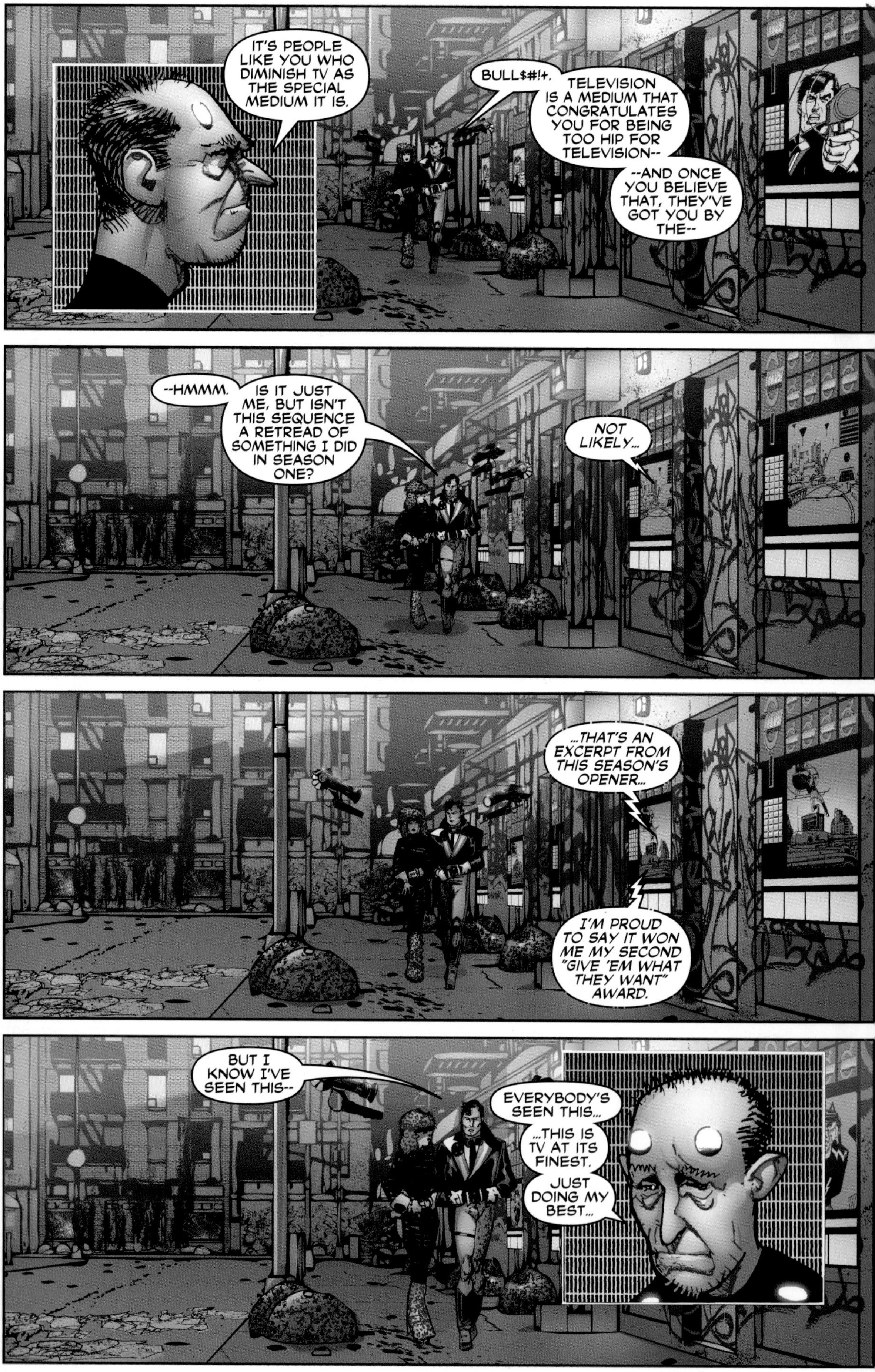

IT'S PEOPLE LIKE YOU WHO DIMINISH TV AS THE SPECIAL MEDIUM IT IS.
BULL$#!+.
TELEVISION IS A MEDIUM THAT CONGRATULATES YOU FOR BEING TOO HIP FOR TELEVISION--
--AND ONCE YOU BELIEVE THAT, THEY'VE GOT YOU BY THE--
--HMMM.
IS IT JUST ME, BUT ISN'T THIS SEQUENCE A RETREAD OF SOMETHING I DID IN SEASON ONE?
NOT LIKELY...
...THAT'S AN EXCERPT FROM THIS SEASON'S OPENER...
I'M PROUD TO SAY IT WON ME MY SECOND "GIVE 'EM WHAT THEY WANT" AWARD.
BUT I KNOW I'VE SEEN THIS--
EVERYBODY'S SEEN THIS...
...THIS IS TV AT ITS FINEST.
JUST DOING MY BEST...

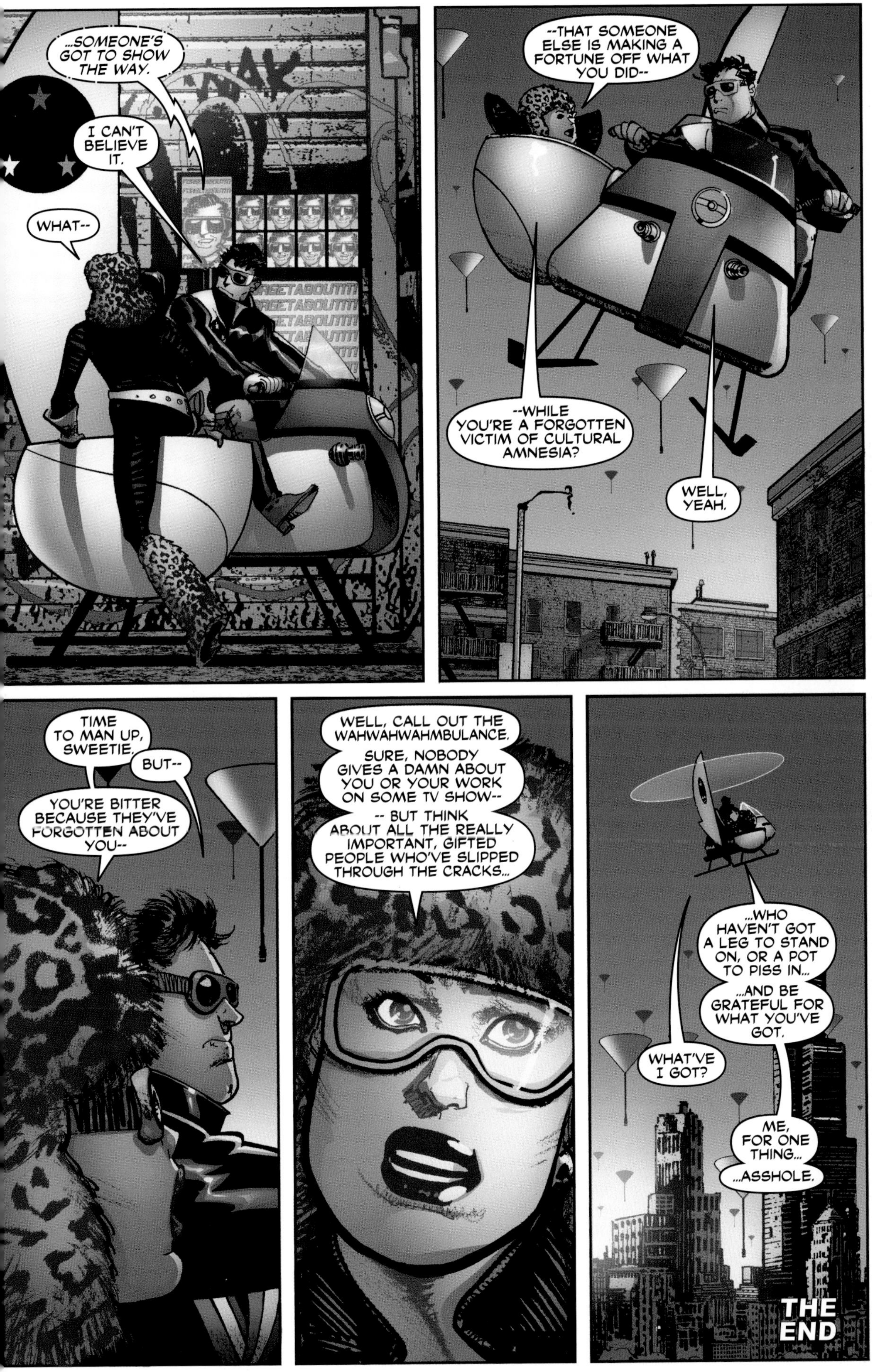
...SOMEONE'S GOT TO SHOW THE WAY.
I CAN'T BELIEVE IT.
WHAT--
--THAT SOMEONE ELSE IS MAKING A FORTUNE OFF WHAT YOU DID--
--WHILE YOU'RE A FORGOTTEN VICTIM OF CULTURAL AMNESIA?
WELL, YEAH.
TIME TO MAN UP, SWEETIE.
BUT--
YOU'RE BITTER BECAUSE THEY'VE FORGOTTEN ABOUT YOU--
WELL, CALL OUT THE WAHWAHWAHMBULANCE.
SURE, NOBODY GIVES A DAMN ABOUT YOU OR YOUR WORK ON SOME TV SHOW--
-- BUT THINK ABOUT ALL THE REALLY IMPORTANT, GIFTED PEOPLE WHO'VE SLIPPED THROUGH THE CRACKS...
...WHO HAVEN'T GOT A LEG TO STAND ON, OR A POT TO PISS IN...
...AND BE GRATEFUL FOR WHAT YOU'VE GOT.
WHAT'VE I GOT?
ME, FOR ONE THING...
...ASSHOLE.
THE END

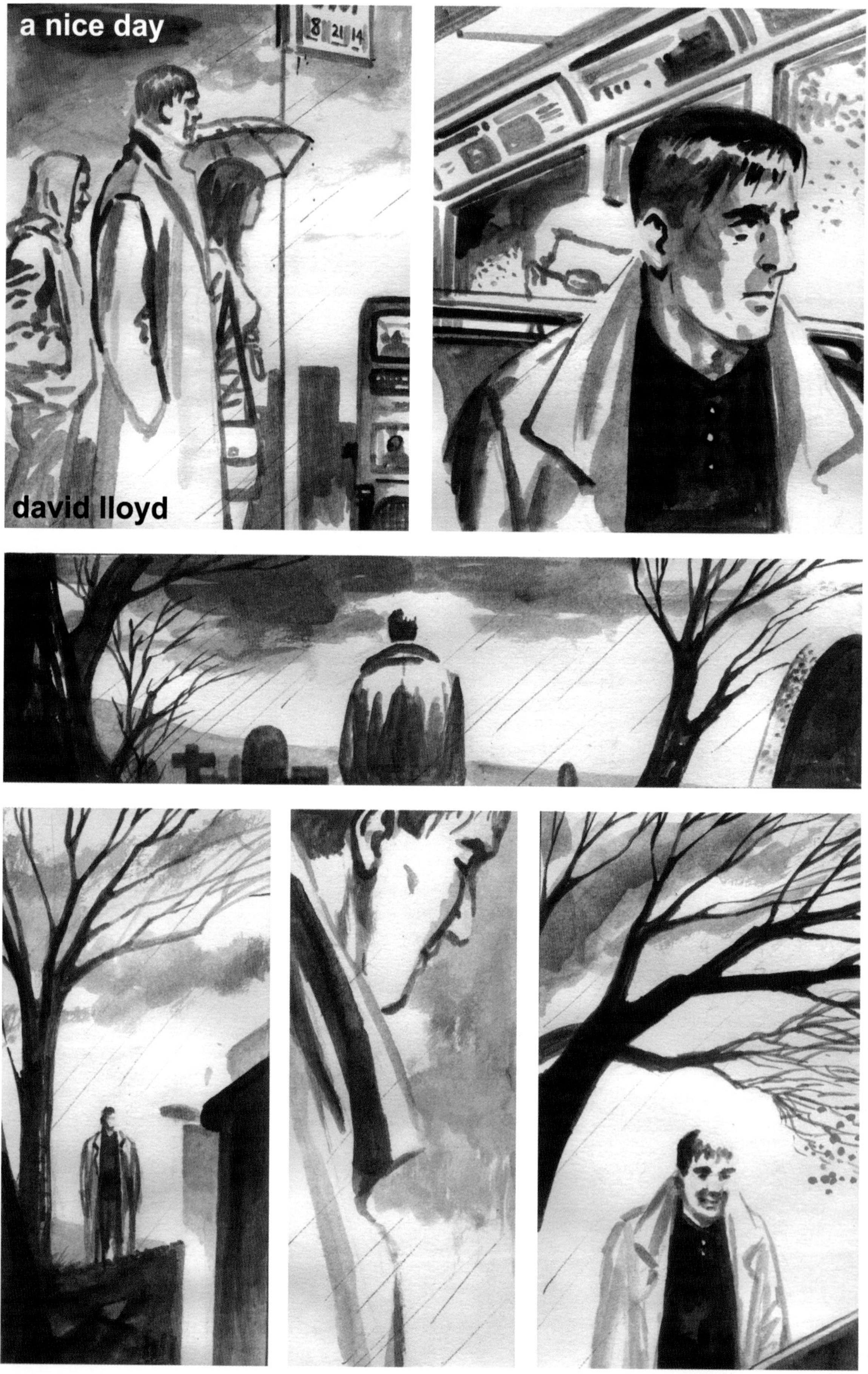
a nice day
8 21 14
david lloyd

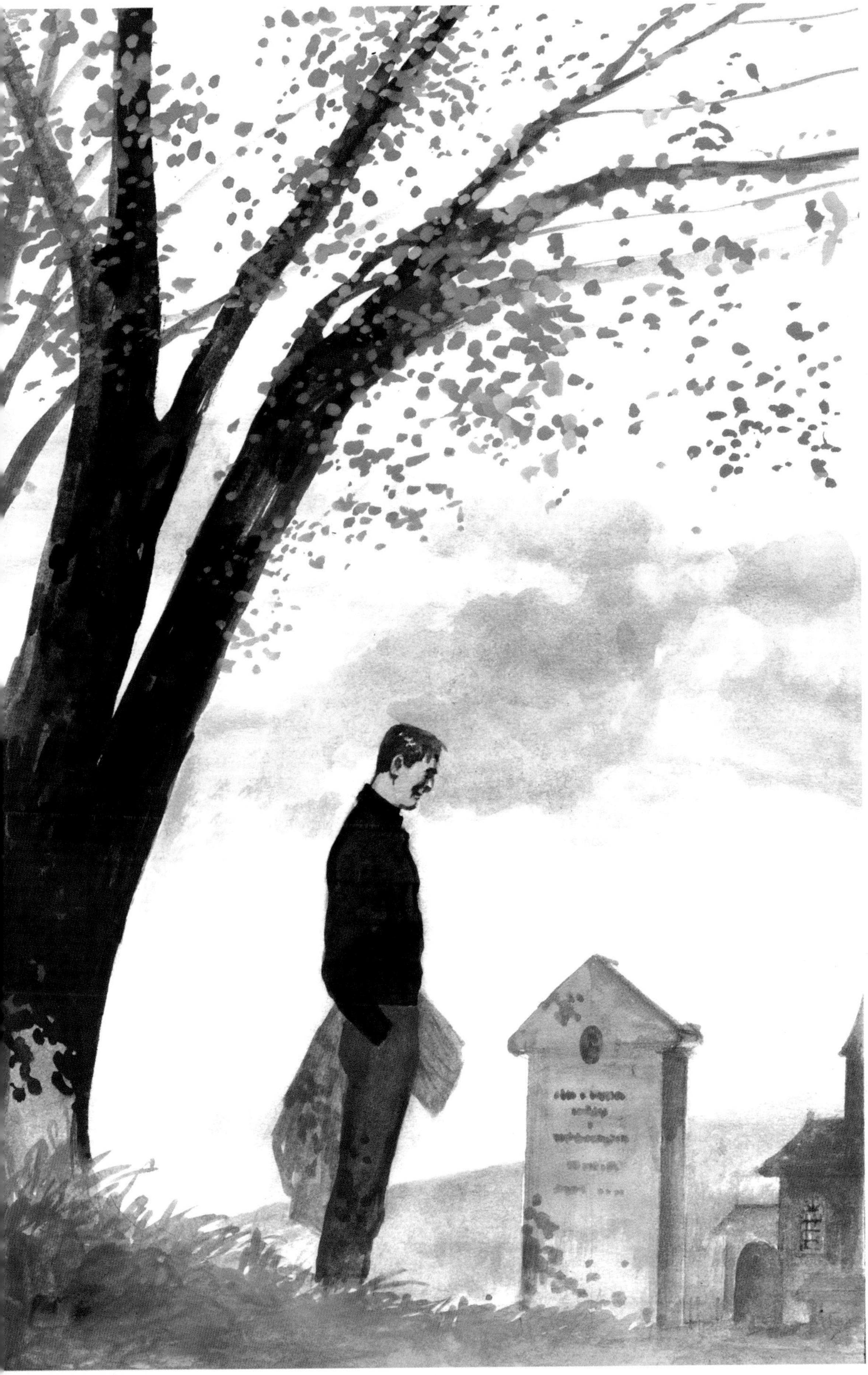

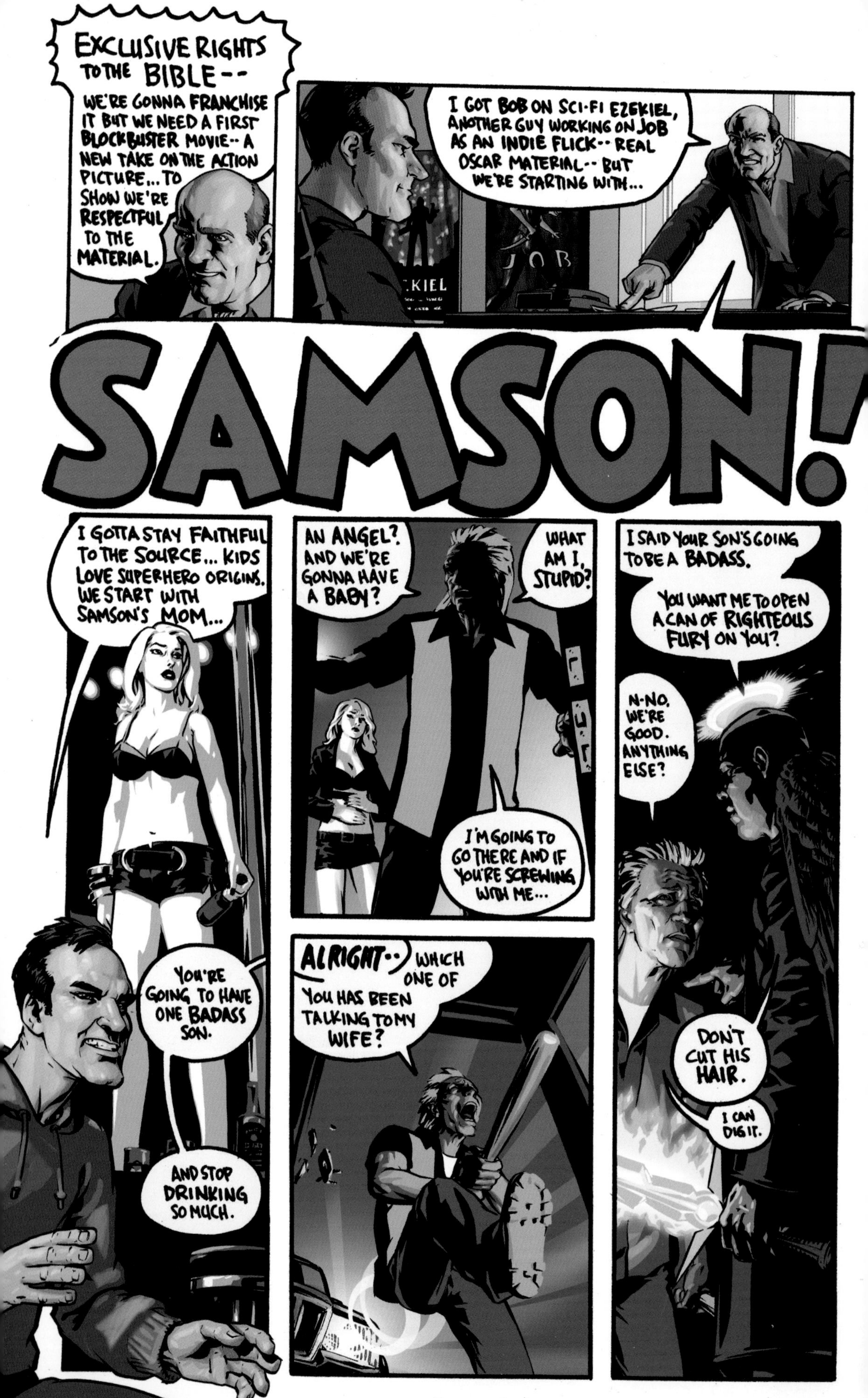
EXCLUSIVE RIGHTS TO THE BIBLE-- WE'RE GONNA FRANCHISE IT BUT WE NEED A FIRST BLOCKBUSTER MOVIE-- A NEW TAKE ON THE ACTION PICTURE... TO SHOW WE'RE RESPECTFUL TO THE MATERIAL.
I GOT BOB ON SCI-FI EZEKIEL, ANOTHER GUY WORKING ON JOB AS AN INDIE FLICK-- REAL OSCAR MATERIAL-- BUT WE'RE STARTING WITH...
JOB
SAMSON!
I GOTTA STAY FAITHFUL TO THE SOURCE... KIDS LOVE SUPERHERO ORIGINS. WE START WITH SAMSON'S MOM...
YOU'RE GOING TO HAVE ONE BADASS SON.
AND STOP DRINKING SO MUCH.
AN ANGEL? AND WE'RE GONNA HAVE A BABY?
WHAT AM I, STUPID?
I'M GOING TO GO THERE AND IF YOU'RE SCREWING WITH ME...
ALRIGHT-- WHICH ONE OF YOU HAS BEEN TALKING TO MY WIFE?
I SAID YOUR SON'S GOING TO BE A BADASS.
YOU WANT ME TO OPEN A CAN OF RIGHTEOUS FURY ON YOU?
N-NO. WE'RE GOOD. ANYTHING ELSE?
DON'T CUT HIS HAIR.
I CAN DIG IT.

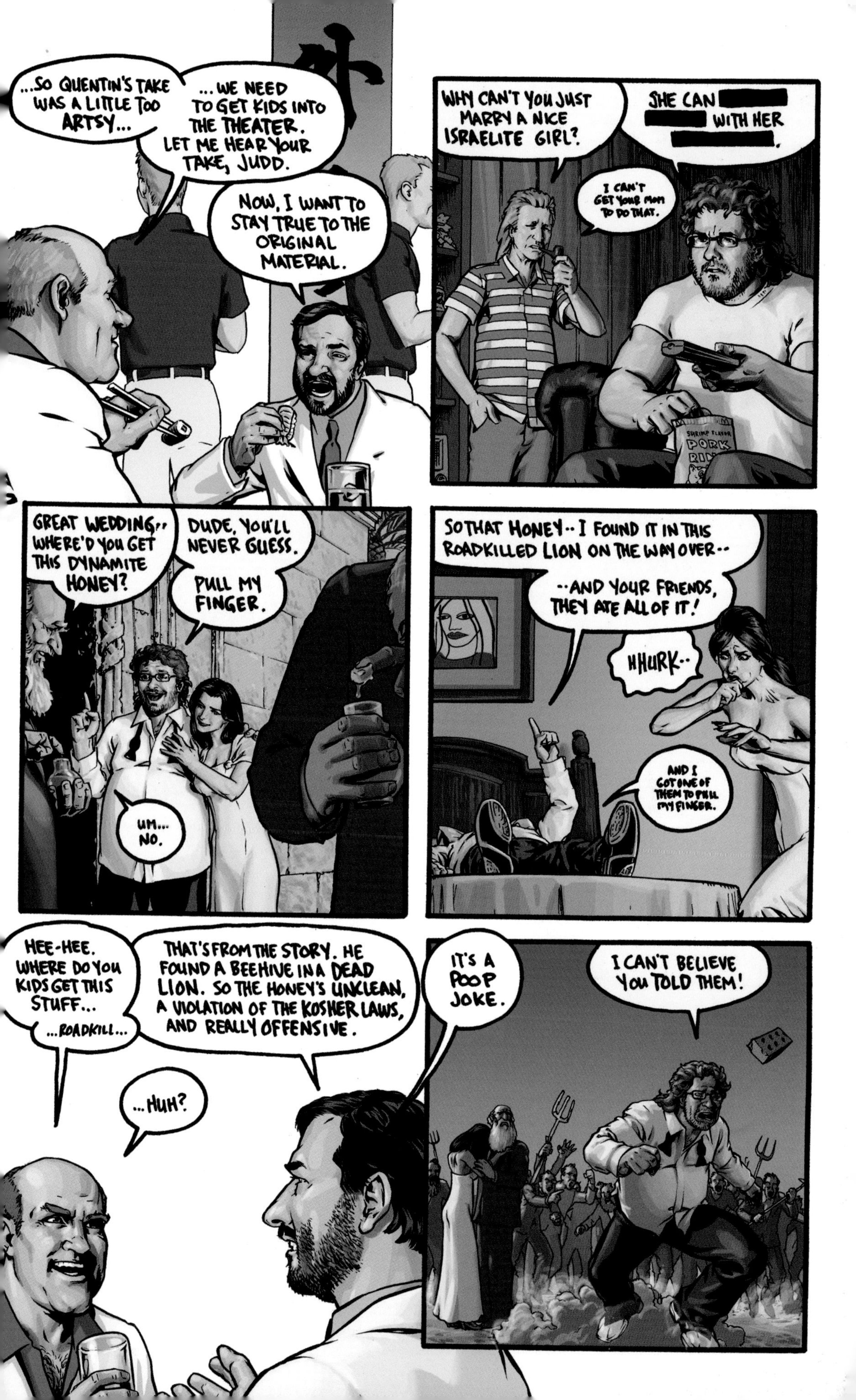
...SO QUENTIN'S TAKE WAS A LITTLE TOO ARTSY...
...WE NEED TO GET KIDS INTO THE THEATER. LET ME HEAR YOUR TAKE, JUDD.
NOW, I WANT TO STAY TRUE TO THE ORIGINAL MATERIAL.
WHY CAN'T YOU JUST MARRY A NICE ISRAELITE GIRL?
SHE CAN [redacted] WITH HER [redacted].
I CAN'T GET YOUR MOM TO DO THAT.
SHRIMP FLAVOR PORK RIN
GREAT WEDDING.. WHERE'D YOU GET THIS DYNAMITE HONEY?
DUDE, YOU'LL NEVER GUESS.
PULL MY FINGER.
UM... NO.
SO THAT HONEY.. I FOUND IT IN THIS ROADKILLED LION ON THE WAY OVER..
..AND YOUR FRIENDS, THEY ATE ALL OF IT!
HHURK..
AND I GOT ONE OF THEM TO PULL MY FINGER.
HEE-HEE. WHERE DO YOU KIDS GET THIS STUFF...
...ROADKILL...
THAT'S FROM THE STORY. HE FOUND A BEEHIVE IN A DEAD LION. SO THE HONEY'S UNCLEAN, A VIOLATION OF THE KOSHER LAWS, AND REALLY OFFENSIVE.
...HUH?
IT'S A POOP JOKE.
I CAN'T BELIEVE YOU TOLD THEM!

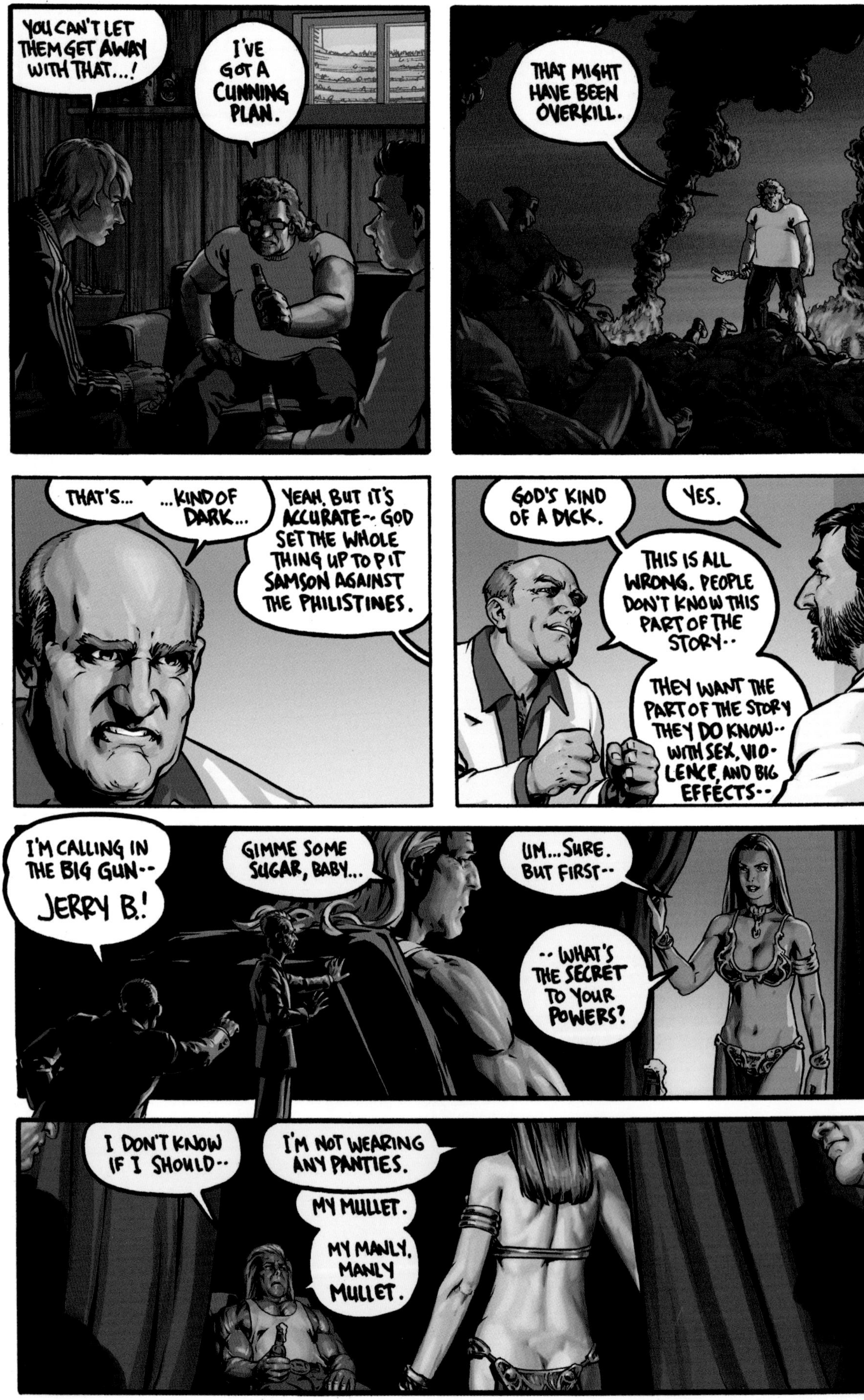
YOU CAN'T LET THEM GET AWAY WITH THAT...!
I'VE GOT A CUNNING PLAN.
THAT MIGHT HAVE BEEN OVERKILL.
THAT'S...
...KIND OF DARK...
YEAH, BUT IT'S ACCURATE-- GOD SET THE WHOLE THING UP TO PIT SAMSON AGAINST THE PHILISTINES.
GOD'S KIND OF A DICK.
YES.
THIS IS ALL WRONG. PEOPLE DON'T KNOW THIS PART OF THE STORY..
THEY WANT THE PART OF THE STORY THEY DO KNOW.. WITH SEX, VIO-LENCE, AND BIG EFFECTS--
I'M CALLING IN THE BIG GUN-- JERRY B.!
GIMME SOME SUGAR, BABY...
UM... SURE. BUT FIRST--
--WHAT'S THE SECRET TO YOUR POWERS?
I DON'T KNOW IF I SHOULD--
I'M NOT WEARING ANY PANTIES.
MY MULLET.
MY MANLY, MANLY MULLET.

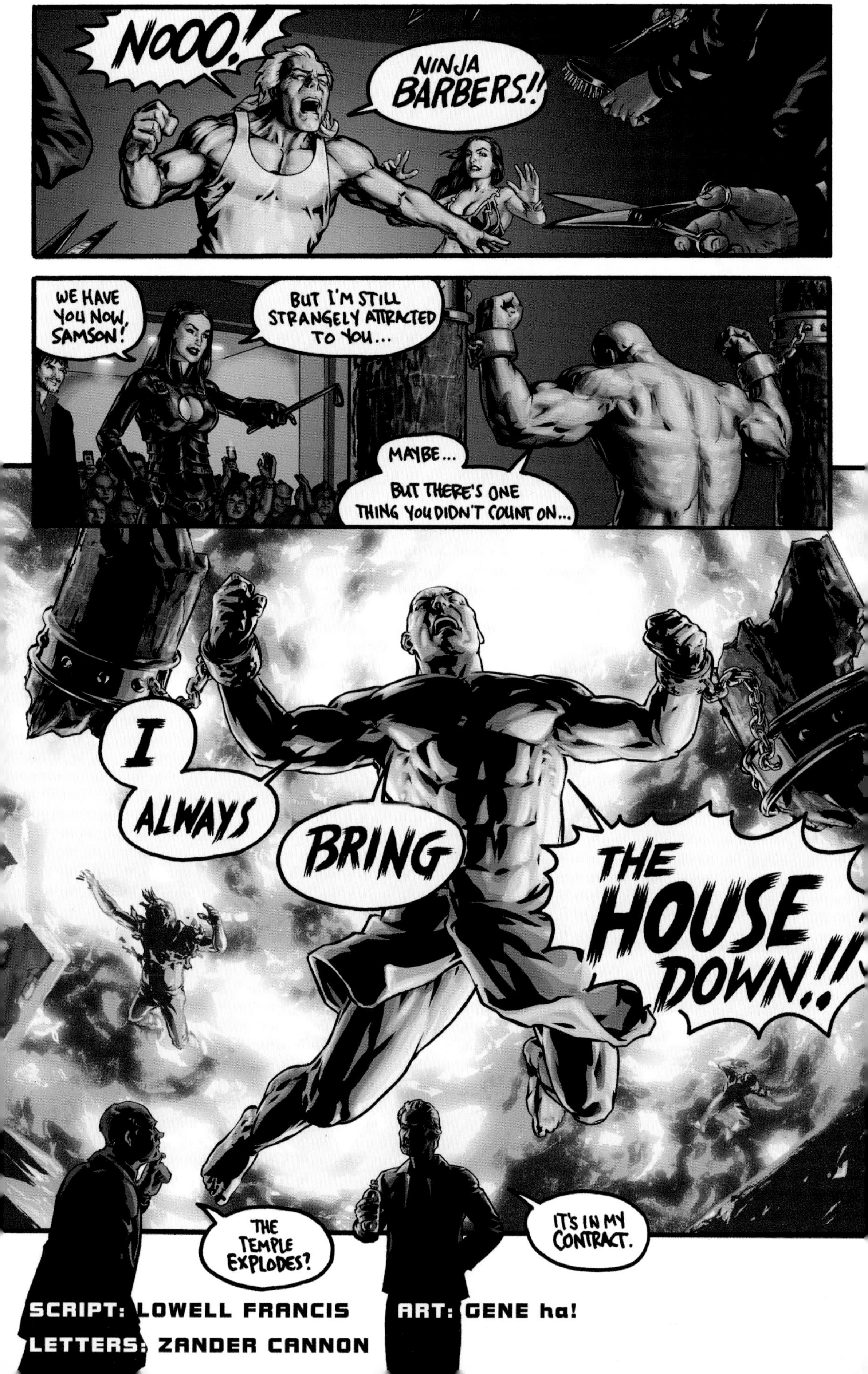
NOOO!
NINJA BARBERS!!
WE HAVE YOU NOW, SAMSON!
BUT I'M STILL STRANGELY ATTRACTED TO YOU...
MAYBE...
BUT THERE'S ONE THING YOU DIDN'T COUNT ON...
I
ALWAYS
BRING
THE HOUSE DOWN!!
THE TEMPLE EXPLODES?
IT'S IN MY CONTRACT.
SCRIPT: LOWELL FRANCIS
ART: GENE ha!
LETTERS: ZANDER CANNON

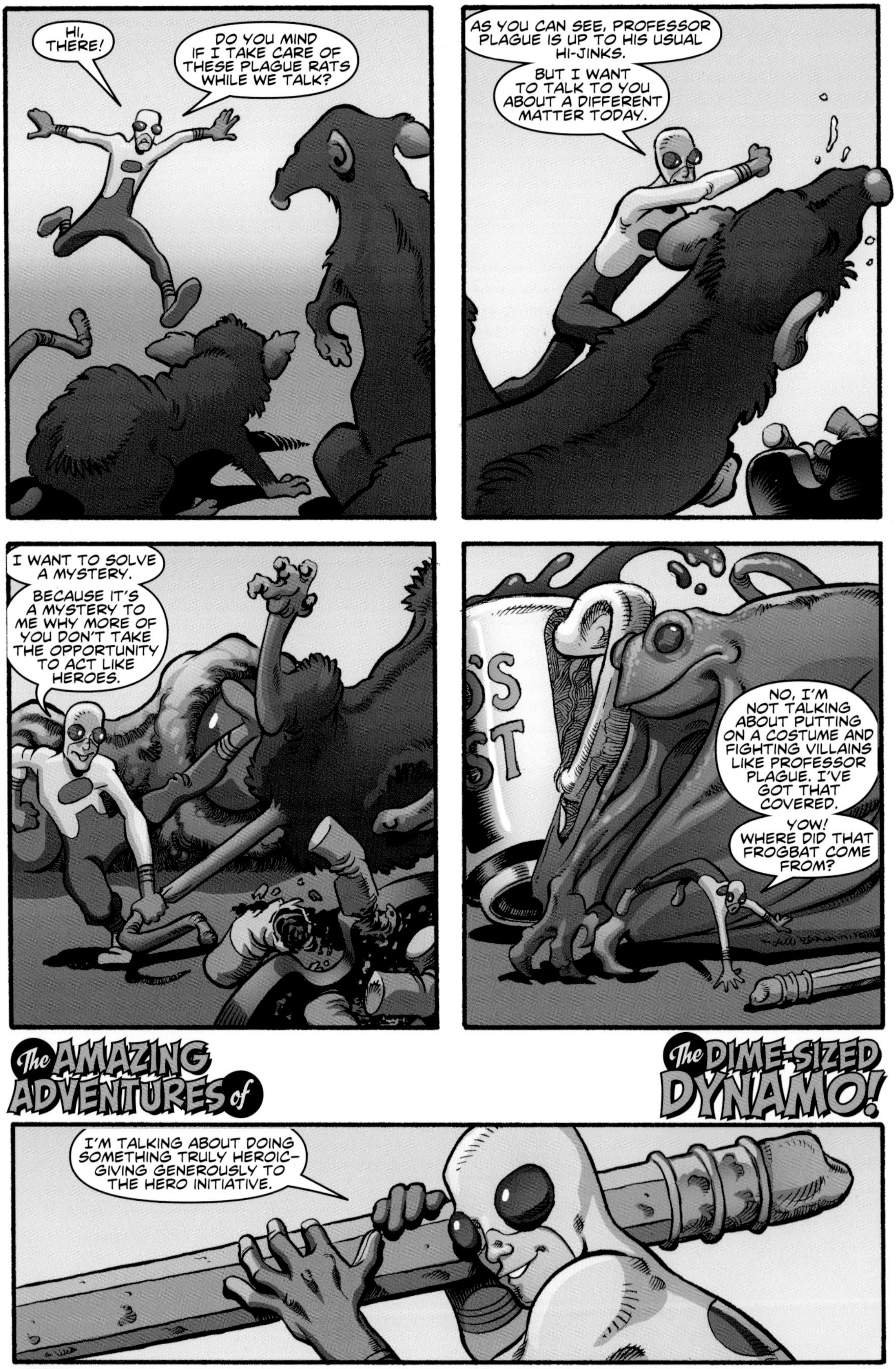
HI, THERE!
DO YOU MIND IF I TAKE CARE OF THESE PLAGUE RATS WHILE WE TALK?
AS YOU CAN SEE, PROFESSOR PLAGUE IS UP TO HIS USUAL HI-JINKS.
BUT I WANT TO TALK TO YOU ABOUT A DIFFERENT MATTER TODAY.
I WANT TO SOLVE A MYSTERY.
BECAUSE IT'S A MYSTERY TO ME WHY MORE OF YOU DON'T TAKE THE OPPORTUNITY TO ACT LIKE HEROES.
NO, I'M NOT TALKING ABOUT PUTTING ON A COSTUME AND FIGHTING VILLAINS LIKE PROFESSOR PLAGUE. I'VE GOT THAT COVERED.
YOW! WHERE DID THAT FROGBAT COME FROM?
The AMAZING ADVENTURES of
The DIME-SIZED DYNAMO!
I'M TALKING ABOUT DOING SOMETHING TRULY HEROIC-GIVING GENEROUSLY TO THE HERO INITIATIVE.
in A TWO-PAGE MYSTERY!
BY BILL WILLINGHAM
COLORED BY LAURA MARTIN
LETTERED BY COMICRAFT

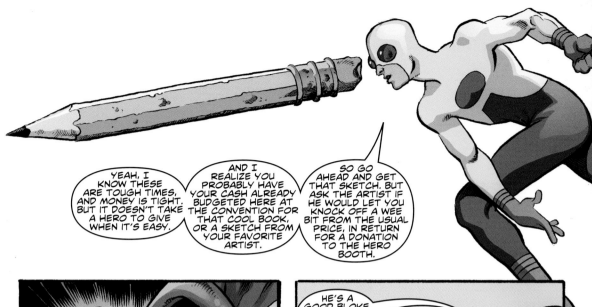

YEAH, I KNOW THESE ARE TOUGH TIMES, AND MONEY IS TIGHT. BUT IT DOESN'T TAKE A HERO TO GIVE WHEN IT'S EASY.

AND I REALIZE YOU PROBABLY HAVE YOUR CASH ALREADY BUDGETED HERE AT THE CONVENTION FOR THAT COOL BOOK, OR A SKETCH FROM YOUR FAVORITE ARTIST.

SO GO AHEAD AND GET THAT SKETCH. BUT ASK THE ARTIST IF HE WOULD LET YOU KNOCK OFF A WEE BIT FROM THE USUAL PRICE, IN RETURN FOR A DONATION TO THE HERO BOOTH.

JUST A COUPLE OF BUCKS.

HE'S A GOOD BLOKE. HE'LL LIKELY AGREE, SINCE IT'S IN SERVICE TO A GOOD CAUSE.

A COUPLE OF BUCKS ISN'T ENOUGH TO HURT, BUT IT'S SURE ENOUGH TO HELP SOMEONE IN NEED.

AND THEN YOU AND THE ARTIST WILL HAVE JOINED TOGETHER TO DO SOME GOOD. JUST LIKE AN OLD-FASHIONED SUPERHERO TEAM-UP!

PRETTY COOL, HUH?

NOW ENJOY THE SHOW, AND KEEP AN EYE OUT FOR MORE OF THE EVIL PROFESSOR'S VERMIN.

FIN

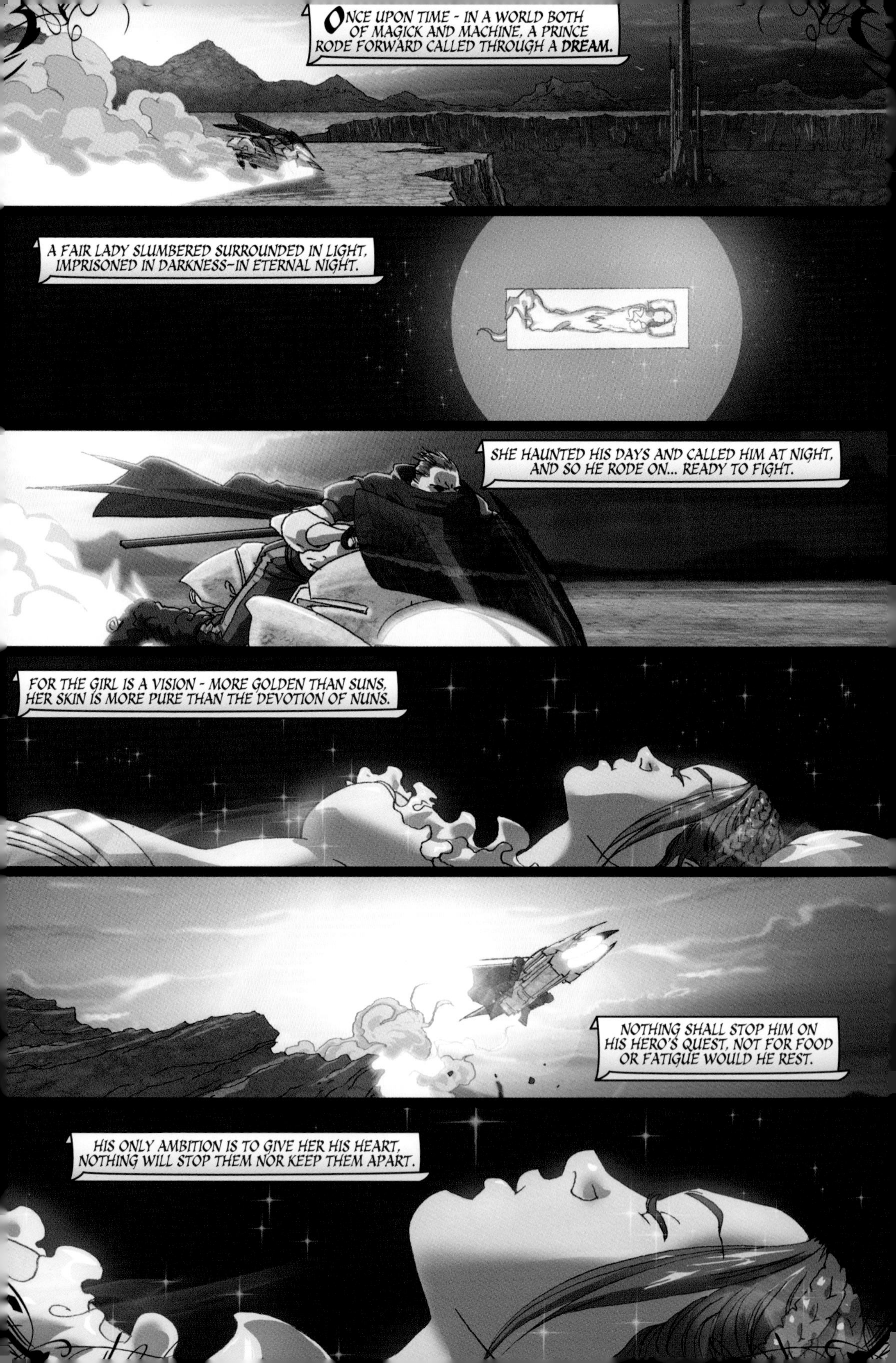
ONCE UPON TIME - IN A WORLD BOTH OF MAGICK AND MACHINE, A PRINCE RODE FORWARD CALLED THROUGH A DREAM.
A FAIR LADY SLUMBERED SURROUNDED IN LIGHT, IMPRISONED IN DARKNESS—IN ETERNAL NIGHT.
SHE HAUNTED HIS DAYS AND CALLED HIM AT NIGHT, AND SO HE RODE ON... READY TO FIGHT.
FOR THE GIRL IS A VISION - MORE GOLDEN THAN SUNS, HER SKIN IS MORE PURE THAN THE DEVOTION OF NUNS.
NOTHING SHALL STOP HIM ON HIS HERO'S QUEST, NOT FOR FOOD OR FATIGUE WOULD HE REST.
HIS ONLY AMBITION IS TO GIVE HER HIS HEART, NOTHING WILL STOP THEM NOR KEEP THEM APART.

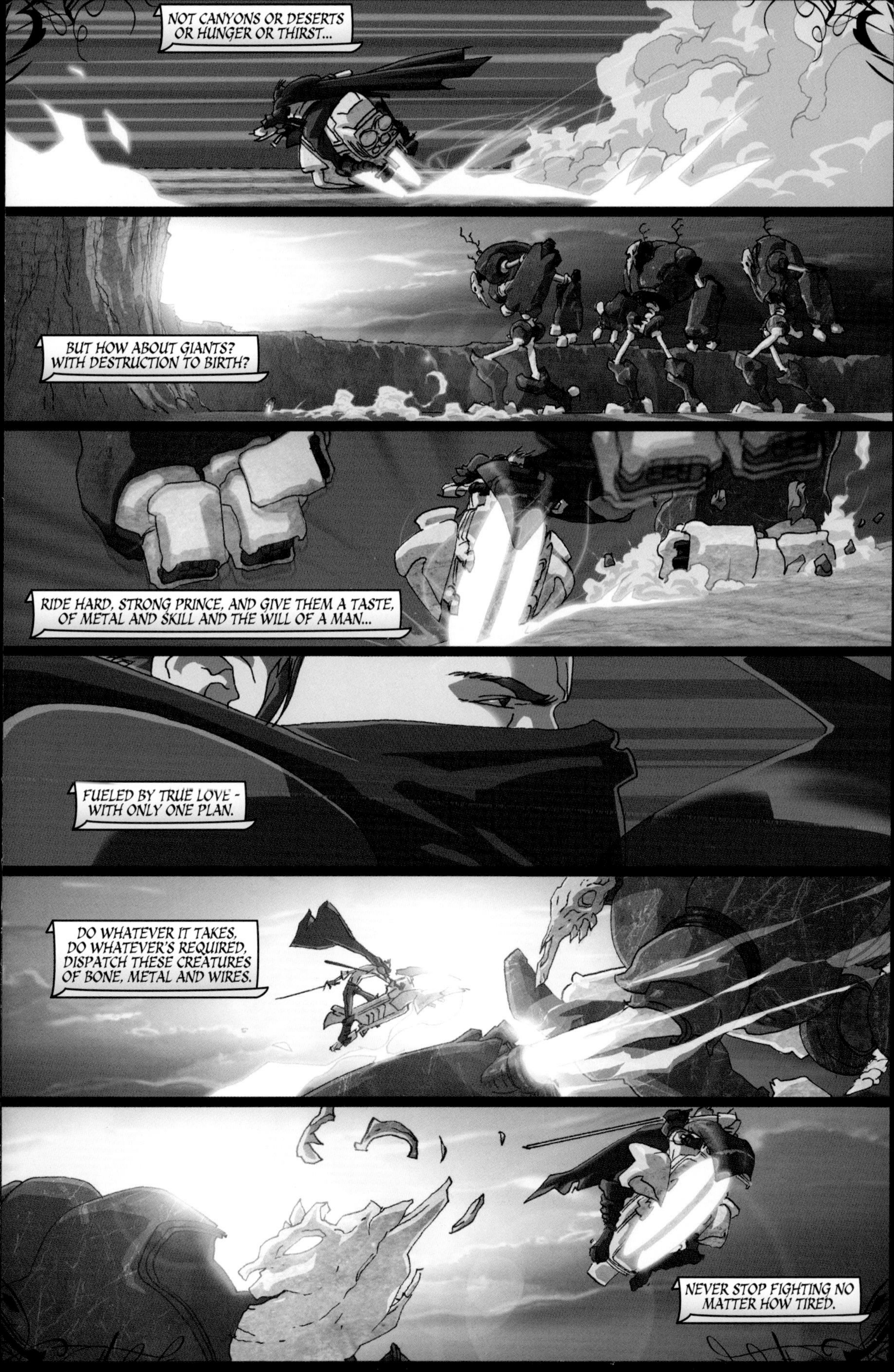
NOT CANYONS OR DESERTS OR HUNGER OR THIRST...
BUT HOW ABOUT GIANTS? WITH DESTRUCTION TO BIRTH?
RIDE HARD, STRONG PRINCE, AND GIVE THEM A TASTE, OF METAL AND SKILL AND THE WILL OF A MAN...
FUELED BY TRUE LOVE - WITH ONLY ONE PLAN.
DO WHATEVER IT TAKES, DO WHATEVER'S REQUIRED, DISPATCH THESE CREATURES OF BONE, METAL AND WIRES.
NEVER STOP FIGHTING NO MATTER HOW TIRED.

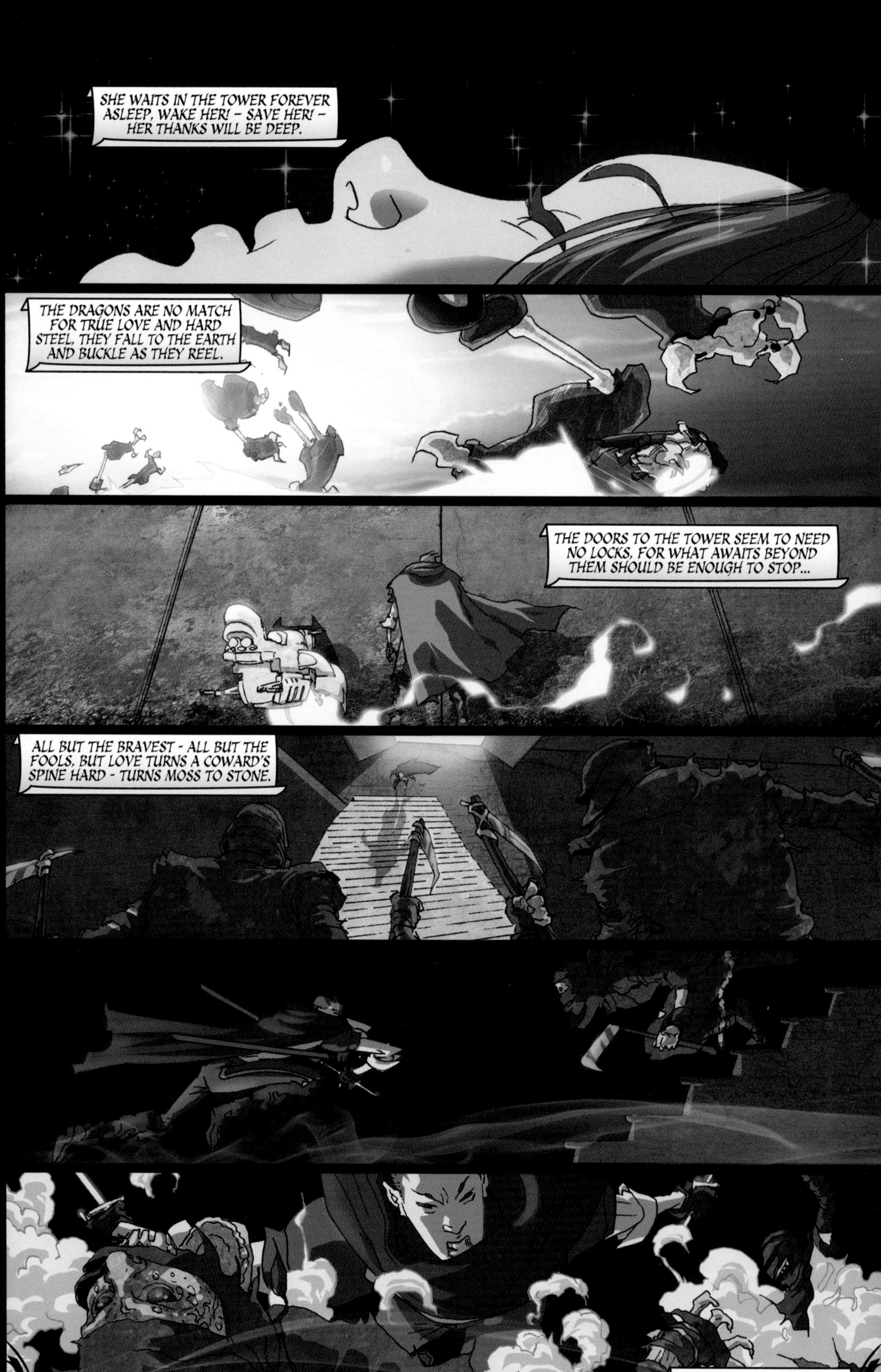
SHE WAITS IN THE TOWER FOREVER ASLEEP, WAKE HER! – SAVE HER! – HER THANKS WILL BE DEEP.
THE DRAGONS ARE NO MATCH FOR TRUE LOVE AND HARD STEEL, THEY FALL TO THE EARTH AND BUCKLE AS THEY REEL.
THE DOORS TO THE TOWER SEEM TO NEED NO LOCKS, FOR WHAT AWAITS BEYOND THEM SHOULD BE ENOUGH TO STOP...
ALL BUT THE BRAVEST - ALL BUT THE FOOLS, BUT LOVE TURNS A COWARD'S SPINE HARD - TURNS MOSS TO STONE.
AND SO HE BREAKS THEIR BODIES AND MAKES DUST OUT OF BONES.

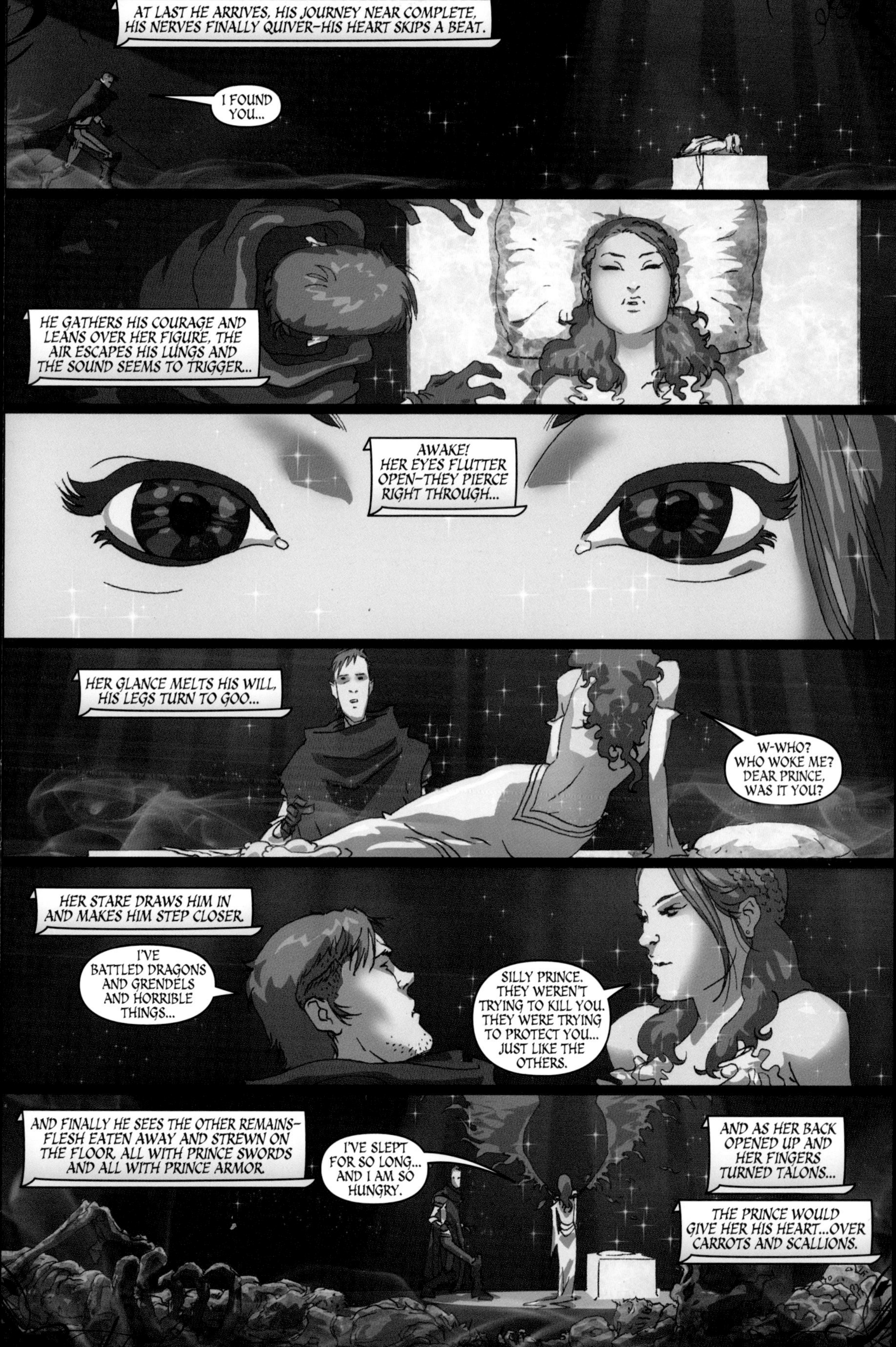

AT LAST HE ARRIVES, HIS JOURNEY NEAR COMPLETE, HIS NERVES FINALLY QUIVER–HIS HEART SKIPS A BEAT.
I FOUND YOU...
HE GATHERS HIS COURAGE AND LEANS OVER HER FIGURE, THE AIR ESCAPES HIS LUNGS AND THE SOUND SEEMS TO TRIGGER...
AWAKE! HER EYES FLUTTER OPEN–THEY PIERCE RIGHT THROUGH...
HER GLANCE MELTS HIS WILL, HIS LEGS TURN TO GOO...
W-WHO? WHO WOKE ME? DEAR PRINCE, WAS IT YOU?
HER STARE DRAWS HIM IN AND MAKES HIM STEP CLOSER.
I'VE BATTLED DRAGONS AND GRENDELS AND HORRIBLE THINGS...
SILLY PRINCE. THEY WEREN'T TRYING TO KILL YOU. THEY WERE TRYING TO PROTECT YOU... JUST LIKE THE OTHERS.
AND FINALLY HE SEES THE OTHER REMAINS–FLESH EATEN AWAY AND STREWN ON THE FLOOR, ALL WITH PRINCE SWORDS AND ALL WITH PRINCE ARMOR.
I'VE SLEPT FOR SO LONG... AND I AM SO HUNGRY.
AND AS HER BACK OPENED UP AND HER FINGERS TURNED TALONS...
THE PRINCE WOULD GIVE HER HIS HEART...OVER CARROTS AND SCALLIONS.

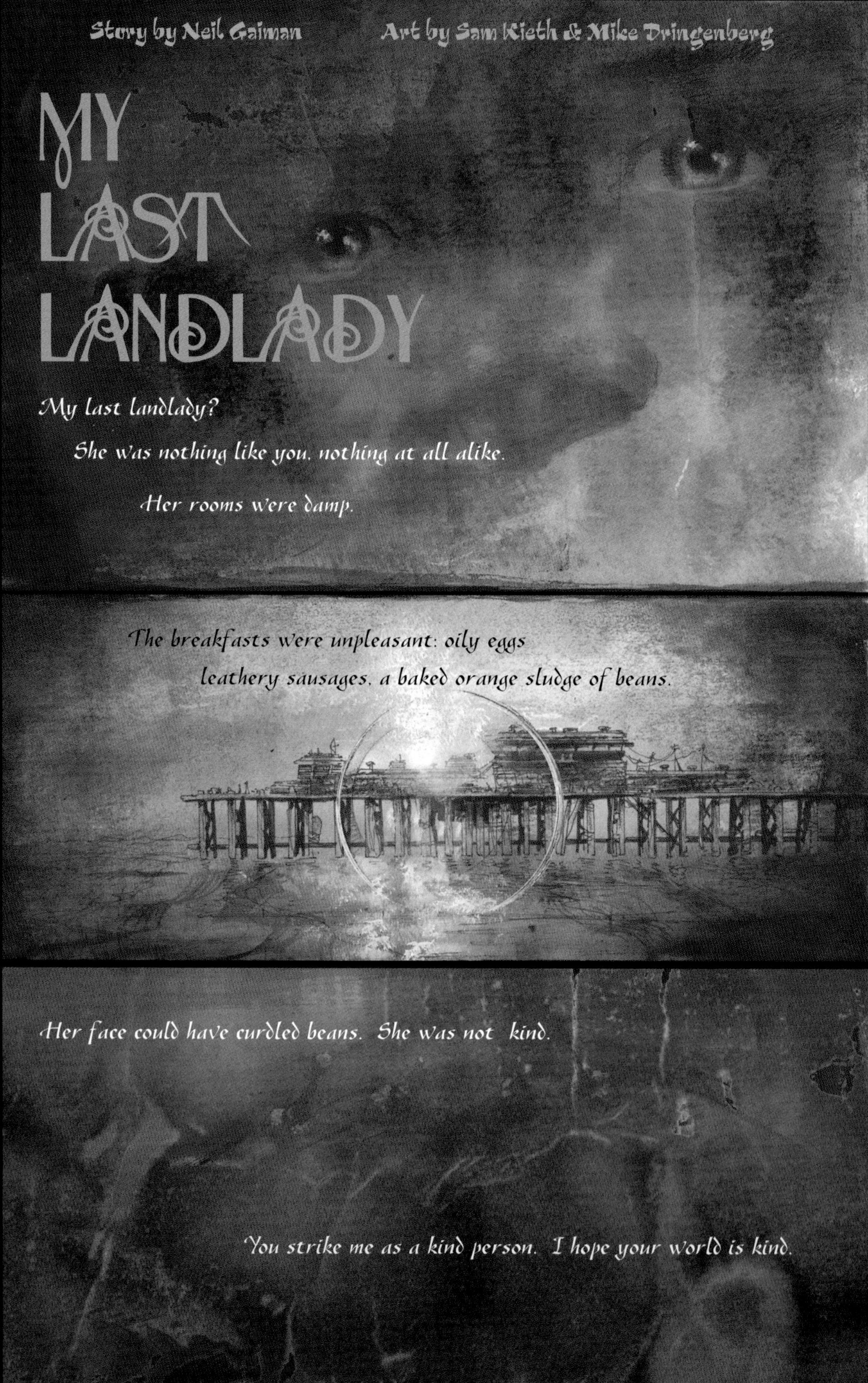
Story by Neil Gaiman
Art by Sam Kieth & Mike Dringenberg
MY LAST LANDLADY
My last landlady?
She was nothing like you, nothing at all alike.
Her rooms were damp.
The breakfasts were unpleasant: oily eggs
leathery sausages, a baked orange sludge of beans.
Her face could have curdled beans. She was not kind.
You strike me as a kind person. I hope your world is kind.

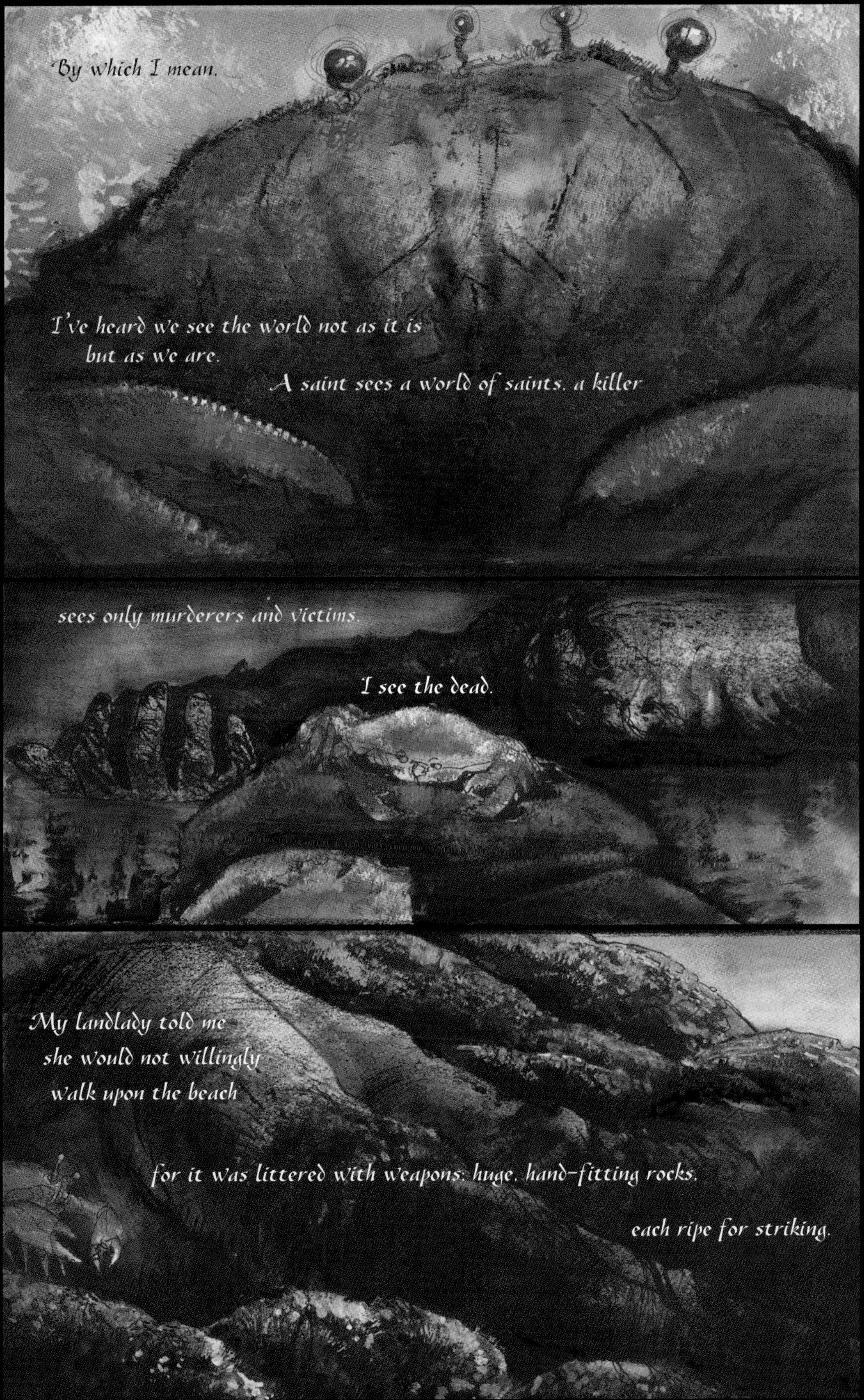
By which I mean.
I've heard we see the world not as it is
but as we are.
A saint sees a world of saints, a killer
sees only murderers and victims.
I see the dead.
My landlady told me
she would not willingly
walk upon the beach
for it was littered with weapons: huge, hand-fitting rocks,
each ripe for striking.

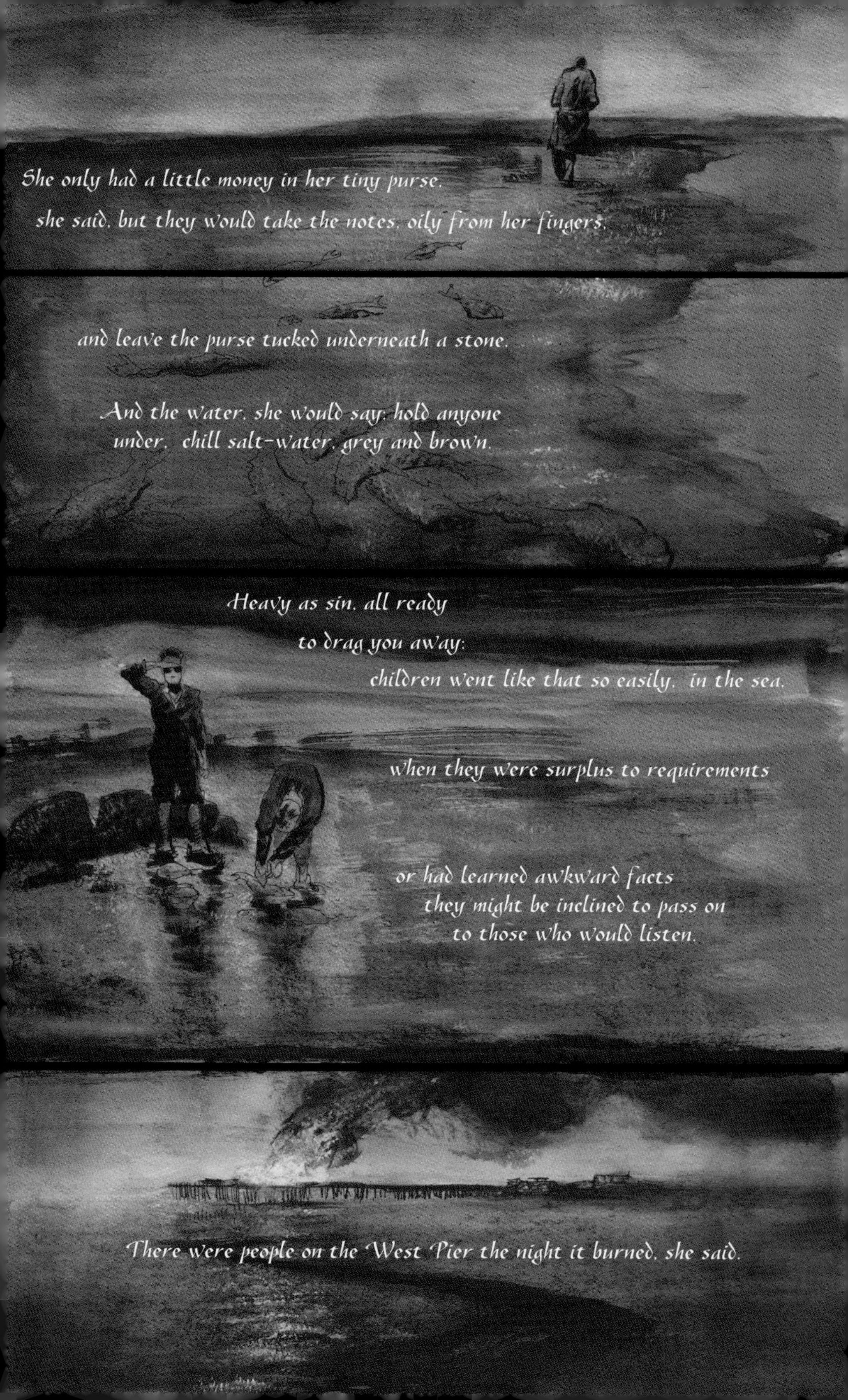
She only had a little money in her tiny purse,
she said, but they would take the notes, oily from her fingers,
and leave the purse tucked underneath a stone.
And the water, she would say, hold anyone under, chill salt-water, grey and brown.
Heavy as sin, all ready
to drag you away:
children went like that so easily, in the sea,
when they were surplus to requirements
or had learned awkward facts they might be inclined to pass on to those who would listen.
There were people on the West Pier the night it burned, she said.

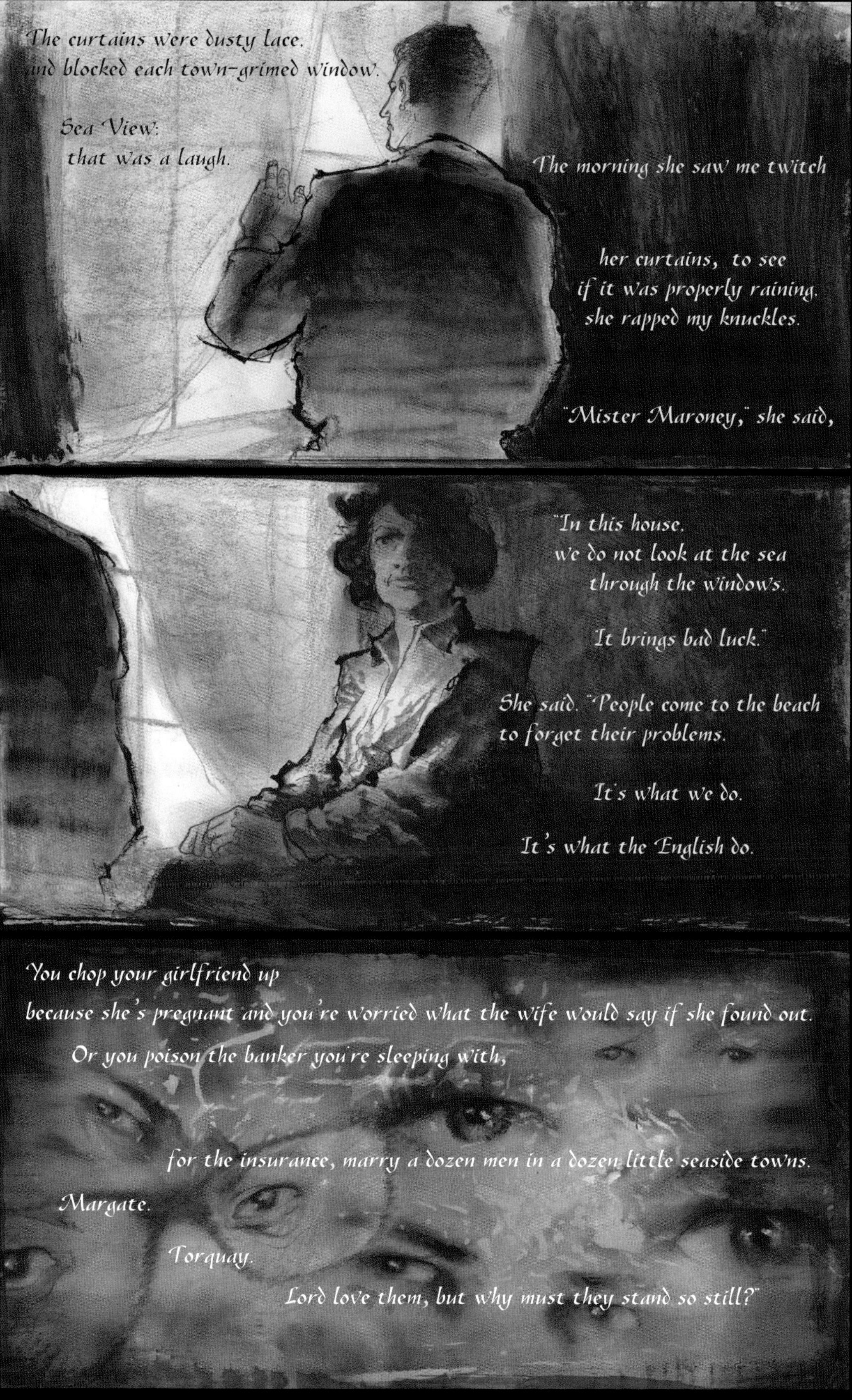
The curtains were dusty lace,
and blocked each town-grimed window.
Sea View:
that was a laugh.
The morning she saw me twitch
her curtains, to see
if it was properly raining,
she rapped my knuckles.
"Mister Maroney," she said,
"In this house,
we do not look at the sea
through the windows.
It brings bad luck."
She said, "People come to the beach
to forget their problems.
It's what we do.
It's what the English do.
You chop your girlfriend up
because she's pregnant and you're worried what the wife would say if she found out.
Or you poison the banker you're sleeping with,
for the insurance, marry a dozen men in a dozen little seaside towns.
Margate.
Torquay.
Lord love them, but why must they stand so still?"

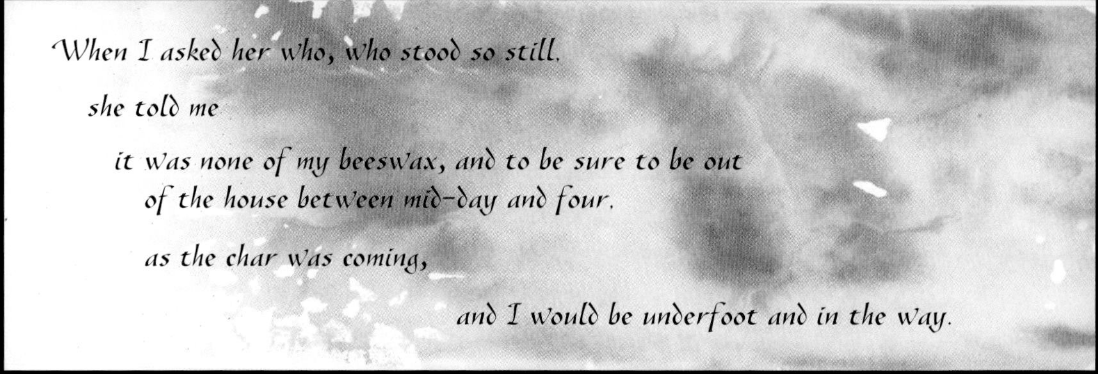
When I asked her who, who stood so still.
she told me
it was none of my beeswax, and to be sure to be out of the house between mid-day and four.
as the char was coming,
and I would be underfoot and in the way.

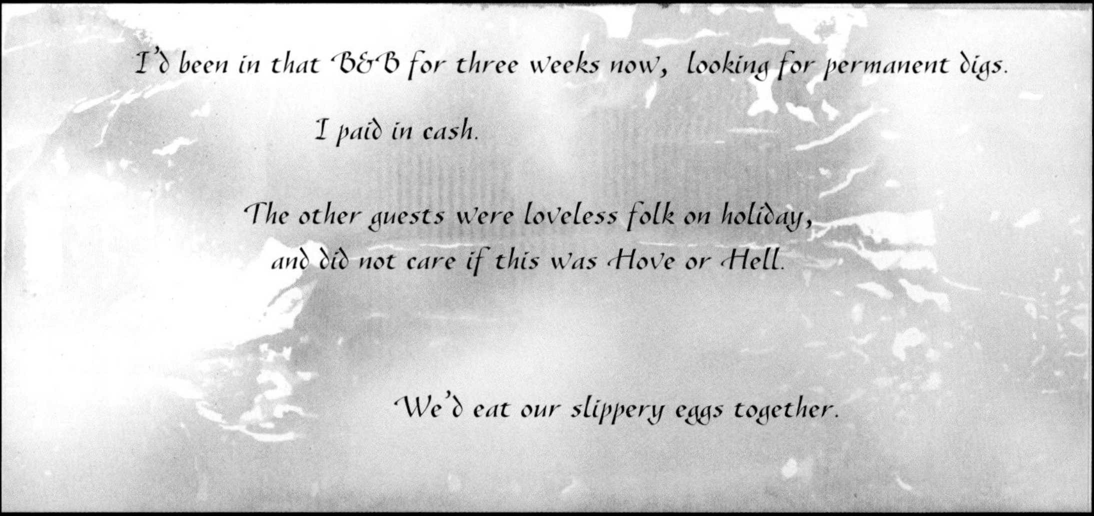
I'd been in that B&B for three weeks now, looking for permanent digs.
I paid in cash.
The other guests were loveless folk on holiday, and did not care if this was Hove or Hell.
We'd eat our slippery eggs together.

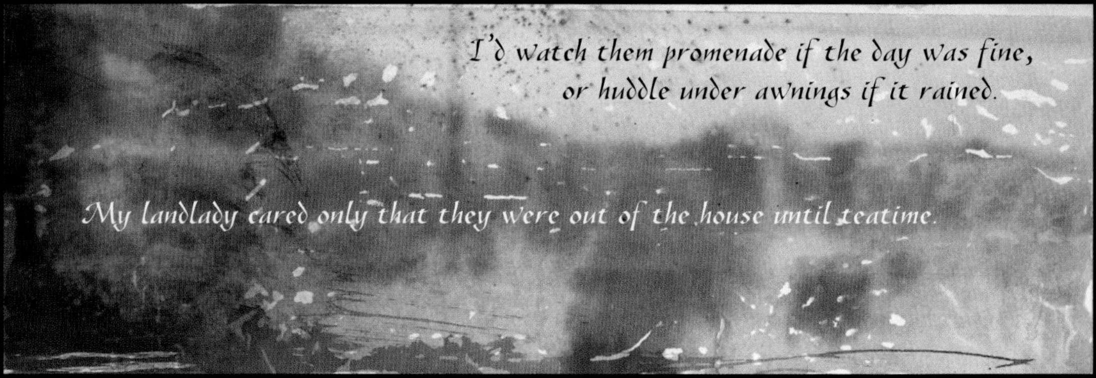
I'd watch them promenade if the day was fine, or huddle under awnings if it rained.
My landlady cared only that they were out of the house until teatime.

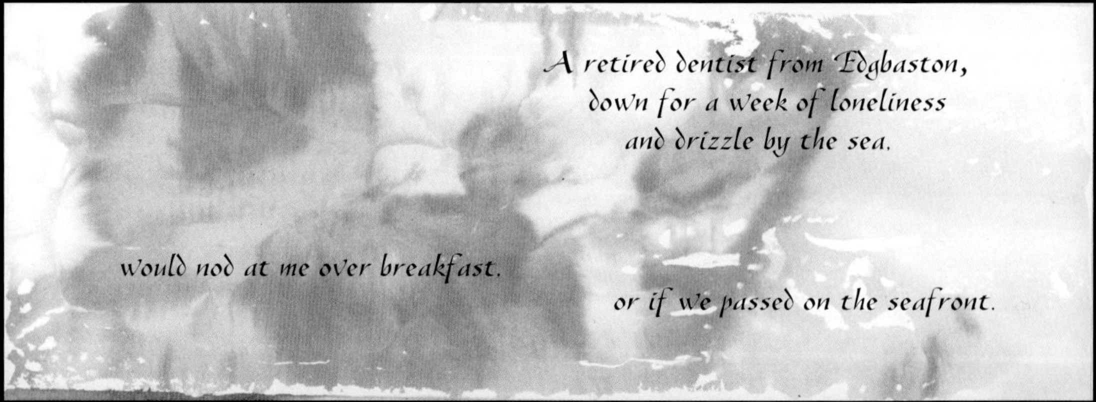
A retired dentist from Edgbaston, down for a week of loneliness and drizzle by the sea.
would nod at me over breakfast.
or if we passed on the seafront.

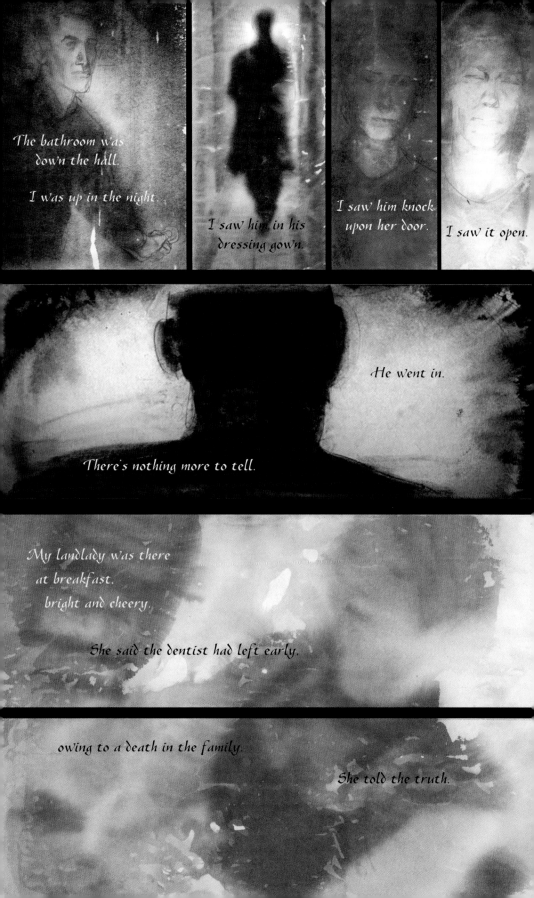

The bathroom was down the hall.

I was up in the night.

I saw him in his dressing gown.

I saw him knock upon her door.

I saw it open.

He went in.

There's nothing more to tell.

My landlady was there at breakfast. bright and cheery.

She said the dentist had left early.

owing to a death in the family.

She told the truth.

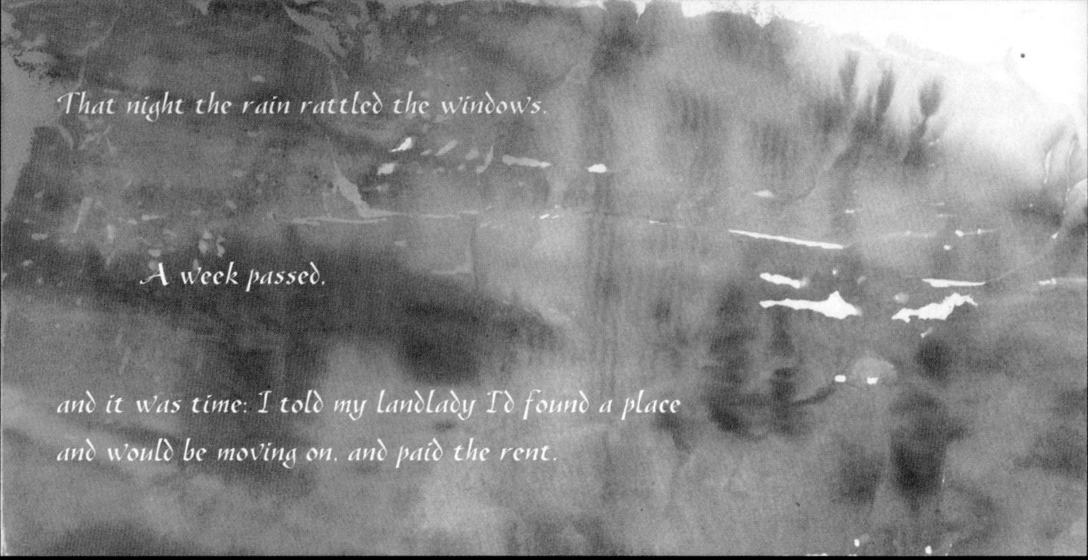
That night the rain rattled the windows.
A week passed.
and it was time: I told my landlady I'd found a place
and would be moving on, and paid the rent.

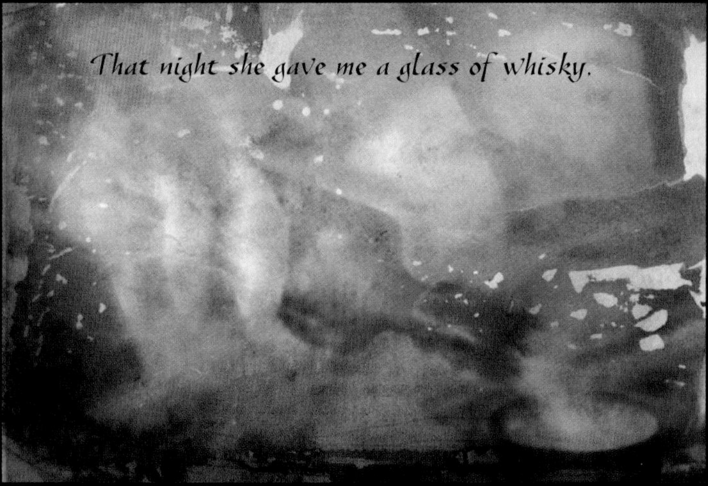
That night she gave me a glass of whisky,

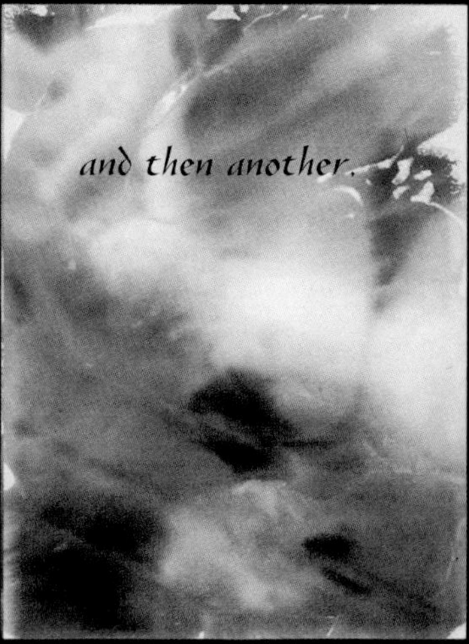
and then another,

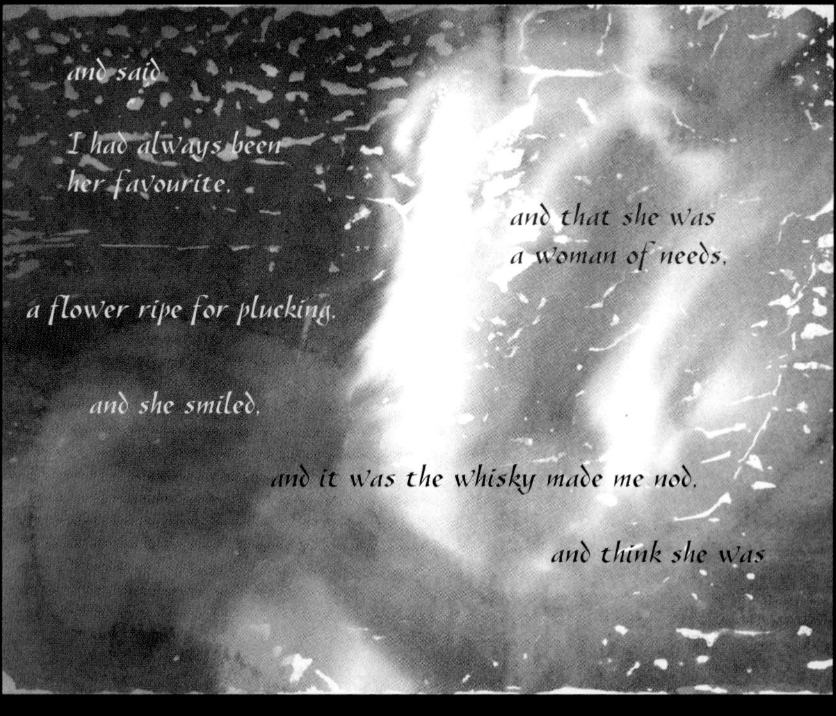
and said
I had always been
her favourite,
and that she was
a woman of needs,
a flower ripe for plucking.
and she smiled.
and it was the whisky made me nod,
and think she was

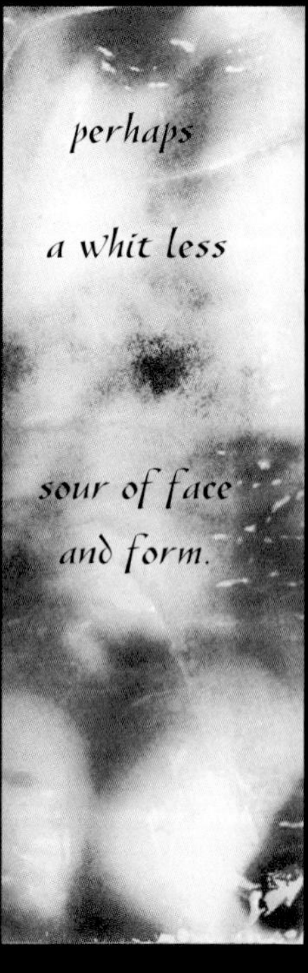
perhaps
a whit less
sour of face
and form.

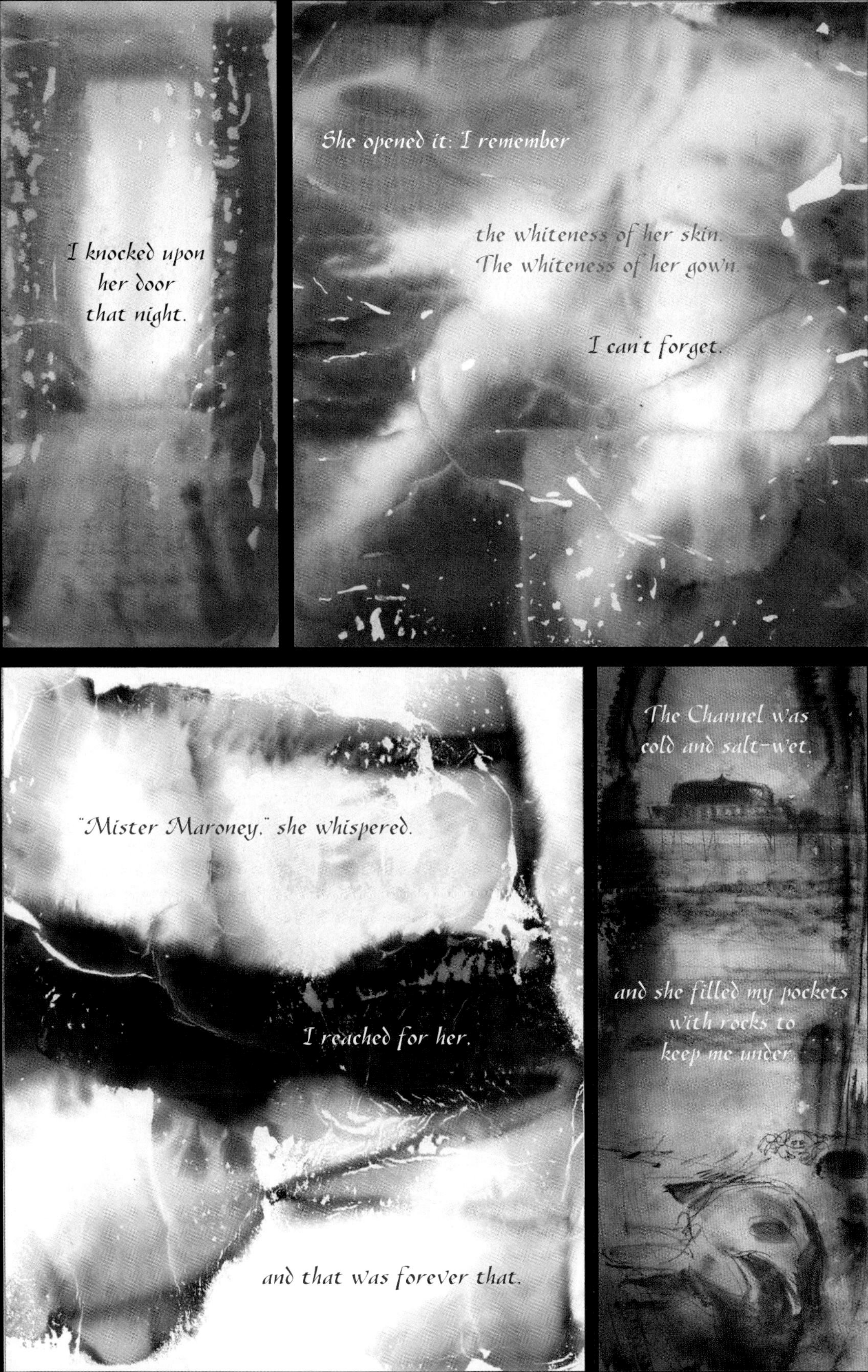
I knocked upon her door that night.
She opened it: I remember
the whiteness of her skin. The whiteness of her gown.
I can't forget.
"Mister Maroney," she whispered.
I reached for her,
and that was forever that.
The Channel was cold and salt-wet,
and she filled my pockets with rocks to keep me under.

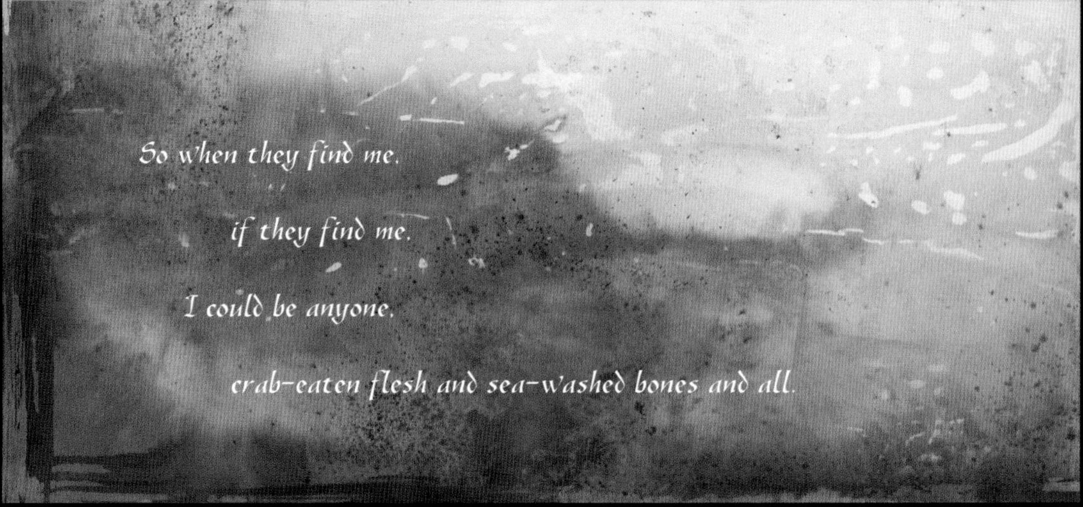
So when they find me,
if they find me,
I could be anyone,
crab-eaten flesh and sea-washed bones and all.

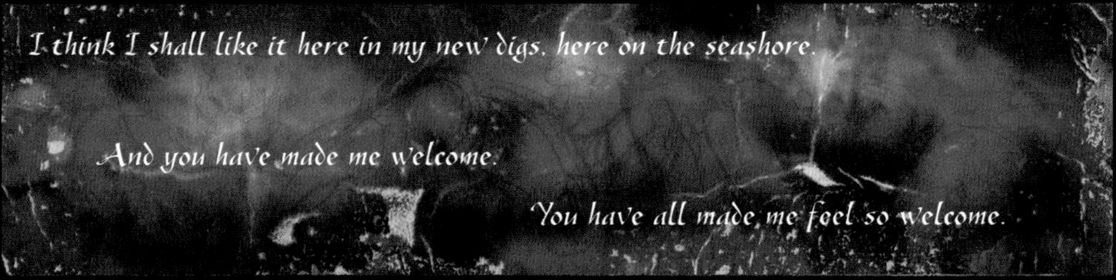
I think I shall like it here in my new digs, here on the seashore.
And you have made me welcome.
You have all made me feel so welcome.

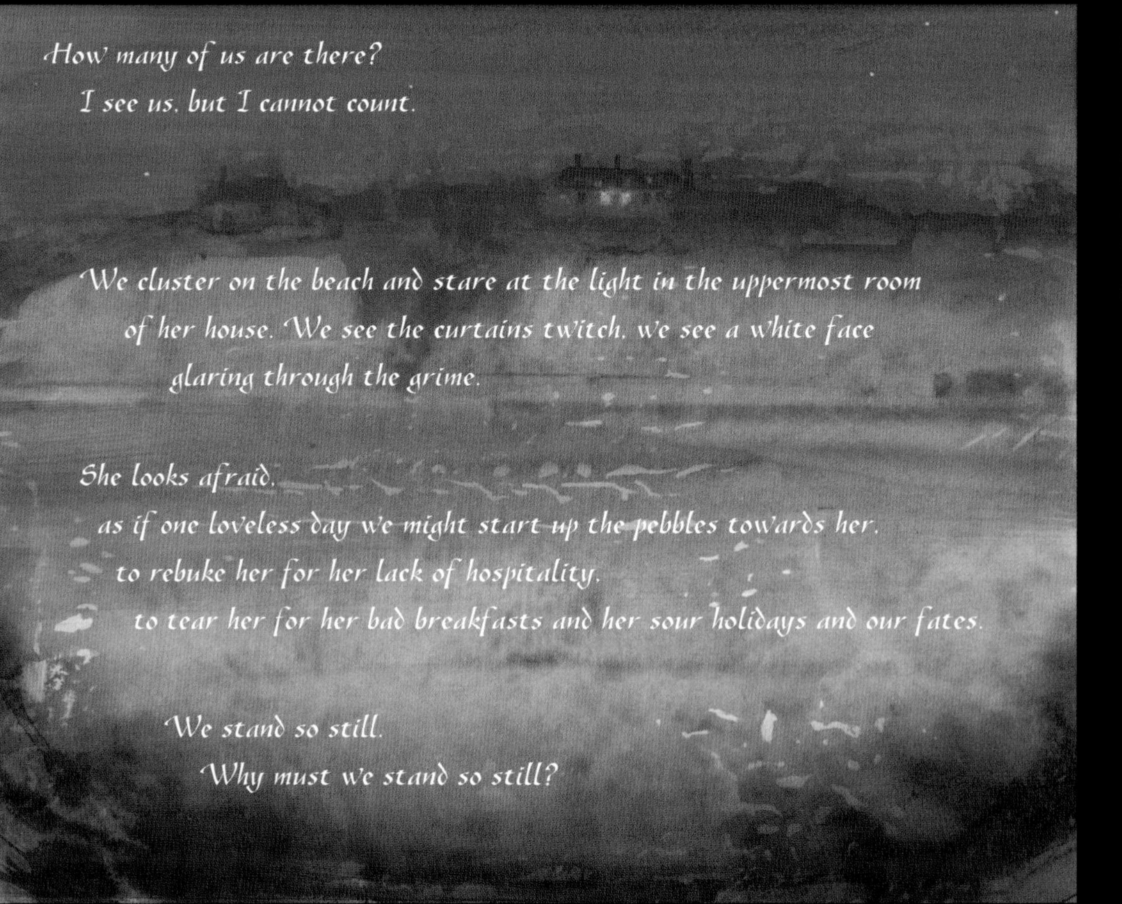
How many of us are there?
I see us, but I cannot count.
We cluster on the beach and stare at the light in the uppermost room of her house. We see the curtains twitch, we see a white face glaring through the grime.
She looks afraid,
as if one loveless day we might start up the pebbles towards her,
to rebuke her for her lack of hospitality,
to tear her for her bad breakfasts and her sour holidays and our fates.
We stand so still.
Why must we stand so still?

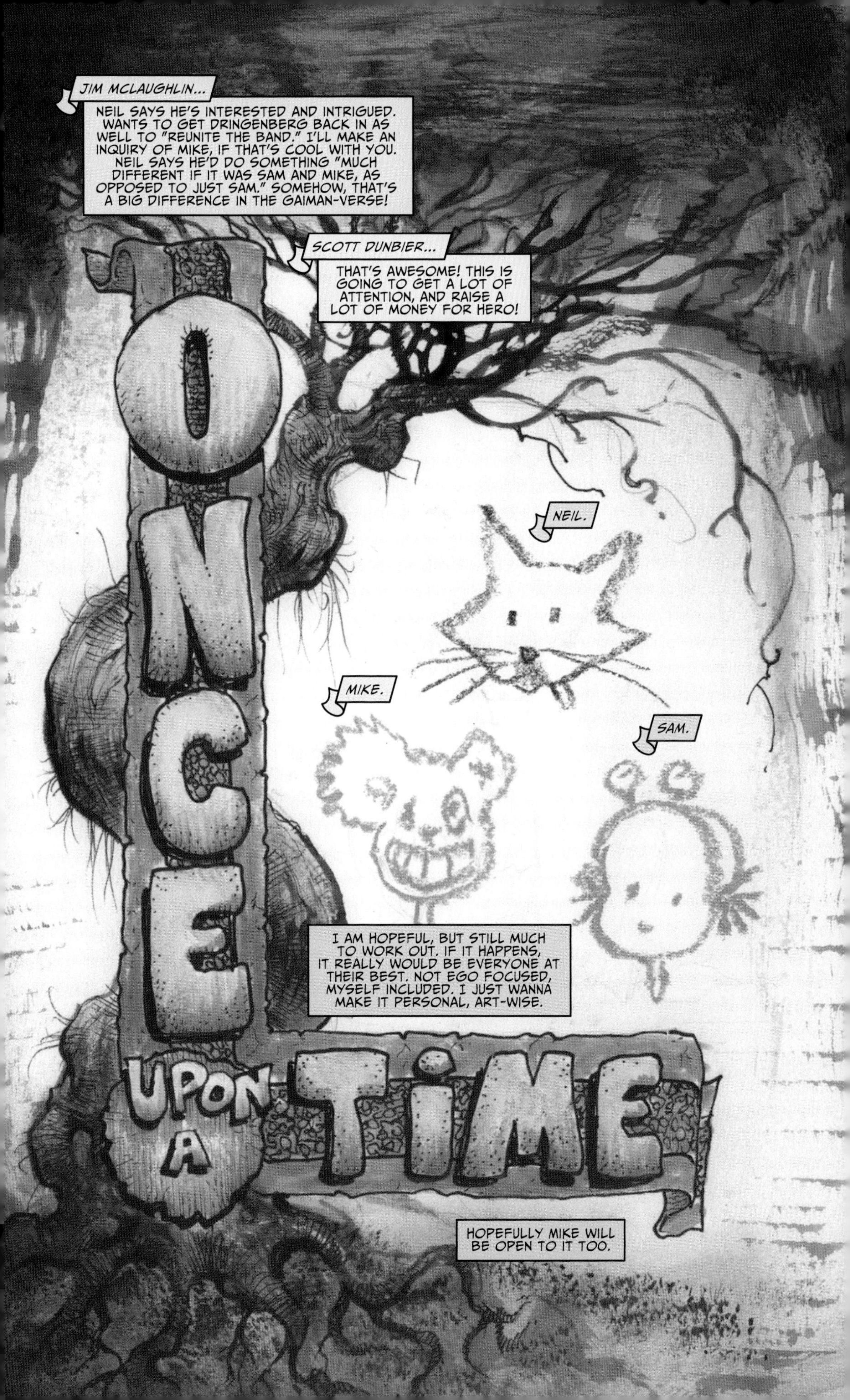
JIM MCLAUGHLIN...
NEIL SAYS HE'S INTERESTED AND INTRIGUED. WANTS TO GET DRINGENBERG BACK IN AS WELL TO "REUNITE THE BAND." I'LL MAKE AN INQUIRY OF MIKE, IF THAT'S COOL WITH YOU. NEIL SAYS HE'D DO SOMETHING "MUCH DIFFERENT IF IT WAS SAM AND MIKE, AS OPPOSED TO JUST SAM." SOMEHOW, THAT'S A BIG DIFFERENCE IN THE GAIMAN-VERSE!
SCOTT DUNBIER...
THAT'S AWESOME! THIS IS GOING TO GET A LOT OF ATTENTION, AND RAISE A LOT OF MONEY FOR HERO!
ONCE
NEIL.
MIKE.
SAM.
I AM HOPEFUL, BUT STILL MUCH TO WORK OUT. IF IT HAPPENS, IT REALLY WOULD BE EVERYONE AT THEIR BEST. NOT EGO FOCUSED, MYSELF INCLUDED. I JUST WANNA MAKE IT PERSONAL, ART-WISE.
UPON A TIME
HOPEFULLY MIKE WILL BE OPEN TO IT TOO.

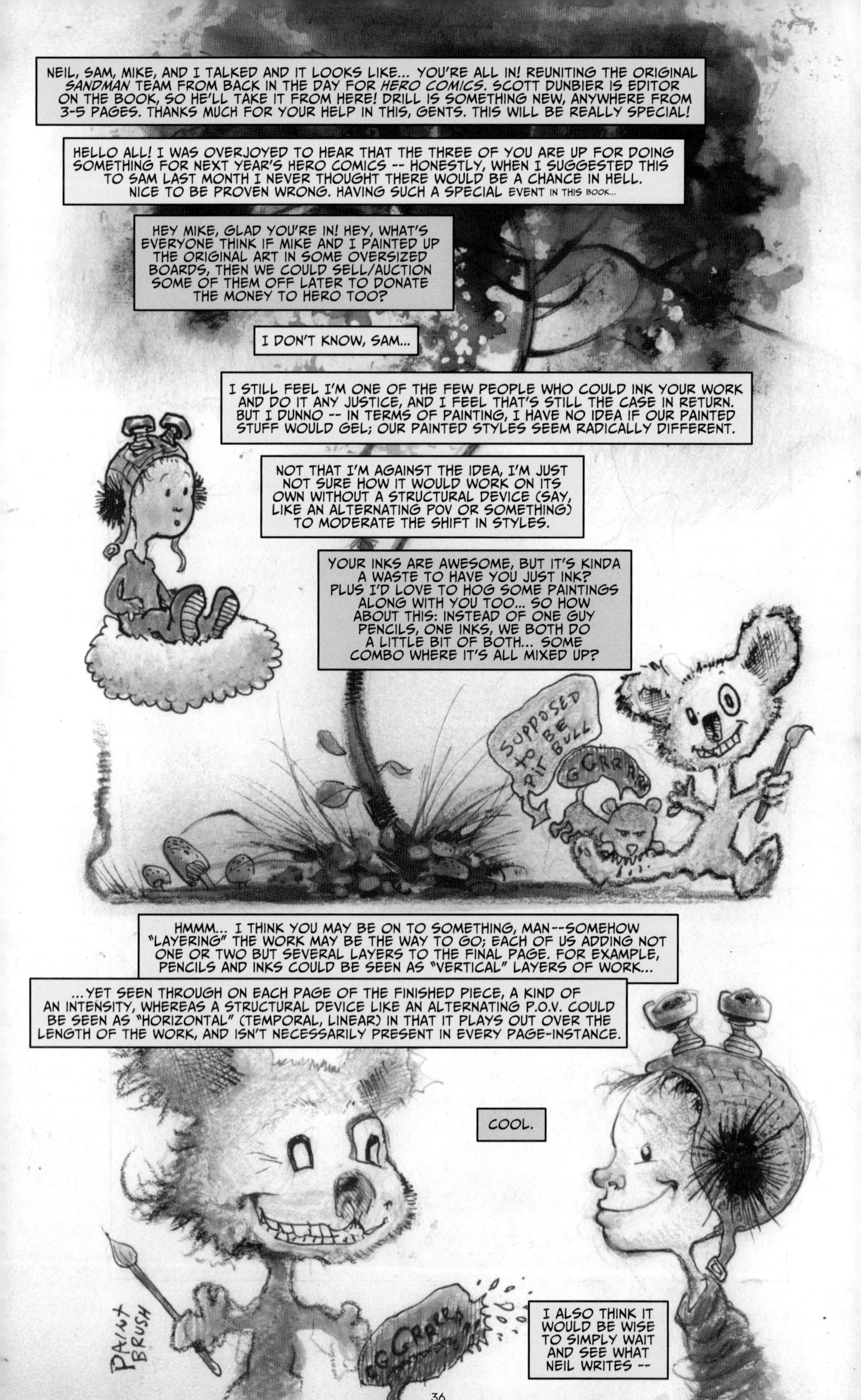
NEIL, SAM, MIKE, AND I TALKED AND IT LOOKS LIKE... YOU'RE ALL IN! REUNITING THE ORIGINAL *SANDMAN* TEAM FROM BACK IN THE DAY FOR *HERO COMICS*. SCOTT DUNBIER IS EDITOR ON THE BOOK, SO HE'LL TAKE IT FROM HERE! DRILL IS SOMETHING NEW, ANYWHERE FROM 3-5 PAGES. THANKS MUCH FOR YOUR HELP IN THIS, GENTS. THIS WILL BE REALLY SPECIAL!
HELLO ALL! I WAS OVERJOYED TO HEAR THAT THE THREE OF YOU ARE UP FOR DOING SOMETHING FOR NEXT YEAR'S HERO COMICS -- HONESTLY, WHEN I SUGGESTED THIS TO SAM LAST MONTH I NEVER THOUGHT THERE WOULD BE A CHANCE IN HELL. NICE TO BE PROVEN WRONG. HAVING SUCH A SPECIAL EVENT IN THIS BOOK...
HEY MIKE, GLAD YOU'RE IN! HEY, WHAT'S EVERYONE THINK IF MIKE AND I PAINTED UP THE ORIGINAL ART IN SOME OVERSIZED BOARDS, THEN WE COULD SELL/AUCTION SOME OF THEM OFF LATER TO DONATE THE MONEY TO HERO TOO?
I DON'T KNOW, SAM...
I STILL FEEL I'M ONE OF THE FEW PEOPLE WHO COULD INK YOUR WORK AND DO IT ANY JUSTICE, AND I FEEL THAT'S STILL THE CASE IN RETURN. BUT I DUNNO -- IN TERMS OF PAINTING, I HAVE NO IDEA IF OUR PAINTED STUFF WOULD GEL; OUR PAINTED STYLES SEEM RADICALLY DIFFERENT.
NOT THAT I'M AGAINST THE IDEA, I'M JUST NOT SURE HOW IT WOULD WORK ON ITS OWN WITHOUT A STRUCTURAL DEVICE (SAY, LIKE AN ALTERNATING POV OR SOMETHING) TO MODERATE THE SHIFT IN STYLES.
YOUR INKS ARE AWESOME, BUT IT'S KINDA A WASTE TO HAVE YOU JUST INK? PLUS I'D LOVE TO HOG SOME PAINTINGS ALONG WITH YOU TOO... SO HOW ABOUT THIS: INSTEAD OF ONE GUY PENCILS, ONE INKS, WE BOTH DO A LITTLE BIT OF BOTH... SOME COMBO WHERE IT'S ALL MIXED UP?
SUPPOSED TO BE PIT BULL
HMMM... I THINK YOU MAY BE ON TO SOMETHING, MAN--SOMEHOW "LAYERING" THE WORK MAY BE THE WAY TO GO; EACH OF US ADDING NOT ONE OR TWO BUT SEVERAL LAYERS TO THE FINAL PAGE. FOR EXAMPLE, PENCILS AND INKS COULD BE SEEN AS "VERTICAL" LAYERS OF WORK...
...YET SEEN THROUGH ON EACH PAGE OF THE FINISHED PIECE, A KIND OF AN INTENSITY, WHEREAS A STRUCTURAL DEVICE LIKE AN ALTERNATING P.O.V. COULD BE SEEN AS "HORIZONTAL" (TEMPORAL, LINEAR) IN THAT IT PLAYS OUT OVER THE LENGTH OF THE WORK, AND ISN'T NECESSARILY PRESENT IN EVERY PAGE-INSTANCE.
COOL.
PAINT BRUSH
I ALSO THINK IT WOULD BE WISE TO SIMPLY WAIT AND SEE WHAT NEIL WRITES --

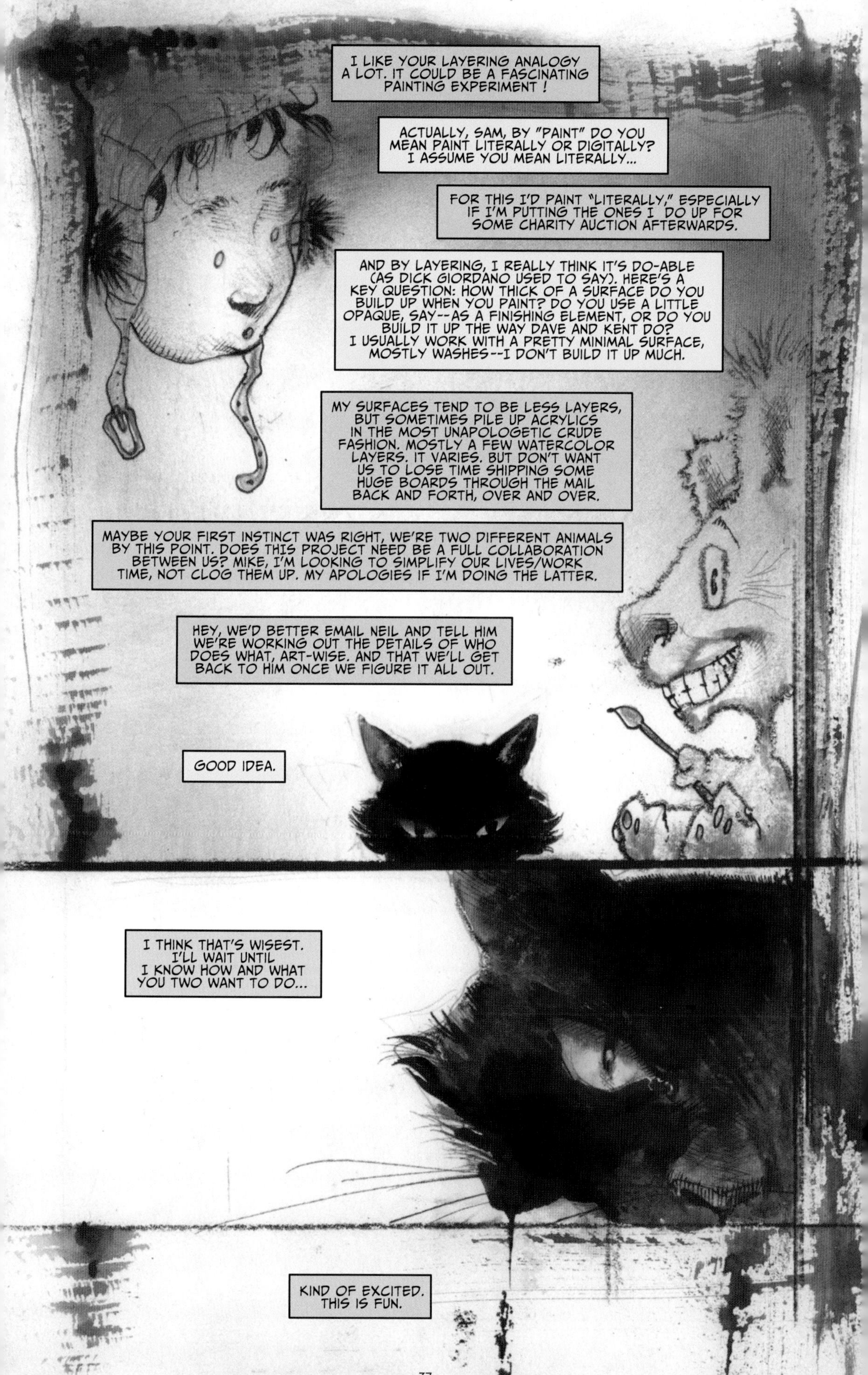
I LIKE YOUR LAYERING ANALOGY A LOT. IT COULD BE A FASCINATING PAINTING EXPERIMENT !
ACTUALLY, SAM, BY "PAINT" DO YOU MEAN PAINT LITERALLY OR DIGITALLY? I ASSUME YOU MEAN LITERALLY...
FOR THIS I'D PAINT "LITERALLY," ESPECIALLY IF I'M PUTTING THE ONES I DO UP FOR SOME CHARITY AUCTION AFTERWARDS.
AND BY LAYERING, I REALLY THINK IT'S DO-ABLE (AS DICK GIORDANO USED TO SAY). HERE'S A KEY QUESTION: HOW THICK OF A SURFACE DO YOU BUILD UP WHEN YOU PAINT? DO YOU USE A LITTLE OPAQUE, SAY--AS A FINISHING ELEMENT, OR DO YOU BUILD IT UP THE WAY DAVE AND KENT DO? I USUALLY WORK WITH A PRETTY MINIMAL SURFACE, MOSTLY WASHES--I DON'T BUILD IT UP MUCH.
MY SURFACES TEND TO BE LESS LAYERS, BUT SOMETIMES PILE UP ACRYLICS IN THE MOST UNAPOLOGETIC CRUDE FASHION. MOSTLY A FEW WATERCOLOR LAYERS. IT VARIES. BUT DON'T WANT US TO LOSE TIME SHIPPING SOME HUGE BOARDS THROUGH THE MAIL BACK AND FORTH, OVER AND OVER.
MAYBE YOUR FIRST INSTINCT WAS RIGHT, WE'RE TWO DIFFERENT ANIMALS BY THIS POINT. DOES THIS PROJECT NEED BE A FULL COLLABORATION BETWEEN US? MIKE, I'M LOOKING TO SIMPLIFY OUR LIVES/WORK TIME, NOT CLOG THEM UP. MY APOLOGIES IF I'M DOING THE LATTER.
HEY, WE'D BETTER EMAIL NEIL AND TELL HIM WE'RE WORKING OUT THE DETAILS OF WHO DOES WHAT, ART-WISE. AND THAT WE'LL GET BACK TO HIM ONCE WE FIGURE IT ALL OUT.
GOOD IDEA.
I THINK THAT'S WISEST. I'LL WAIT UNTIL I KNOW HOW AND WHAT YOU TWO WANT TO DO...
KIND OF EXCITED. THIS IS FUN.

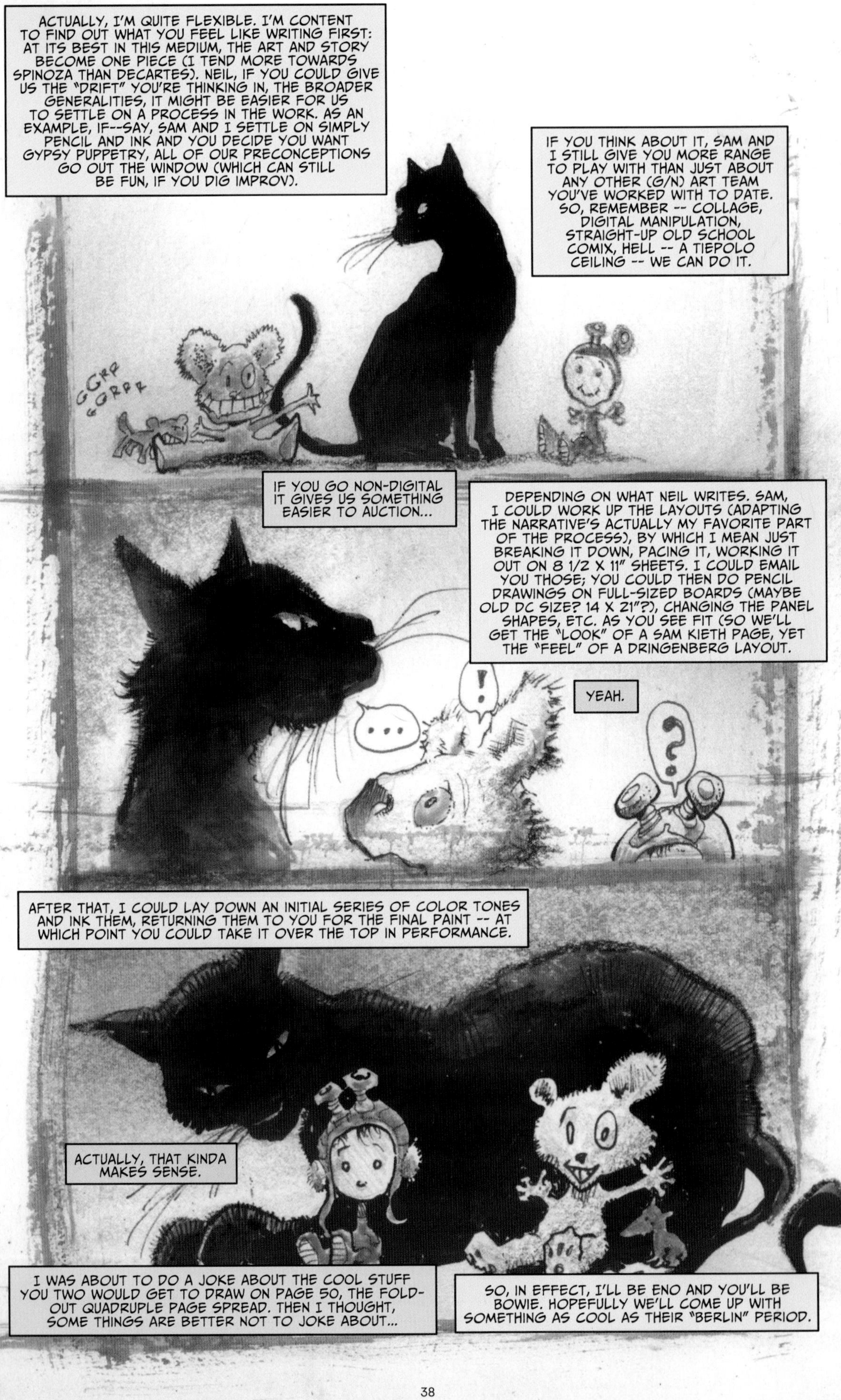
ACTUALLY, I'M QUITE FLEXIBLE. I'M CONTENT TO FIND OUT WHAT YOU FEEL LIKE WRITING FIRST: AT ITS BEST IN THIS MEDIUM, THE ART AND STORY BECOME ONE PIECE (I TEND MORE TOWARDS SPINOZA THAN DECARTES). NEIL, IF YOU COULD GIVE US THE "DRIFT" YOU'RE THINKING IN, THE BROADER GENERALITIES, IT MIGHT BE EASIER FOR US TO SETTLE ON A PROCESS IN THE WORK. AS AN EXAMPLE, IF--SAY, SAM AND I SETTLE ON SIMPLY PENCIL AND INK AND YOU DECIDE YOU WANT GYPSY PUPPETRY, ALL OF OUR PRECONCEPTIONS GO OUT THE WINDOW (WHICH CAN STILL BE FUN, IF YOU DIG IMPROV).
IF YOU THINK ABOUT IT, SAM AND I STILL GIVE YOU MORE RANGE TO PLAY WITH THAN JUST ABOUT ANY OTHER (G/N) ART TEAM YOU'VE WORKED WITH TO DATE. SO, REMEMBER -- COLLAGE, DIGITAL MANIPULATION, STRAIGHT-UP OLD SCHOOL COMIX, HELL -- A TIEPOLO CEILING -- WE CAN DO IT.
GGRR GGRRR
IF YOU GO NON-DIGITAL IT GIVES US SOMETHING EASIER TO AUCTION...
DEPENDING ON WHAT NEIL WRITES. SAM, I COULD WORK UP THE LAYOUTS (ADAPTING THE NARRATIVE'S ACTUALLY MY FAVORITE PART OF THE PROCESS), BY WHICH I MEAN JUST BREAKING IT DOWN, PACING IT, WORKING IT OUT ON 8 1/2 X 11" SHEETS. I COULD EMAIL YOU THOSE; YOU COULD THEN DO PENCIL DRAWINGS ON FULL-SIZED BOARDS (MAYBE OLD DC SIZE? 14 X 21"?), CHANGING THE PANEL SHAPES, ETC. AS YOU SEE FIT (SO WE'LL GET THE "LOOK" OF A SAM KIETH PAGE, YET THE "FEEL" OF A DRINGENBERG LAYOUT.
...
!
YEAH.
?
AFTER THAT, I COULD LAY DOWN AN INITIAL SERIES OF COLOR TONES AND INK THEM, RETURNING THEM TO YOU FOR THE FINAL PAINT -- AT WHICH POINT YOU COULD TAKE IT OVER THE TOP IN PERFORMANCE.
ACTUALLY, THAT KINDA MAKES SENSE.
I WAS ABOUT TO DO A JOKE ABOUT THE COOL STUFF YOU TWO WOULD GET TO DRAW ON PAGE 50, THE FOLD-OUT QUADRUPLE PAGE SPREAD. THEN I THOUGHT, SOME THINGS ARE BETTER NOT TO JOKE ABOUT...
SO, IN EFFECT, I'LL BE ENO AND YOU'LL BE BOWIE. HOPEFULLY WE'LL COME UP WITH SOMETHING AS COOL AS THEIR "BERLIN" PERIOD.

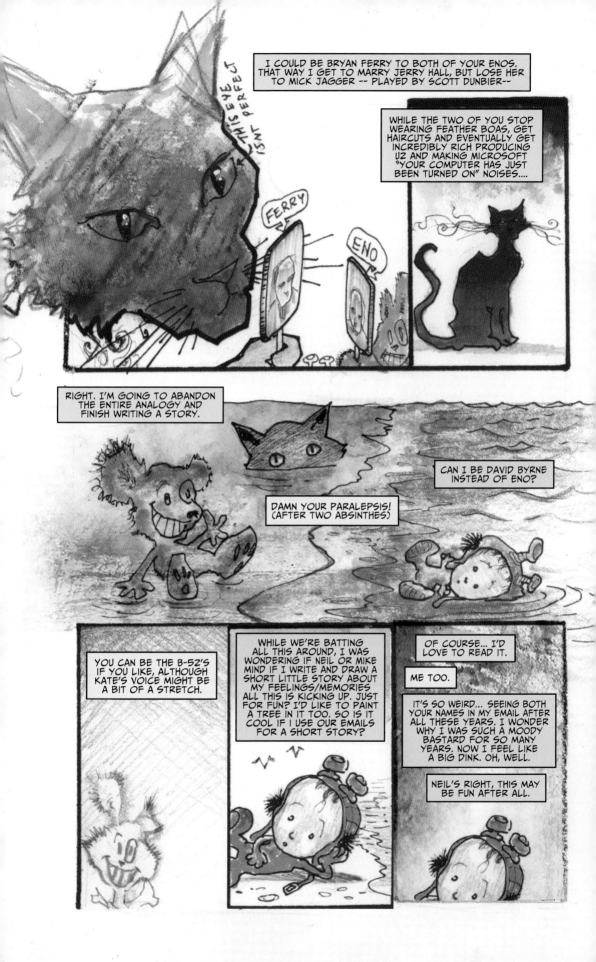

I COULD BE BRYAN FERRY TO BOTH OF YOUR ENOS. THAT WAY I GET TO MARRY JERRY HALL, BUT LOSE HER TO MICK JAGGER -- PLAYED BY SCOTT DUNBIER--

WHILE THE TWO OF YOU STOP WEARING FEATHER BOAS, GET HAIRCUTS AND EVENTUALLY GET INCREDIBLY RICH PRODUCING U2 AND MAKING MICROSOFT "YOUR COMPUTER HAS JUST BEEN TURNED ON" NOISES....

THIS EYE ISN'T PERFECT

FERRY

ENO

RIGHT. I'M GOING TO ABANDON THE ENTIRE ANALOGY AND FINISH WRITING A STORY.

CAN I BE DAVID BYRNE INSTEAD OF ENO?

DAMN YOUR PARALEPSIS! (AFTER TWO ABSINTHES)

YOU CAN BE THE B-52'S IF YOU LIKE, ALTHOUGH KATE'S VOICE MIGHT BE A BIT OF A STRETCH.

WHILE WE'RE BATTING ALL THIS AROUND, I WAS WONDERING IF NEIL OR MIKE MIND IF I WRITE AND DRAW A SHORT LITTLE STORY ABOUT MY FEELINGS/MEMORIES ALL THIS IS KICKING UP. JUST FOR FUN? I'D LIKE TO PAINT A TREE IN IT TOO. SO IS IT COOL IF I USE OUR EMAILS FOR A SHORT STORY?

OF COURSE... I'D LOVE TO READ IT.

ME TOO.

IT'S SO WEIRD... SEEING BOTH YOUR NAMES IN MY EMAIL AFTER ALL THESE YEARS. I WONDER WHY I WAS SUCH A MOODY BASTARD FOR SO MANY YEARS. NOW I FEEL LIKE A BIG DINK. OH, WELL.

NEIL'S RIGHT, THIS MAY BE FUN AFTER ALL.

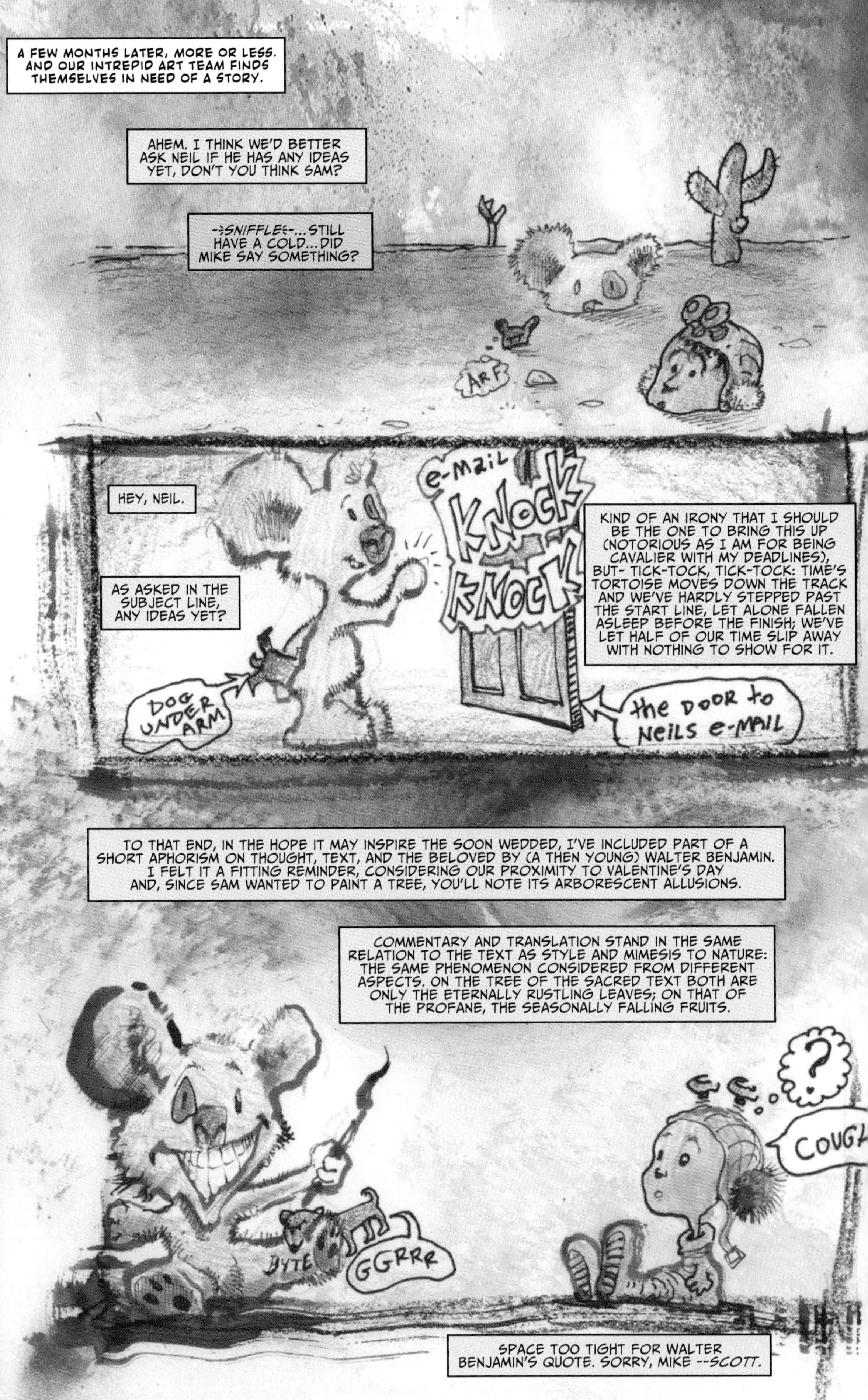

A FEW MONTHS LATER, MORE OR LESS. AND OUR INTREPID ART TEAM FINDS THEMSELVES IN NEED OF A STORY.
AHEM. I THINK WE'D BETTER ASK NEIL IF HE HAS ANY IDEAS YET, DON'T YOU THINK SAM?
-SNIFFLE-...STILL HAVE A COLD...DID MIKE SAY SOMETHING?
ARF
HEY, NEIL.
AS ASKED IN THE SUBJECT LINE, ANY IDEAS YET?
e-MAIL
KNOCK KNOCK
KIND OF AN IRONY THAT I SHOULD BE THE ONE TO BRING THIS UP (NOTORIOUS AS I AM FOR BEING CAVALIER WITH MY DEADLINES), BUT- TICK-TOCK, TICK-TOCK: TIME'S TORTOISE MOVES DOWN THE TRACK AND WE'VE HARDLY STEPPED PAST THE START LINE, LET ALONE FALLEN ASLEEP BEFORE THE FINISH; WE'VE LET HALF OF OUR TIME SLIP AWAY WITH NOTHING TO SHOW FOR IT.
DOG UNDER ARM
the DOOR to NEILS e-MAIL
TO THAT END, IN THE HOPE IT MAY INSPIRE THE SOON WEDDED, I'VE INCLUDED PART OF A SHORT APHORISM ON THOUGHT, TEXT, AND THE BELOVED BY (A THEN YOUNG) WALTER BENJAMIN. I FELT IT A FITTING REMINDER, CONSIDERING OUR PROXIMITY TO VALENTINE'S DAY AND, SINCE SAM WANTED TO PAINT A TREE, YOU'LL NOTE ITS ARBORESCENT ALLUSIONS.
COMMENTARY AND TRANSLATION STAND IN THE SAME RELATION TO THE TEXT AS STYLE AND MIMESIS TO NATURE: THE SAME PHENOMENON CONSIDERED FROM DIFFERENT ASPECTS. ON THE TREE OF THE SACRED TEXT BOTH ARE ONLY THE ETERNALLY RUSTLING LEAVES; ON THAT OF THE PROFANE, THE SEASONALLY FALLING FRUITS.
?
COUG
BYTE
GGRRR
SPACE TOO TIGHT FOR WALTER BENJAMIN'S QUOTE. SORRY, MIKE --SCOTT.

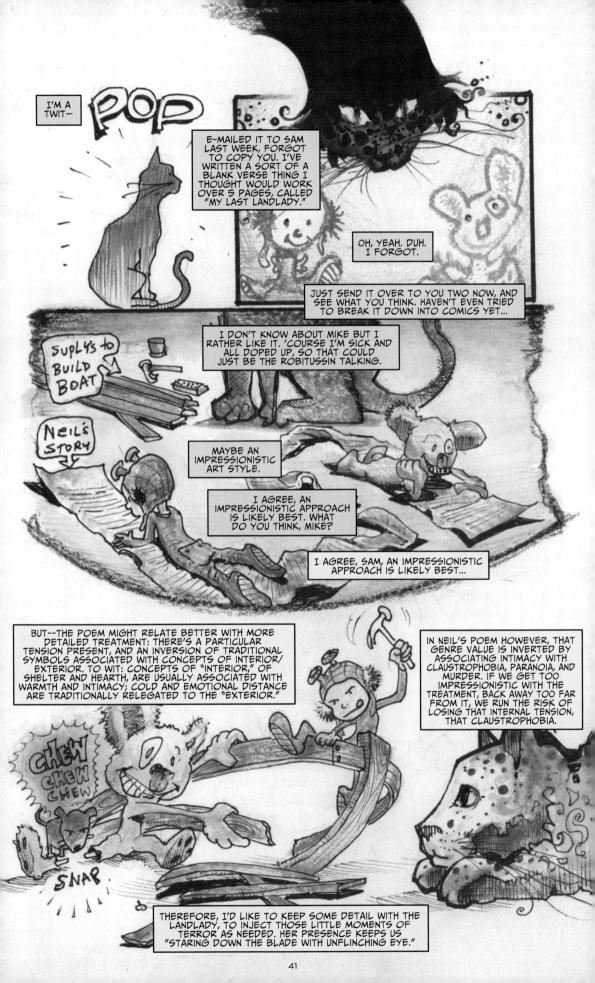

I'M A TWIT—

POP

E-MAILED IT TO SAM LAST WEEK, FORGOT TO COPY YOU. I'VE WRITTEN A SORT OF A BLANK VERSE THING I THOUGHT WOULD WORK OVER 5 PAGES, CALLED "MY LAST LANDLADY."

OH, YEAH. DUH. I FORGOT.

JUST SEND IT OVER TO YOU TWO NOW, AND SEE WHAT YOU THINK. HAVEN'T EVEN TRIED TO BREAK IT DOWN INTO COMICS YET...

I DON'T KNOW ABOUT MIKE BUT I RATHER LIKE IT. 'COURSE I'M SICK AND ALL DOPED UP, SO THAT COULD JUST BE THE ROBITUSSIN TALKING.

SUPLY's to BUILD BOAT

NEIL'S STORY

MAYBE AN IMPRESSIONISTIC ART STYLE.

I AGREE, AN IMPRESSIONISTIC APPROACH IS LIKELY BEST. WHAT DO YOU THINK, MIKE?

I AGREE, SAM, AN IMPRESSIONISTIC APPROACH IS LIKELY BEST...

BUT--THE POEM MIGHT RELATE BETTER WITH MORE DETAILED TREATMENT: THERE'S A PARTICULAR TENSION PRESENT, AND AN INVERSION OF TRADITIONAL SYMBOLS ASSOCIATED WITH CONCEPTS OF INTERIOR/EXTERIOR. TO WIT: CONCEPTS OF "INTERIOR," OF SHELTER AND HEARTH, ARE USUALLY ASSOCIATED WITH WARMTH AND INTIMACY; COLD AND EMOTIONAL DISTANCE ARE TRADITIONALLY RELEGATED TO THE "EXTERIOR."

IN NEIL'S POEM HOWEVER, THAT GENRE VALUE IS INVERTED BY ASSOCIATING INTIMACY WITH CLAUSTROPHOBIA, PARANOIA, AND MURDER. IF WE GET TOO IMPRESSIONISTIC WITH THE TREATMENT, BACK AWAY TOO FAR FROM IT, WE RUN THE RISK OF LOSING THAT INTERNAL TENSION, THAT CLAUSTROPHOBIA.

CHEW CHEW CHEW

SNAP

THEREFORE, I'D LIKE TO KEEP SOME DETAIL WITH THE LANDLADY, TO INJECT THOSE LITTLE MOMENTS OF TERROR AS NEEDED. HER PRESENCE KEEPS US "STARING DOWN THE BLADE WITH UNFLINCHING EYE."

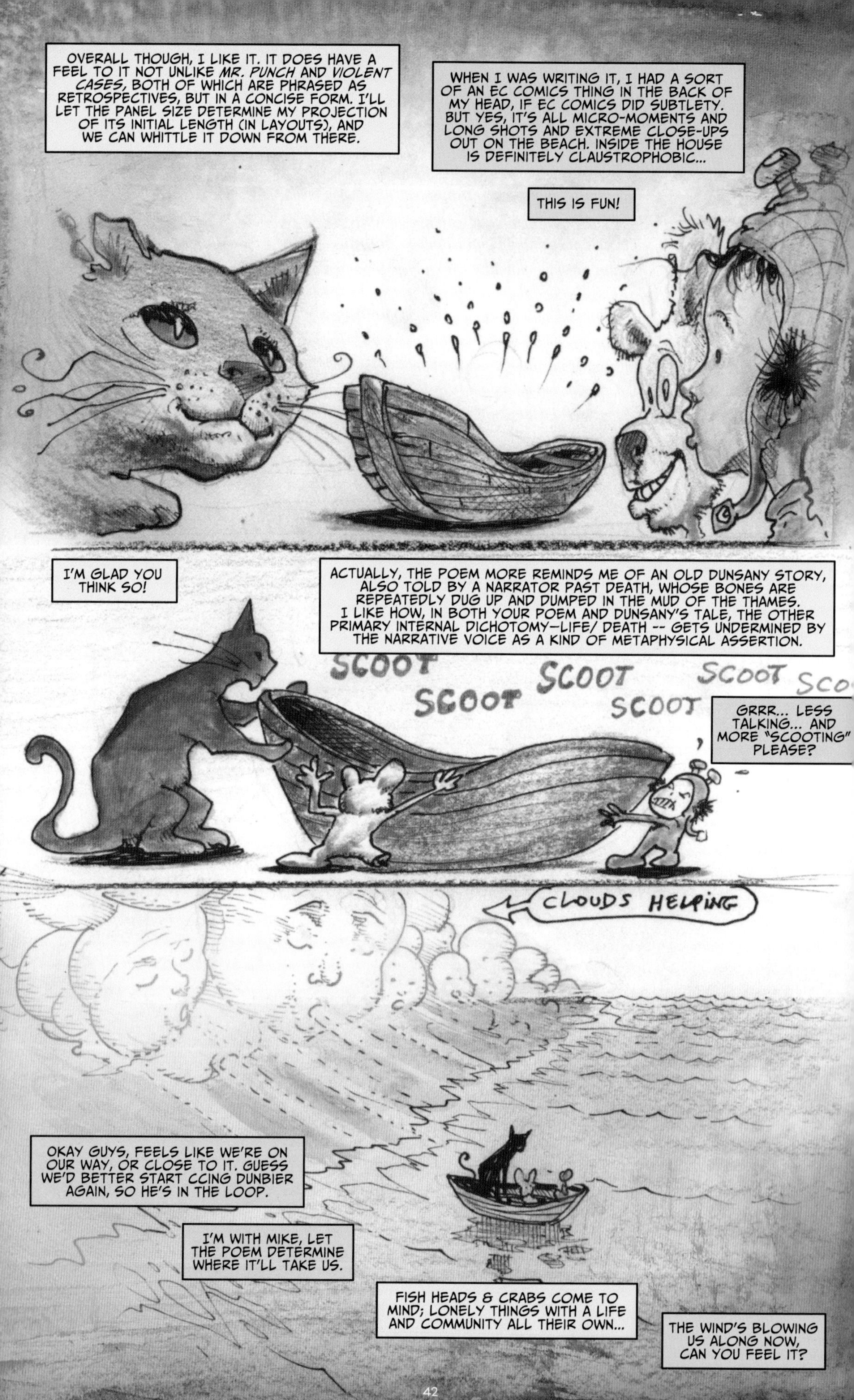
OVERALL THOUGH, I LIKE IT. IT DOES HAVE A FEEL TO IT NOT UNLIKE *MR. PUNCH* AND *VIOLENT CASES*, BOTH OF WHICH ARE PHRASED AS RETROSPECTIVES, BUT IN A CONCISE FORM. I'LL LET THE PANEL SIZE DETERMINE MY PROJECTION OF ITS INITIAL LENGTH (IN LAYOUTS), AND WE CAN WHITTLE IT DOWN FROM THERE.
WHEN I WAS WRITING IT, I HAD A SORT OF AN EC COMICS THING IN THE BACK OF MY HEAD, IF EC COMICS DID SUBTLETY. BUT YES, IT'S ALL MICRO-MOMENTS AND LONG SHOTS AND EXTREME CLOSE-UPS OUT ON THE BEACH. INSIDE THE HOUSE IS DEFINITELY CLAUSTROPHOBIC...
THIS IS FUN!
I'M GLAD YOU THINK SO!
ACTUALLY, THE POEM MORE REMINDS ME OF AN OLD DUNSANY STORY, ALSO TOLD BY A NARRATOR PAST DEATH, WHOSE BONES ARE REPEATEDLY DUG UP AND DUMPED IN THE MUD OF THE THAMES. I LIKE HOW, IN BOTH YOUR POEM AND DUNSANY'S TALE, THE OTHER PRIMARY INTERNAL DICHOTOMY—LIFE/ DEATH -- GETS UNDERMINED BY THE NARRATIVE VOICE AS A KIND OF METAPHYSICAL ASSERTION.
SCOOT
SCOOT
SCOOT
SCOOT
SCOOT
GRRR... LESS TALKING... AND MORE "SCOOTING" PLEASE?
CLOUDS HELPING
OKAY GUYS, FEELS LIKE WE'RE ON OUR WAY, OR CLOSE TO IT. GUESS WE'D BETTER START CCING DUNBIER AGAIN, SO HE'S IN THE LOOP.
I'M WITH MIKE, LET THE POEM DETERMINE WHERE IT'LL TAKE US.
FISH HEADS & CRABS COME TO MIND; LONELY THINGS WITH A LIFE AND COMMUNITY ALL THEIR OWN...
THE WIND'S BLOWING US ALONG NOW, CAN YOU FEEL IT?

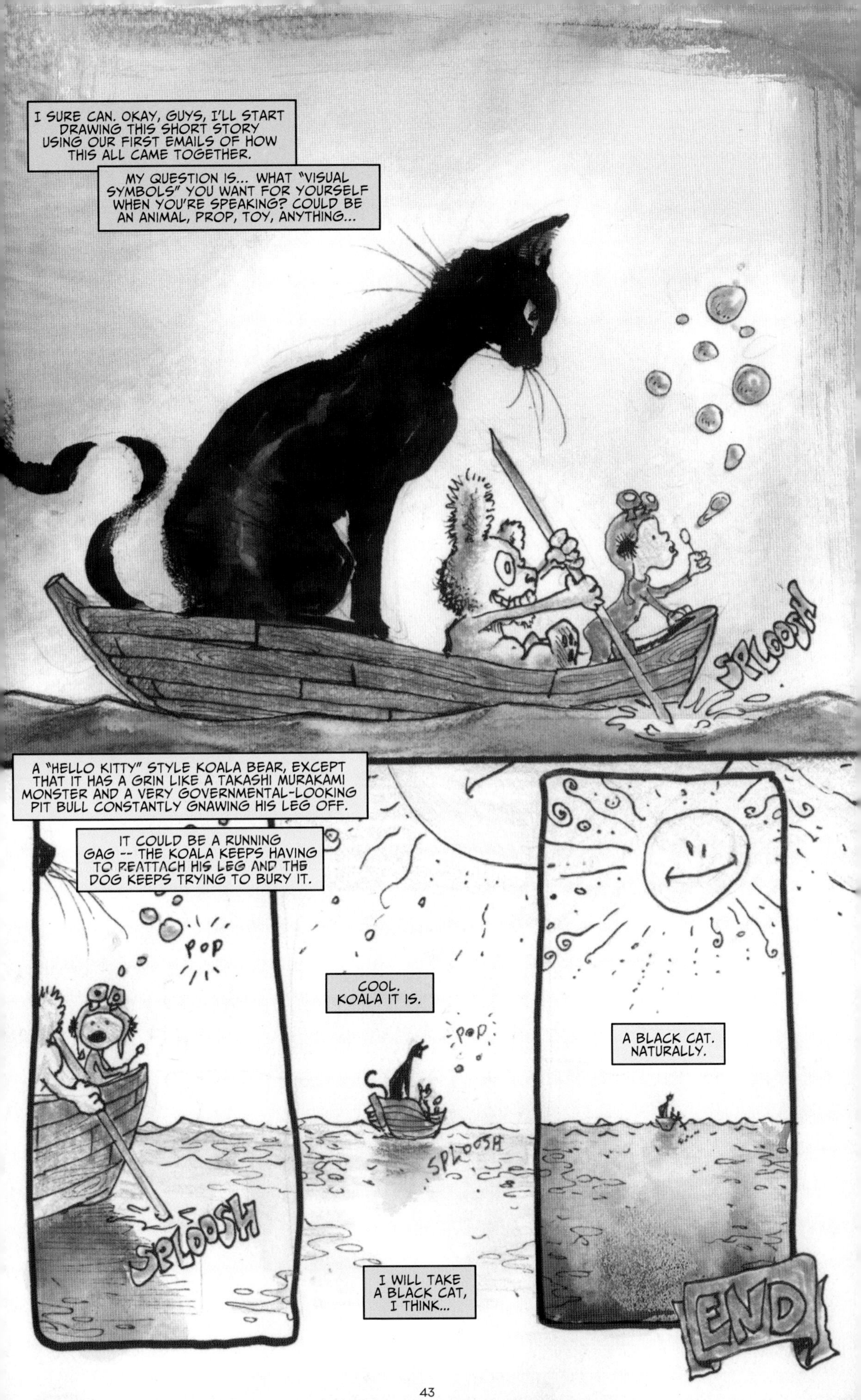

I SURE CAN. OKAY, GUYS, I'LL START DRAWING THIS SHORT STORY USING OUR FIRST EMAILS OF HOW THIS ALL CAME TOGETHER.
MY QUESTION IS... WHAT "VISUAL SYMBOLS" YOU WANT FOR YOURSELF WHEN YOU'RE SPEAKING? COULD BE AN ANIMAL, PROP, TOY, ANYTHING...
SPLOOSH
A "HELLO KITTY" STYLE KOALA BEAR, EXCEPT THAT IT HAS A GRIN LIKE A TAKASHI MURAKAMI MONSTER AND A VERY GOVERNMENTAL-LOOKING PIT BULL CONSTANTLY GNAWING HIS LEG OFF.
IT COULD BE A RUNNING GAG -- THE KOALA KEEPS HAVING TO REATTACH HIS LEG AND THE DOG KEEPS TRYING TO BURY IT.
POP
SPLOOSH
COOL. KOALA IT IS.
POP
SPLOOSH
I WILL TAKE A BLACK CAT, I THINK...
A BLACK CAT. NATURALLY.
END

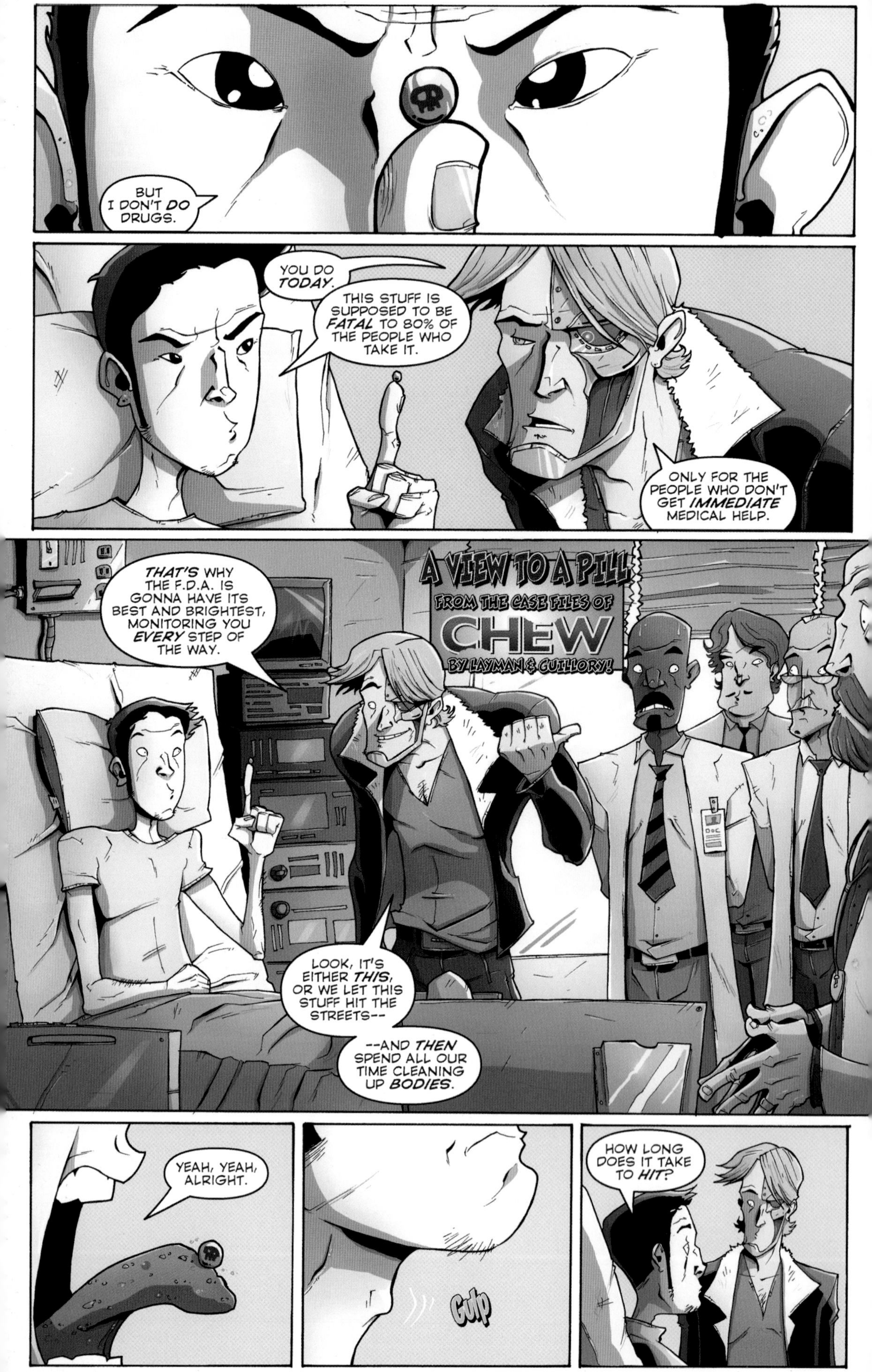
BUT I DON'T DO DRUGS.
YOU DO TODAY.
THIS STUFF IS SUPPOSED TO BE FATAL TO 80% OF THE PEOPLE WHO TAKE IT.
ONLY FOR THE PEOPLE WHO DON'T GET IMMEDIATE MEDICAL HELP.
THAT'S WHY THE F.D.A. IS GONNA HAVE ITS BEST AND BRIGHTEST, MONITORING YOU EVERY STEP OF THE WAY.
A VIEW TO A PILL
FROM THE CASE FILES OF
CHEW
BY LAYMAN & GUILLORY!
LOOK, IT'S EITHER THIS, OR WE LET THIS STUFF HIT THE STREETS--
--AND THEN SPEND ALL OUR TIME CLEANING UP BODIES.
YEAH, YEAH, ALRIGHT.
Gulp
HOW LONG DOES IT TAKE TO HIT?

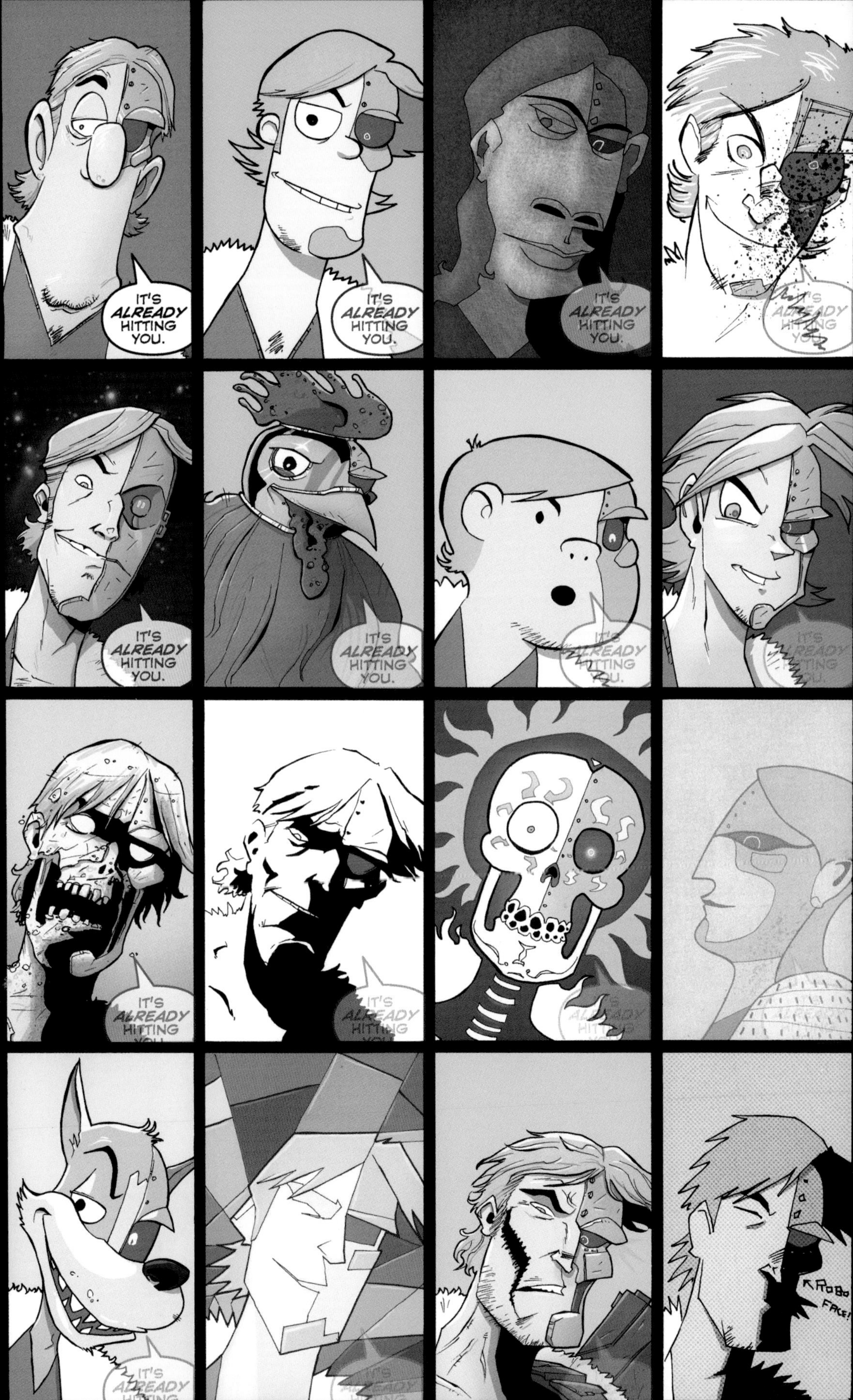
IT'S ALREADY HITTING YOU.
IT'S ALREADY HITTING YOU.
IT'S ALREADY HITTING YOU.
IT'S ALREADY HITTING YOU.
IT'S ALREADY HITTING YOU.
IT'S ALREADY
ROBO FACE!

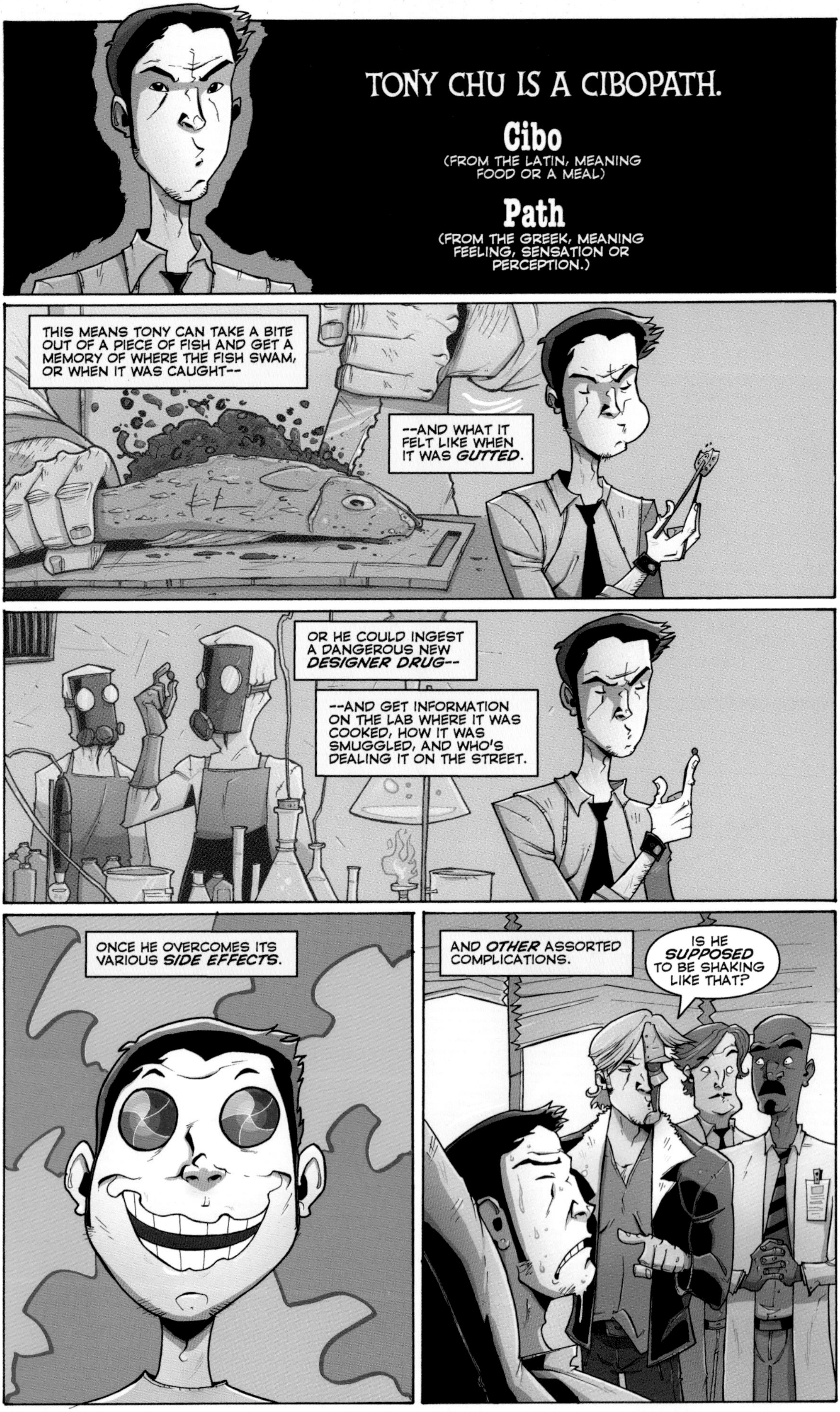
TONY CHU IS A CIBOPATH.
Cibo
(FROM THE LATIN, MEANING FOOD OR A MEAL)
Path
(FROM THE GREEK, MEANING FEELING, SENSATION OR PERCEPTION.)
THIS MEANS TONY CAN TAKE A BITE OUT OF A PIECE OF FISH AND GET A MEMORY OF WHERE THE FISH SWAM, OR WHEN IT WAS CAUGHT--
--AND WHAT IT FELT LIKE WHEN IT WAS GUTTED.
OR HE COULD INGEST A DANGEROUS NEW DESIGNER DRUG--
--AND GET INFORMATION ON THE LAB WHERE IT WAS COOKED, HOW IT WAS SMUGGLED, AND WHO'S DEALING IT ON THE STREET.
ONCE HE OVERCOMES ITS VARIOUS SIDE EFFECTS.
AND OTHER ASSORTED COMPLICATIONS.
IS HE SUPPOSED TO BE SHAKING LIKE THAT?

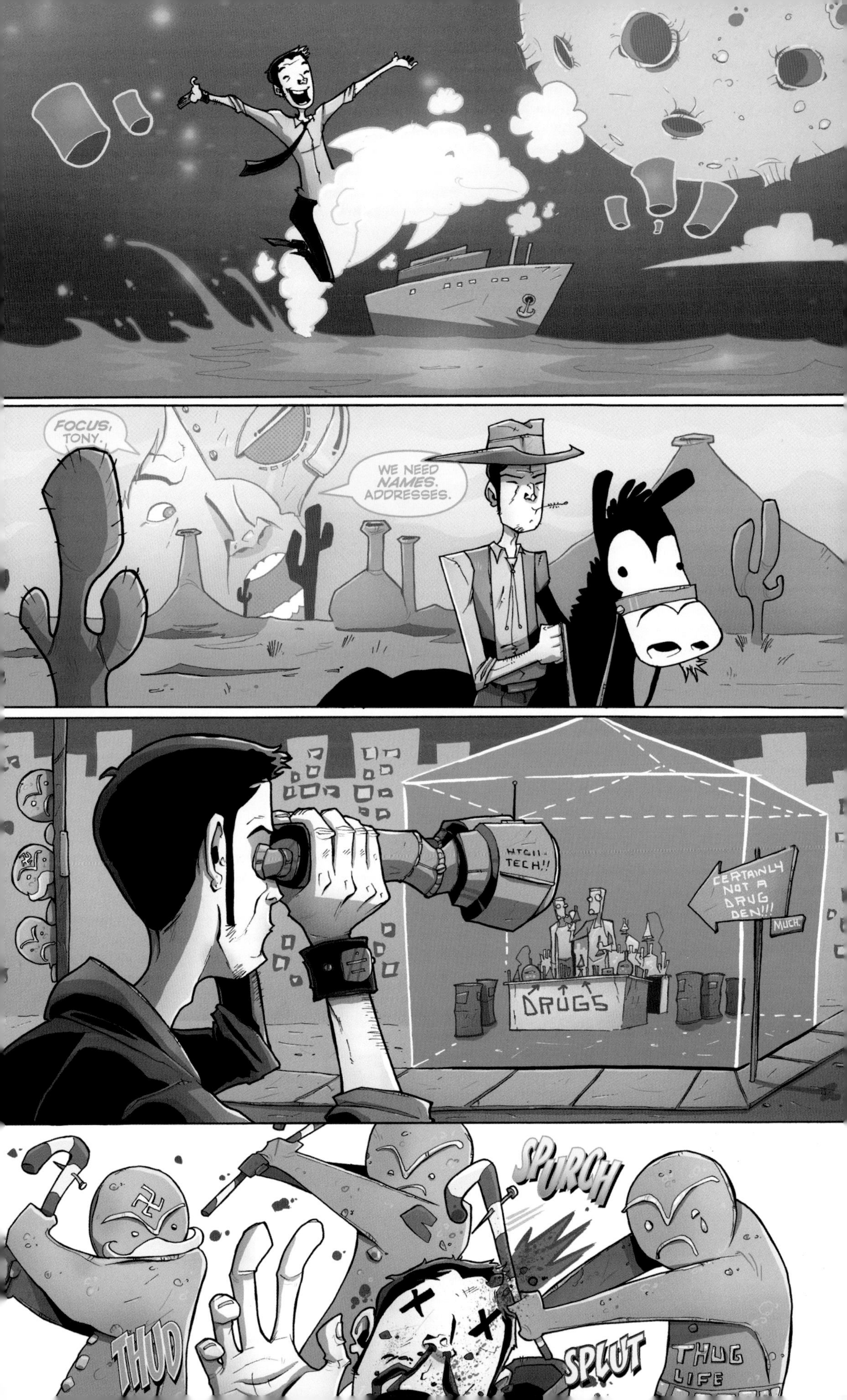
FOCUS, TONY.
WE NEED NAMES. ADDRESSES.
HIGH-TECH!!
CERTAINLY NOT A DRUG DEN!!!
MUCH.
DRUGS
SPURCH
THUD
SPLUT
THUG LIFE

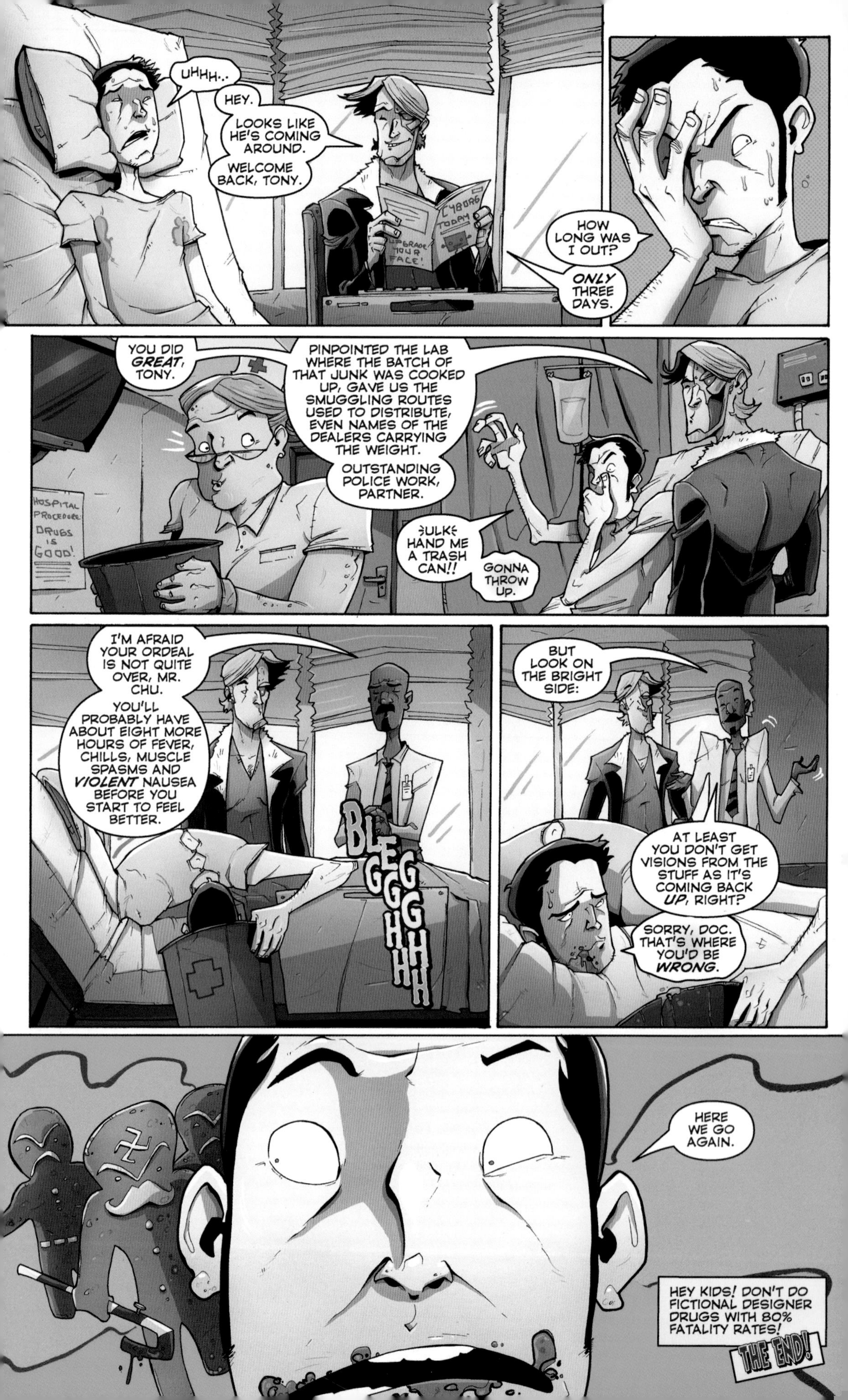
UHHH...
HEY.
LOOKS LIKE HE'S COMING AROUND.
WELCOME BACK, TONY.
CYBORG TODAY
UPGRADE YOUR FACE!
HOW LONG WAS I OUT?
ONLY THREE DAYS.
YOU DID *GREAT*, TONY.
PINPOINTED THE LAB WHERE THE BATCH OF THAT JUNK WAS COOKED UP, GAVE US THE SMUGGLING ROUTES USED TO DISTRIBUTE, EVEN NAMES OF THE DEALERS CARRYING THE WEIGHT.
OUTSTANDING POLICE WORK, PARTNER.
HOSPITAL PROCEDURE: DRUGS IS GOOD!
ULK
HAND ME A TRASH CAN!!
GONNA THROW UP.
I'M AFRAID YOUR ORDEAL IS NOT QUITE OVER, MR. CHU.
YOU'LL PROBABLY HAVE ABOUT EIGHT MORE HOURS OF FEVER, CHILLS, MUSCLE SPASMS AND *VIOLENT* NAUSEA BEFORE YOU START TO FEEL BETTER.
BLEGGGHHHH
BUT LOOK ON THE BRIGHT SIDE:
AT LEAST YOU DON'T GET VISIONS FROM THE STUFF AS IT'S COMING BACK *UP*, RIGHT?
SORRY, DOC. THAT'S WHERE YOU'D BE *WRONG*.
HERE WE GO AGAIN.
HEY KIDS! DON'T DO FICTIONAL DESIGNER DRUGS WITH 80% FATALITY RATES!
THE END!

WESTWOOD · CALIFORNIA · 2259

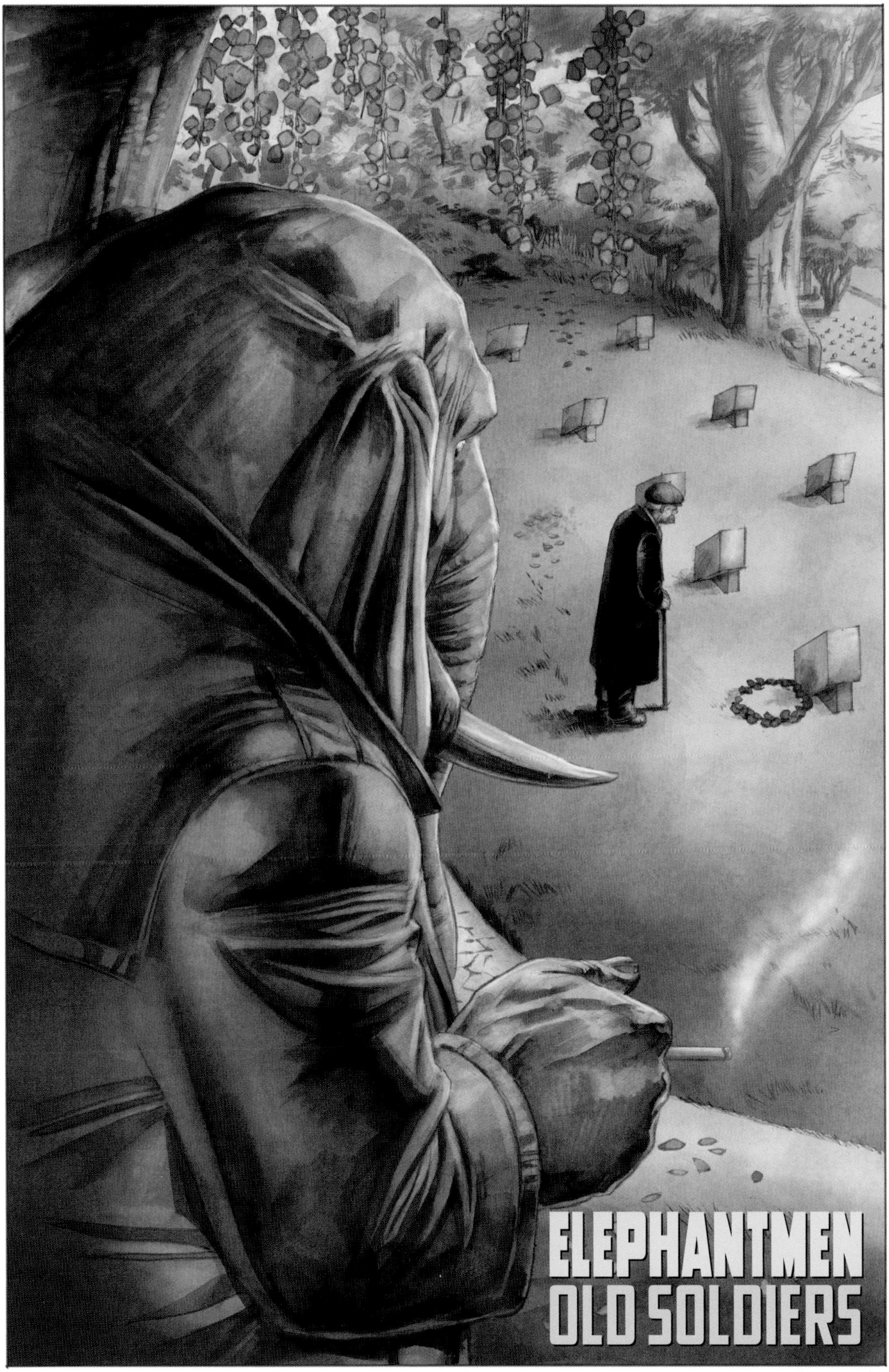
ELEPHANTMEN
OLD SOLDIERS

By Richard Starkings & Dougie Braithwaite with Ulises Arreola

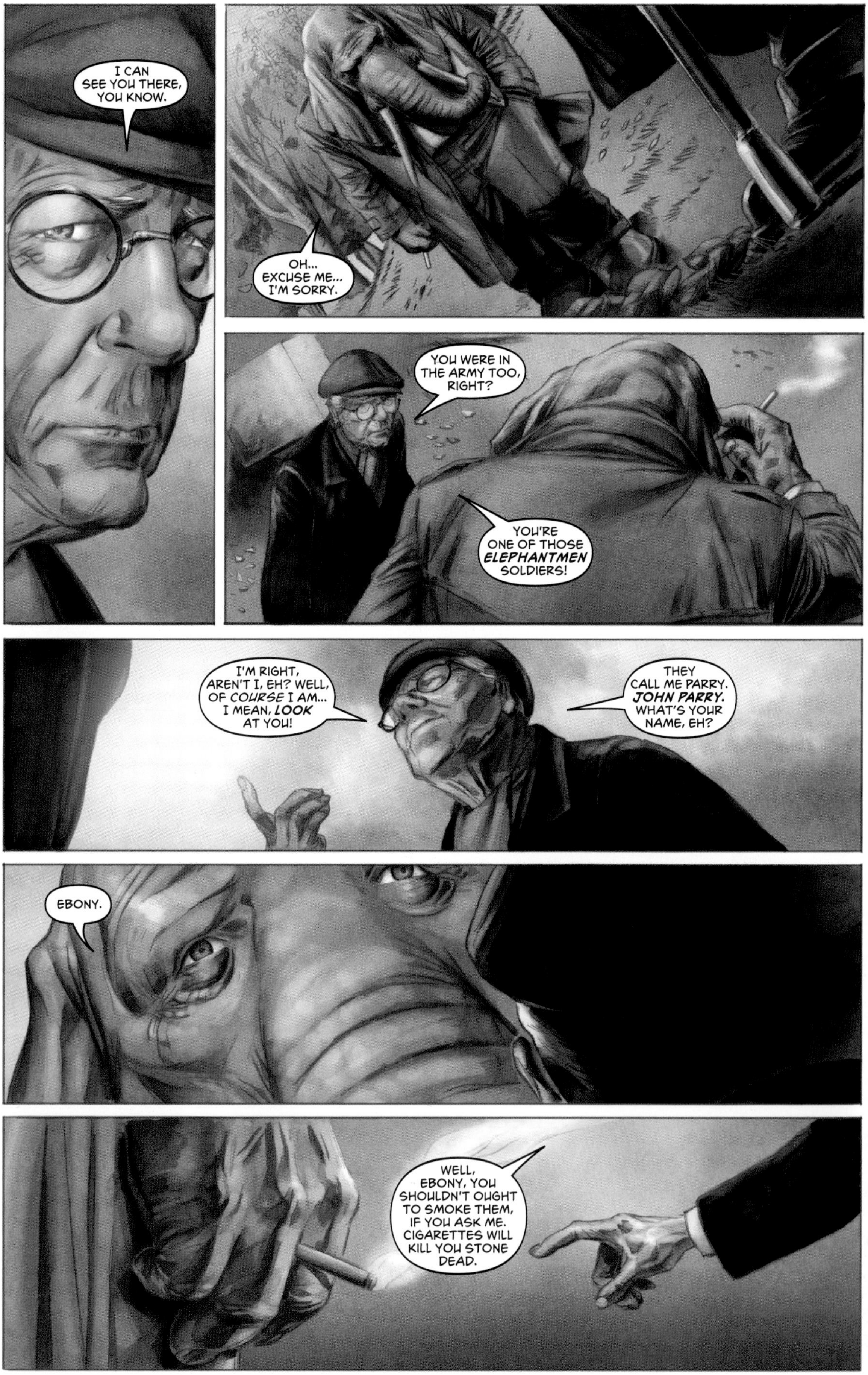
I CAN SEE YOU THERE, YOU KNOW.
OH... EXCUSE ME... I'M SORRY.
YOU WERE IN THE ARMY TOO, RIGHT?
YOU'RE ONE OF THOSE *ELEPHANTMEN* SOLDIERS!
I'M RIGHT, AREN'T I, EH? WELL, OF *COURSE* I AM... I MEAN, *LOOK* AT YOU!
THEY CALL ME PARRY. *JOHN PARRY.* WHAT'S YOUR NAME, EH?
EBONY.
WELL, EBONY, YOU SHOULDN'T OUGHT TO SMOKE THEM, IF YOU ASK ME. CIGARETTES WILL KILL YOU STONE DEAD.

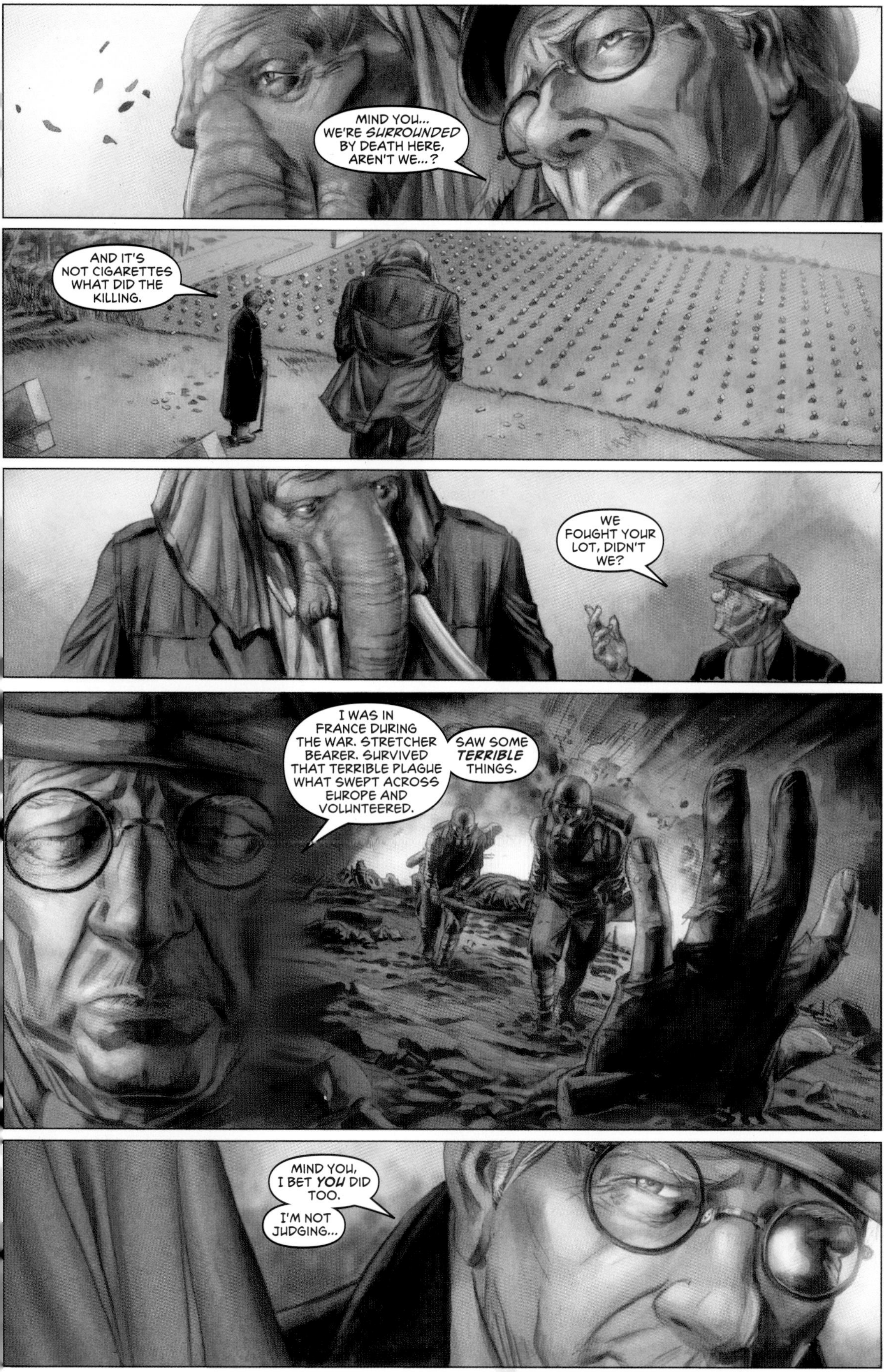
MIND YOU... WE'RE SURROUNDED BY DEATH HERE, AREN'T WE...?
AND IT'S NOT CIGARETTES WHAT DID THE KILLING.
WE FOUGHT YOUR LOT, DIDN'T WE?
I WAS IN FRANCE DURING THE WAR. STRETCHER BEARER. SURVIVED THAT TERRIBLE PLAGUE WHAT SWEPT ACROSS EUROPE AND VOLUNTEERED.
SAW SOME TERRIBLE THINGS.
MIND YOU, I BET YOU DID TOO.
I'M NOT JUDGING...

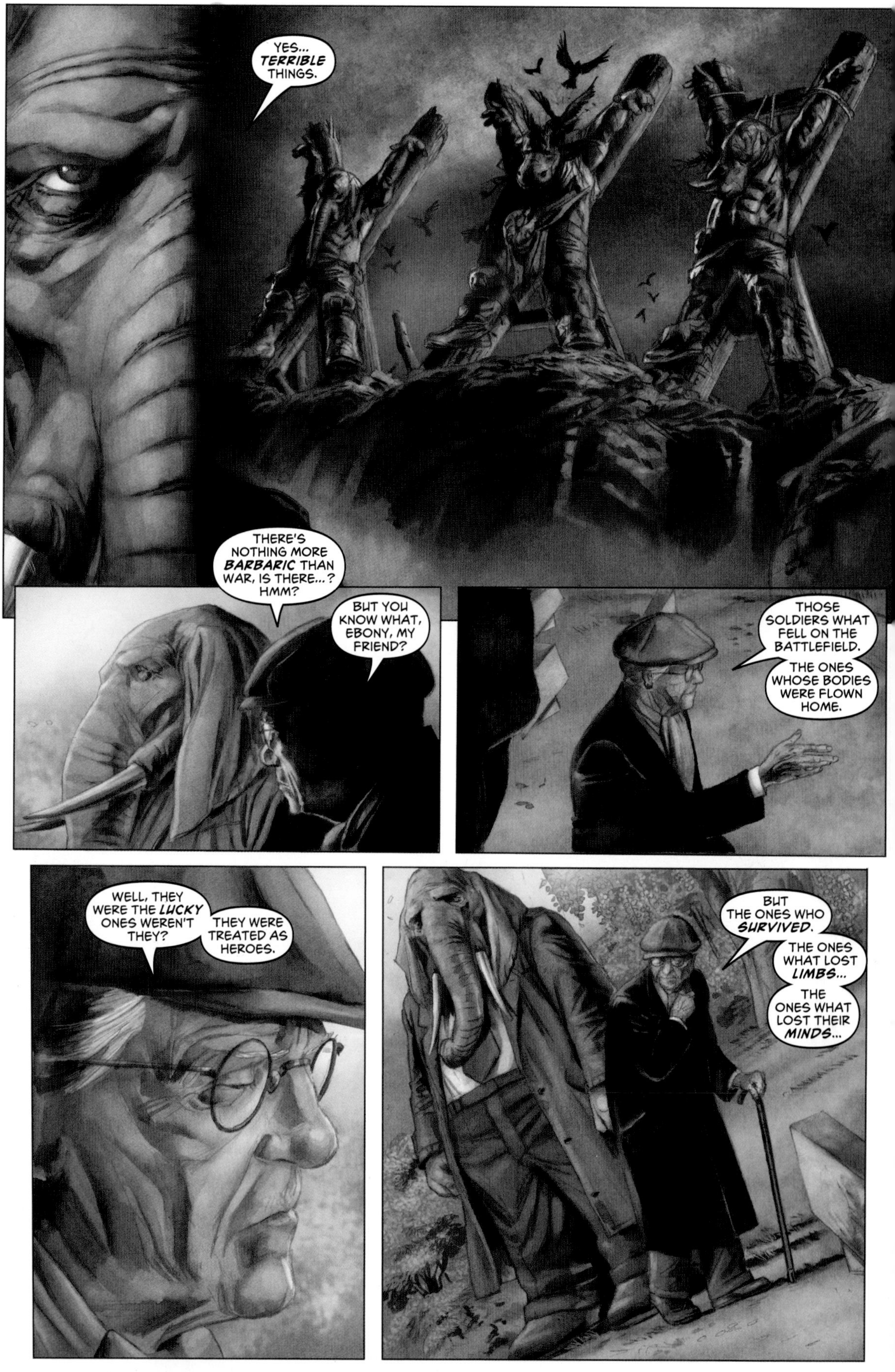
YES... TERRIBLE THINGS.
THERE'S NOTHING MORE BARBARIC THAN WAR, IS THERE...? HMM?
BUT YOU KNOW WHAT, EBONY, MY FRIEND?
THOSE SOLDIERS WHAT FELL ON THE BATTLEFIELD.
THE ONES WHOSE BODIES WERE FLOWN HOME.
WELL, THEY WERE THE LUCKY ONES WEREN'T THEY?
THEY WERE TREATED AS HEROES.
BUT THE ONES WHO SURVIVED.
THE ONES WHAT LOST LIMBS...
THE ONES WHAT LOST THEIR MINDS...

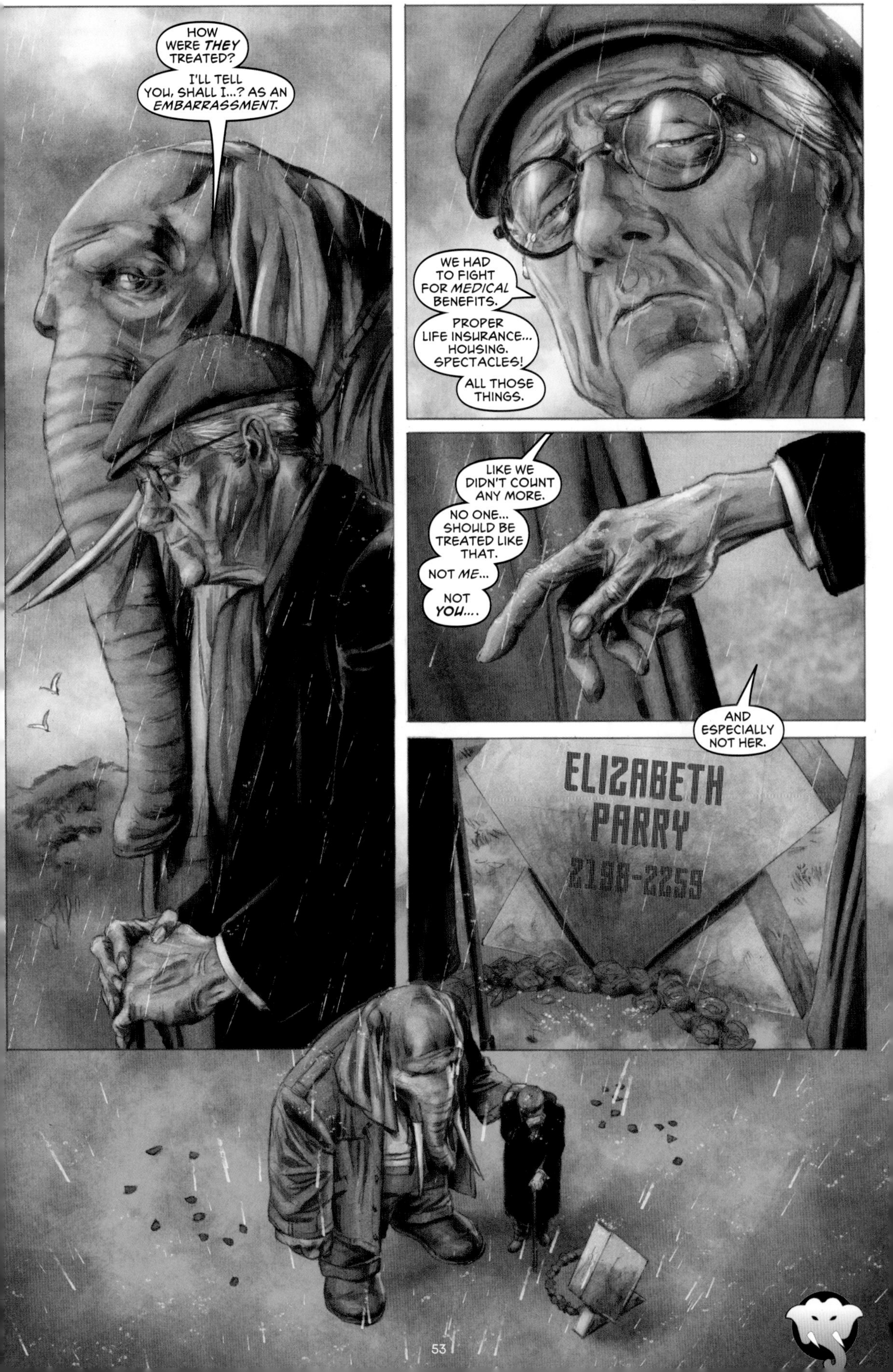
HOW WERE *THEY* TREATED?
I'LL TELL YOU, SHALL I...? AS AN *EMBARRASSMENT*.
WE HAD TO FIGHT FOR *MEDICAL* BENEFITS.
PROPER LIFE INSURANCE... HOUSING. SPECTACLES!
ALL THOSE THINGS.
LIKE WE DIDN'T COUNT ANY MORE.
NO ONE... SHOULD BE TREATED LIKE THAT.
NOT *ME*...
NOT *YOU*....
AND ESPECIALLY NOT HER.
ELIZABETH PARRY
2198-2259

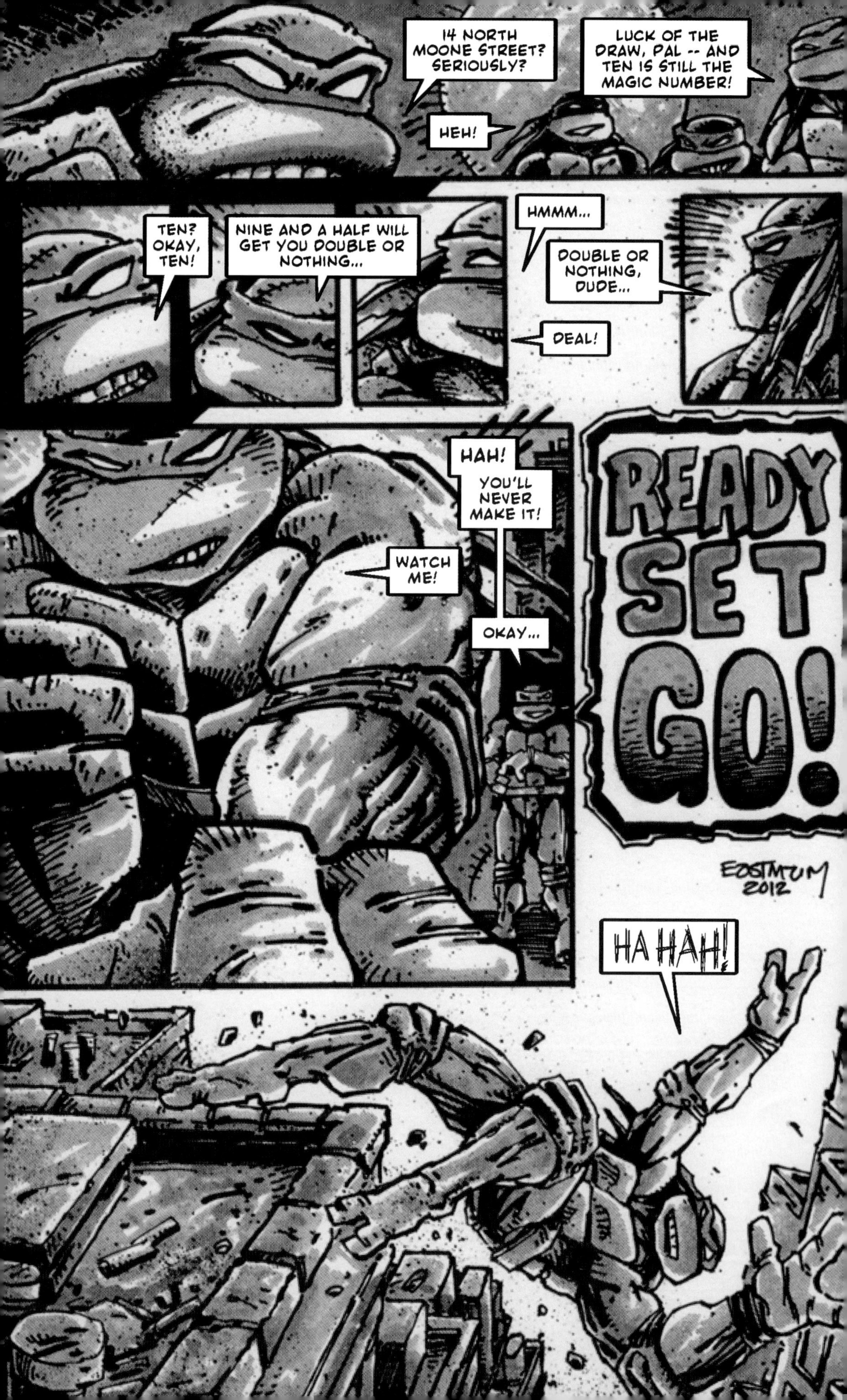

14 NORTH MOONE STREET? SERIOUSLY?
HEH!
LUCK OF THE DRAW, PAL -- AND TEN IS STILL THE MAGIC NUMBER!
TEN? OKAY, TEN!
NINE AND A HALF WILL GET YOU DOUBLE OR NOTHING...
HMMM...
DEAL!
DOUBLE OR NOTHING, DUDE...
HAH!
YOU'LL NEVER MAKE IT!
WATCH ME!
OKAY...
READY SET GO!
EASTMAN 2012
HA HAH!

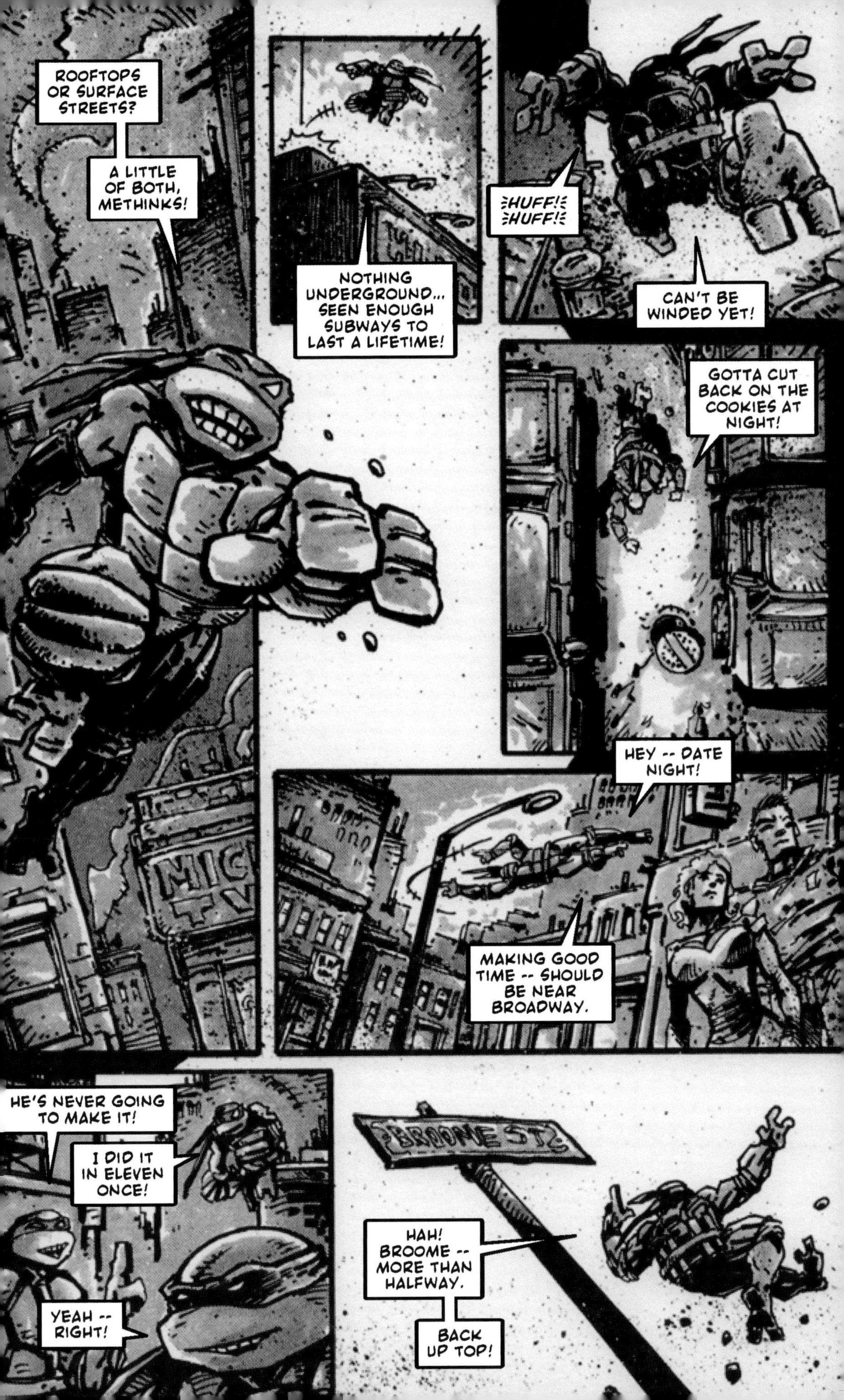
ROOFTOPS OR SURFACE STREETS?
A LITTLE OF BOTH, METHINKS!
NOTHING UNDERGROUND... SEEN ENOUGH SUBWAYS TO LAST A LIFETIME!
HUFF! HUFF!
CAN'T BE WINDED YET!
GOTTA CUT BACK ON THE COOKIES AT NIGHT!
HEY -- DATE NIGHT!
MAKING GOOD TIME -- SHOULD BE NEAR BROADWAY.
HE'S NEVER GOING TO MAKE IT!
I DID IT IN ELEVEN ONCE!
YEAH -- RIGHT!
BROOME ST
HAH! BROOME -- MORE THAN HALFWAY.
BACK UP TOP!

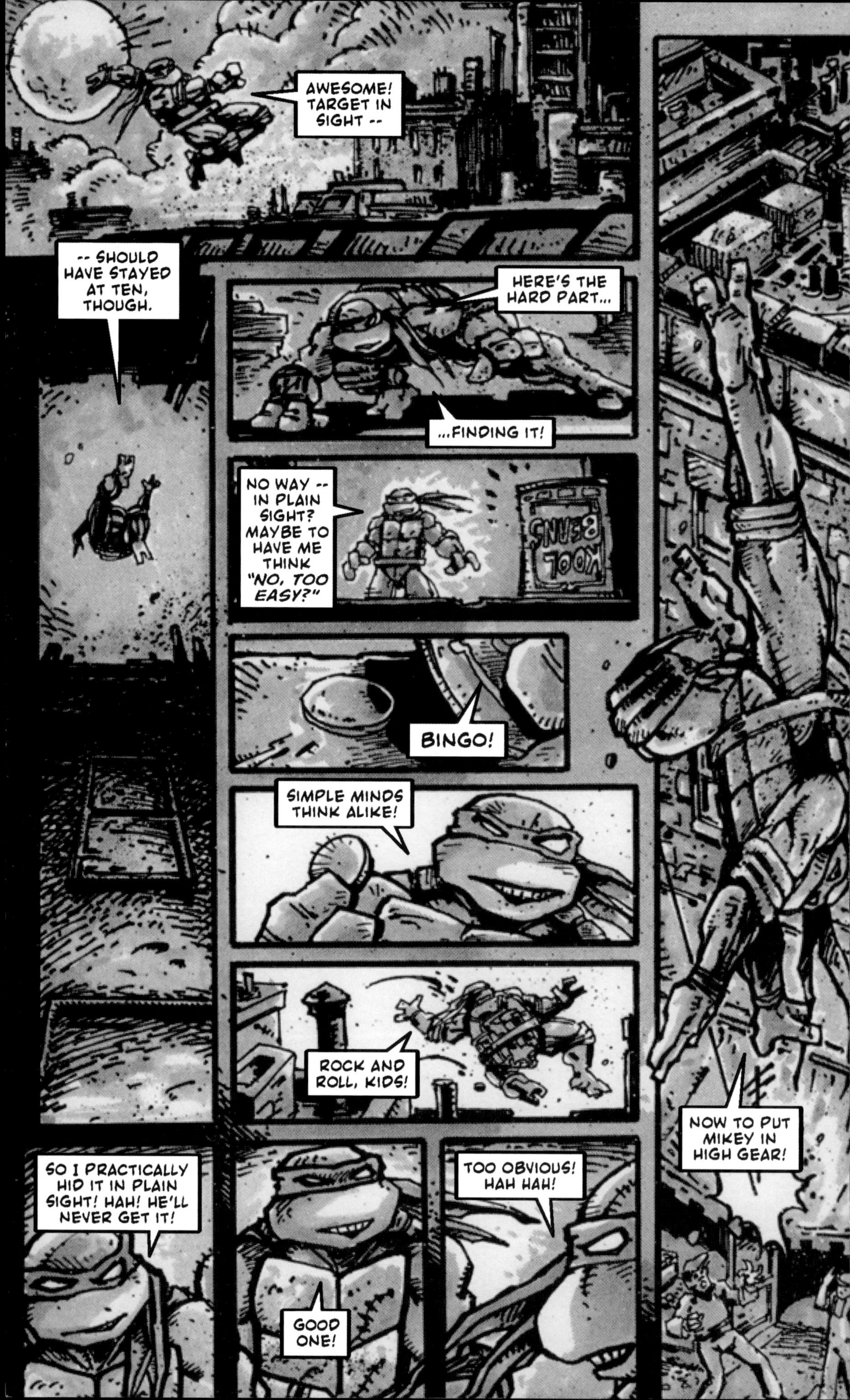
AWESOME! TARGET IN SIGHT --
-- SHOULD HAVE STAYED AT TEN, THOUGH.
HERE'S THE HARD PART...
...FINDING IT!
NO WAY -- IN PLAIN SIGHT? MAYBE TO HAVE ME THINK "NO, TOO EASY?"
BINGO!
SIMPLE MINDS THINK ALIKE!
ROCK AND ROLL, KIDS!
NOW TO PUT MIKEY IN HIGH GEAR!
SO I PRACTICALLY HID IT IN PLAIN SIGHT! HAH! HE'LL NEVER GET IT!
GOOD ONE!
TOO OBVIOUS! HAH HAH!

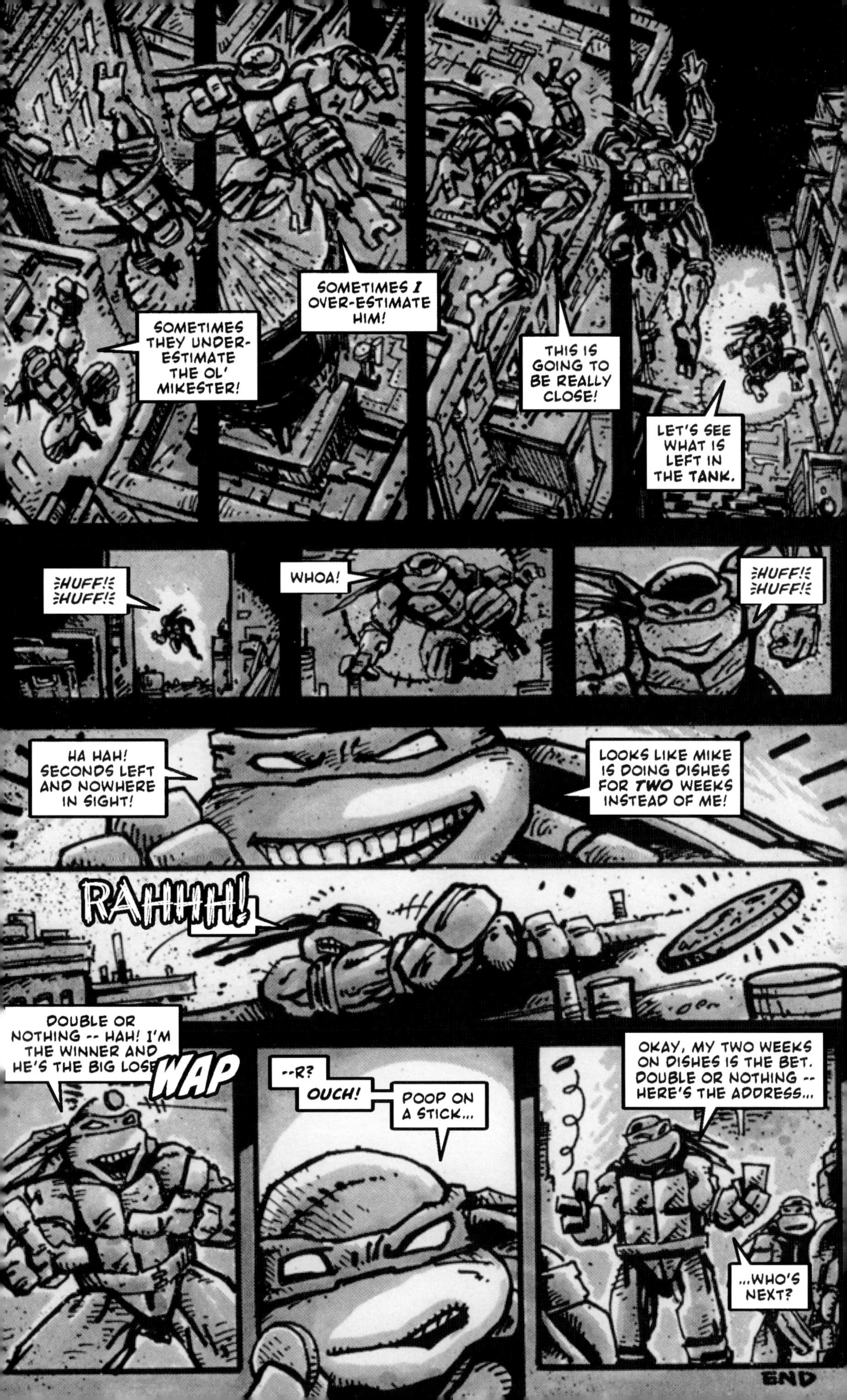
SOMETIMES THEY UNDER-ESTIMATE THE OL' MIKESTER!
SOMETIMES I OVER-ESTIMATE HIM!
THIS IS GOING TO BE REALLY CLOSE!
LET'S SEE WHAT IS LEFT IN THE TANK.
HUFF! HUFF!
WHOA!
HUFF! HUFF!
HA HAH! SECONDS LEFT AND NOWHERE IN SIGHT!
LOOKS LIKE MIKE IS DOING DISHES FOR TWO WEEKS INSTEAD OF ME!
RAHHHH!
DOUBLE OR NOTHING -- HAH! I'M THE WINNER AND HE'S THE BIG LOSE
WAP
--R? OUCH!
POOP ON A STICK...
OKAY, MY TWO WEEKS ON DISHES IS THE BET. DOUBLE OR NOTHING -- HERE'S THE ADDRESS...
...WHO'S NEXT?
END

ZOMBIES VS ROBOTS

FOUR FINE DAYS DURING THE ZOMBIE ROBOT WAR

BY CHRIS RYALL + ASHLEY WOOD

ONE DAY IN A LABORATORY

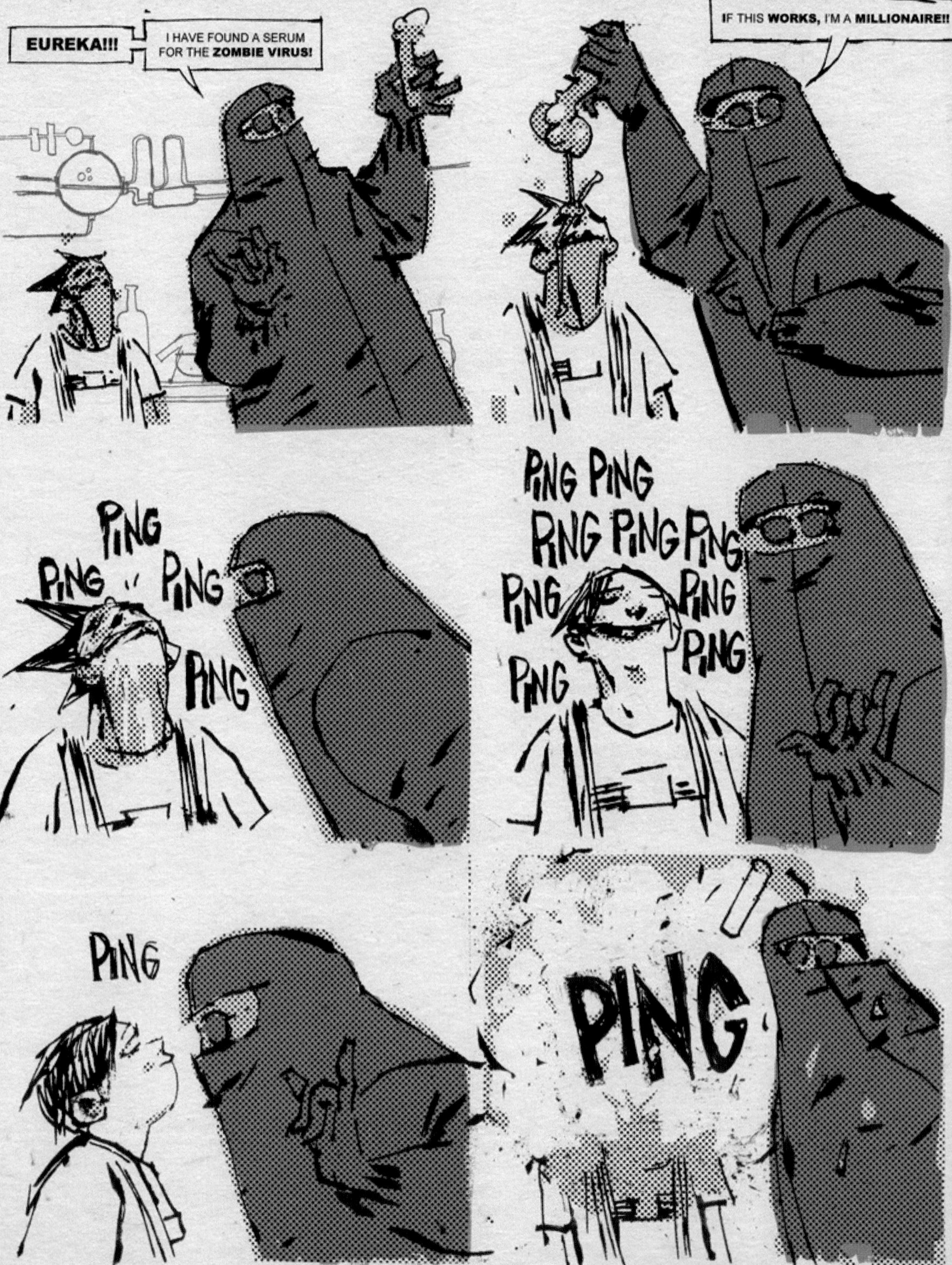
EUREKA!!!
I HAVE FOUND A SERUM FOR THE ZOMBIE VIRUS!
IF THIS WORKS, I'M A MILLIONAIRE!!
PING
PING
PING
PING
PING PING
PING PING PING
PING
PING
PING
PING
PING
PING
PING

MR MARTIN, RYALL MADE ME DO IT — W

ONE DAY IN R&D

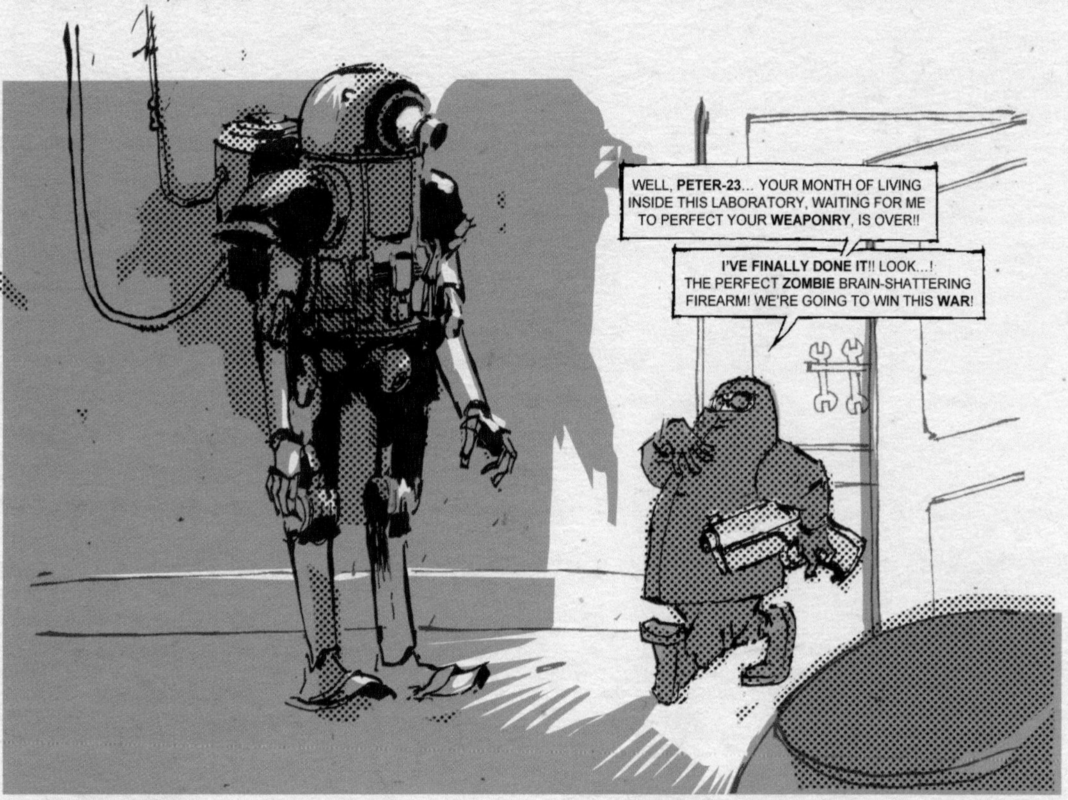
WELL, PETER-23... YOUR MONTH OF LIVING INSIDE THIS LABORATORY, WAITING FOR ME TO PERFECT YOUR WEAPONRY, IS OVER!!
I'VE FINALLY DONE IT!! LOOK...! THE PERFECT ZOMBIE BRAIN-SHATTERING FIREARM! WE'RE GOING TO WIN THIS WAR!

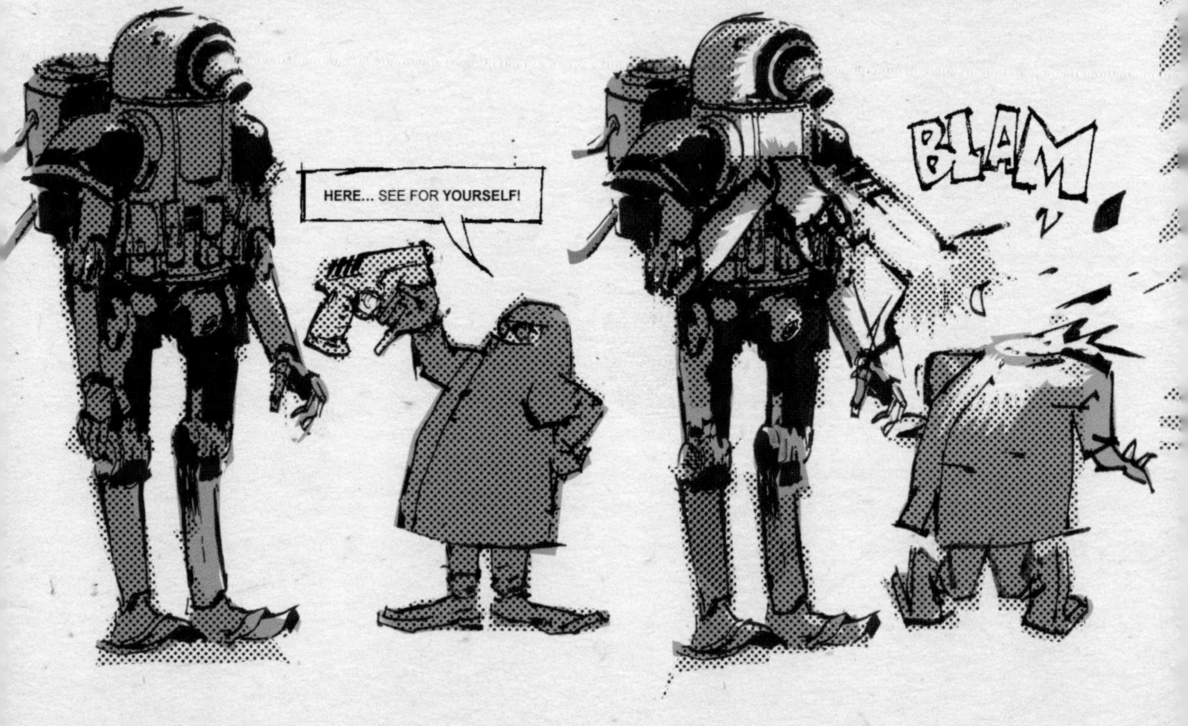
HERE... SEE FOR YOURSELF!
BLAM

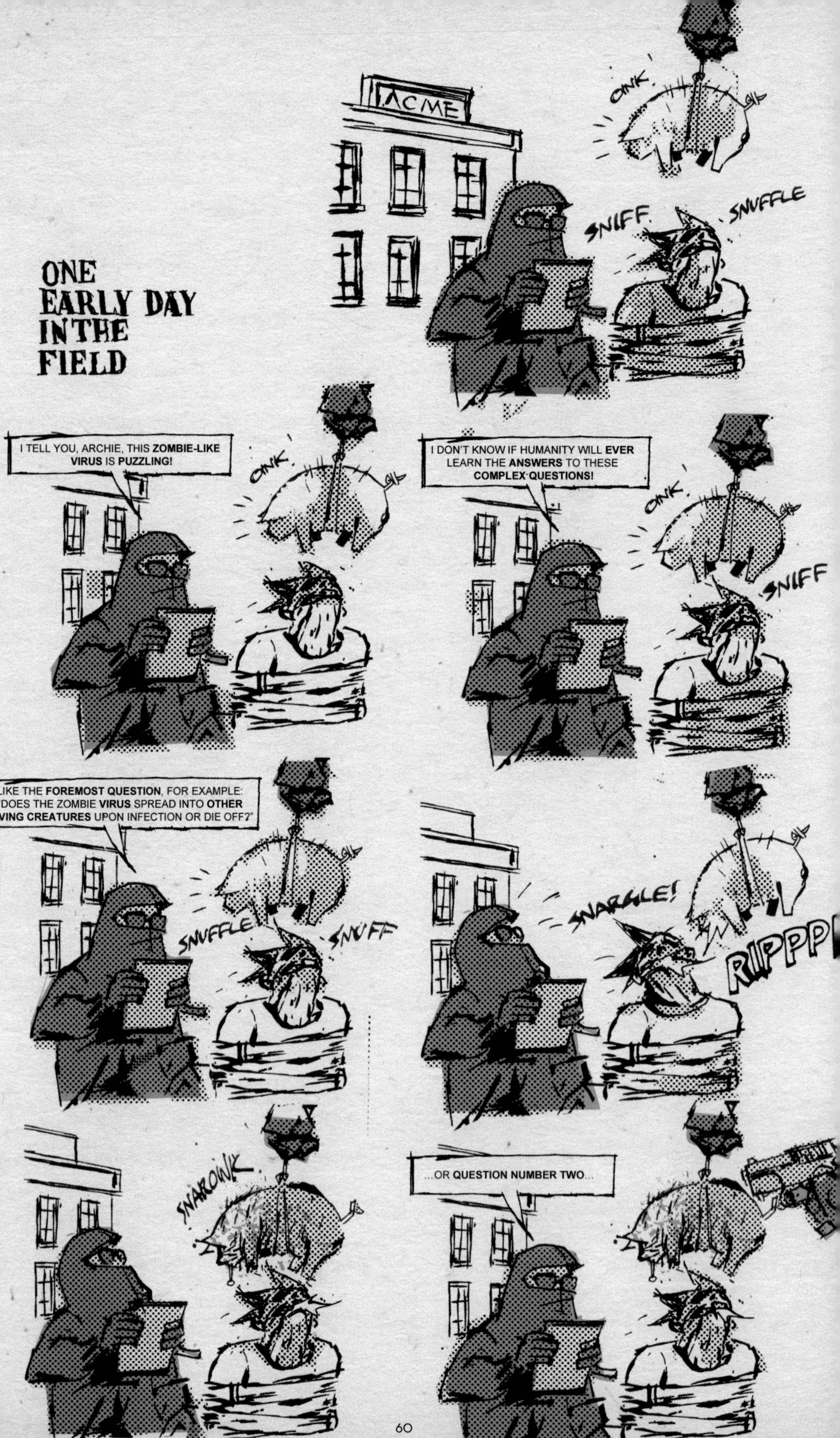
ONE EARLY DAY IN THE FIELD
ACME
OINK
SNIFF
SNUFFLE
I TELL YOU, ARCHIE, THIS ZOMBIE-LIKE VIRUS IS PUZZLING!
OINK
I DON'T KNOW IF HUMANITY WILL EVER LEARN THE ANSWERS TO THESE COMPLEX QUESTIONS!
OINK
SNIFF
LIKE THE FOREMOST QUESTION, FOR EXAMPLE: "DOES THE ZOMBIE VIRUS SPREAD INTO OTHER LIVING CREATURES UPON INFECTION OR DIE OFF?"
SNUFFLE
SNUFF
SNARGLE!
RIPPP
SNAROWK
...OR QUESTION NUMBER TWO...

ONE DAY ON THE ASSEMBLY LINE

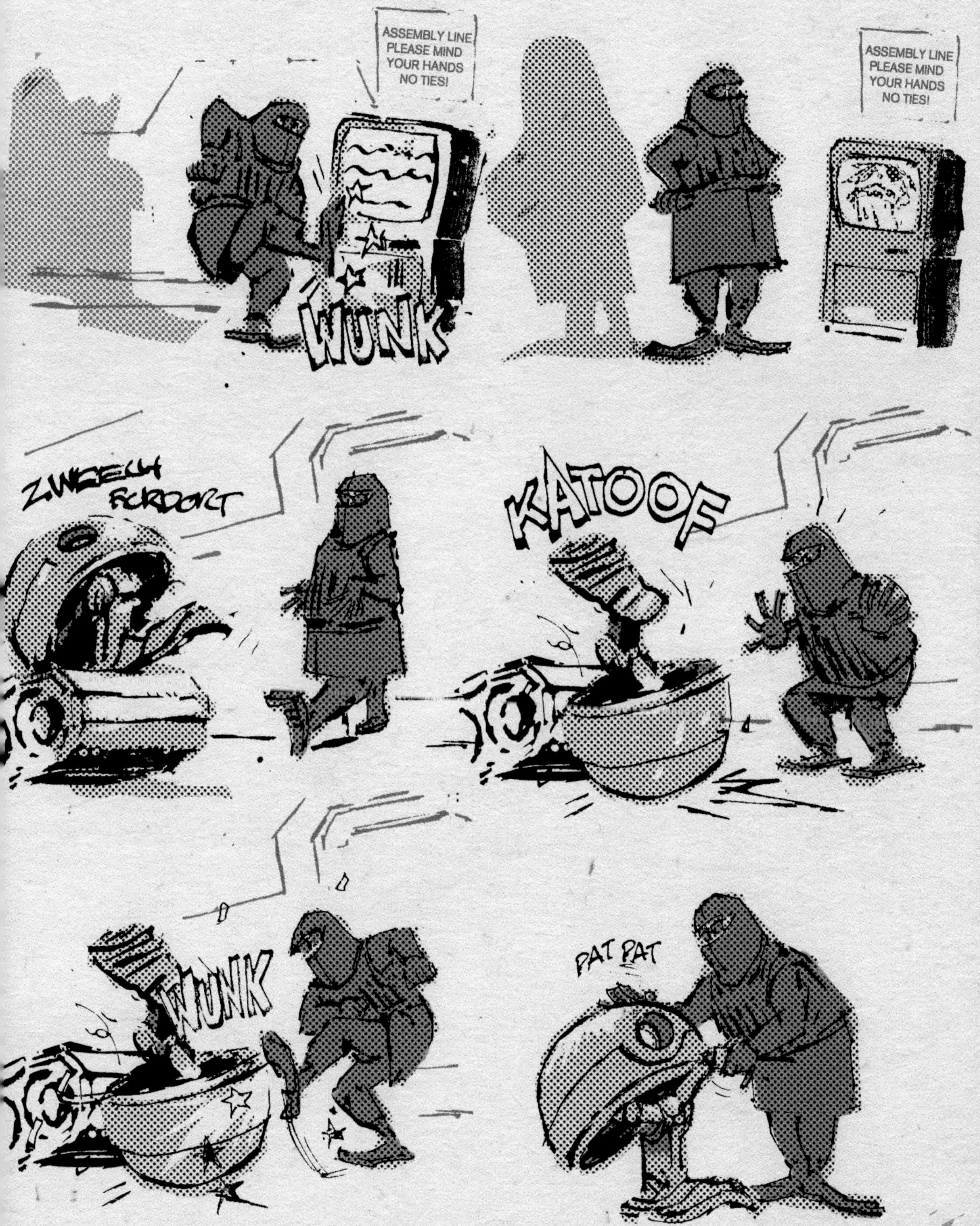
ASSEMBLY LINE
PLEASE MIND
YOUR HANDS
NO TIES!
WUNK
ASSEMBLY LINE
PLEASE MIND
YOUR HANDS
NO TIES!
ZWEECH
FCRDORT
KATOOF
WUNK
PAT PAT

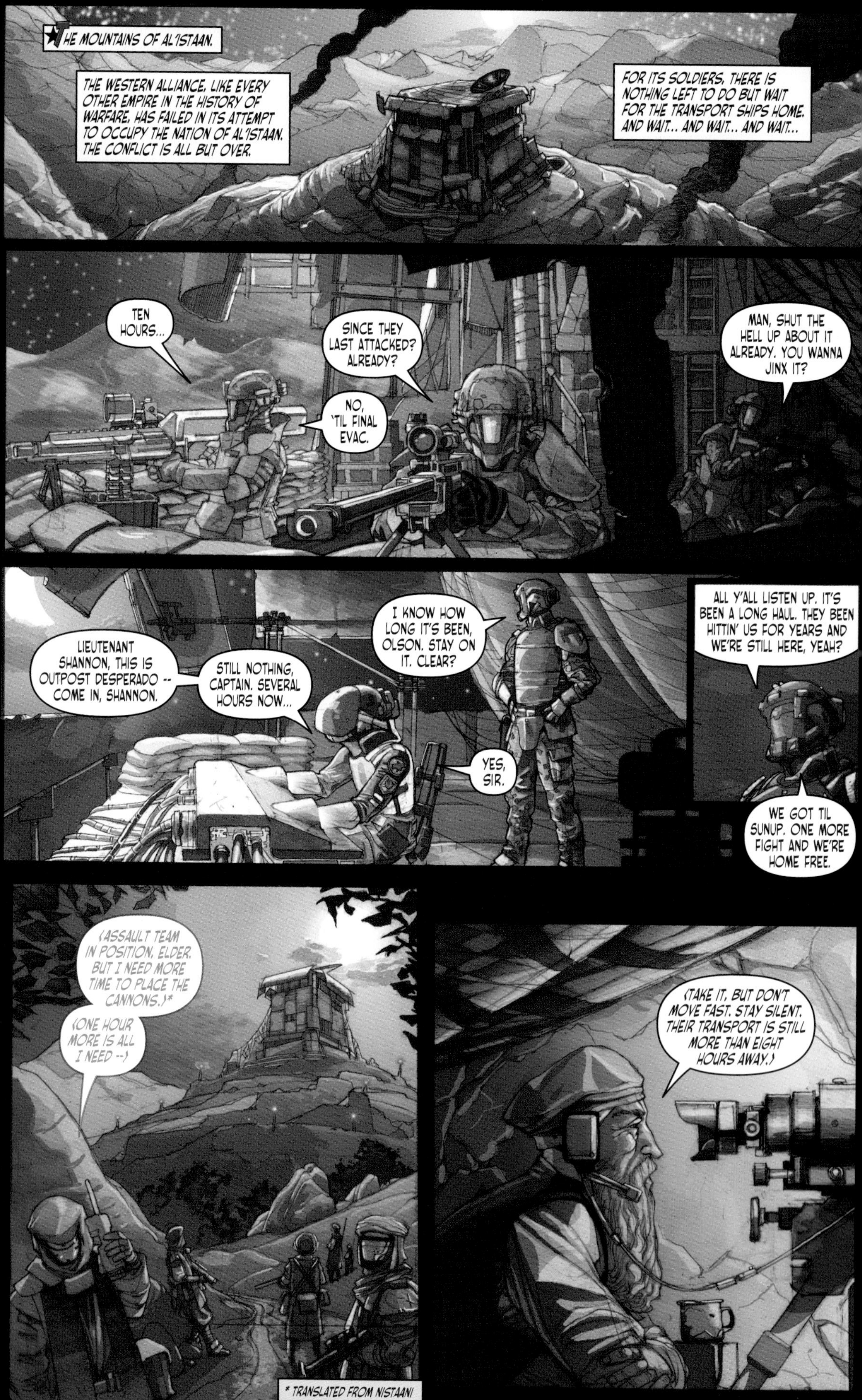
THE MOUNTAINS OF AL'ISTAAN.
THE WESTERN ALLIANCE, LIKE EVERY OTHER EMPIRE IN THE HISTORY OF WARFARE, HAS FAILED IN ITS ATTEMPT TO OCCUPY THE NATION OF AL'ISTAAN. THE CONFLICT IS ALL BUT OVER.
FOR ITS SOLDIERS, THERE IS NOTHING LEFT TO DO BUT WAIT FOR THE TRANSPORT SHIPS HOME. AND WAIT... AND WAIT... AND WAIT...
TEN HOURS...
SINCE THEY LAST ATTACKED? ALREADY?
NO, 'TIL FINAL EVAC.
MAN, SHUT THE HELL UP ABOUT IT ALREADY. YOU WANNA JINX IT?
LIEUTENANT SHANNON, THIS IS OUTPOST DESPERADO -- COME IN, SHANNON.
STILL NOTHING, CAPTAIN. SEVERAL HOURS NOW...
I KNOW HOW LONG IT'S BEEN, OLSON. STAY ON IT. CLEAR?
YES, SIR.
ALL Y'ALL LISTEN UP. IT'S BEEN A LONG HAUL. THEY BEEN HITTIN' US FOR YEARS AND WE'RE STILL HERE, YEAH?
WE GOT TIL SUNUP. ONE MORE FIGHT AND WE'RE HOME FREE.
‹ASSAULT TEAM IN POSITION, ELDER. BUT I NEED MORE TIME TO PLACE THE CANNONS.›*
‹ONE HOUR MORE IS ALL I NEED --›
‹TAKE IT, BUT DON'T MOVE FAST. STAY SILENT. THEIR TRANSPORT IS STILL MORE THAN EIGHT HOURS AWAY.›
* TRANSLATED FROM NISTAANI

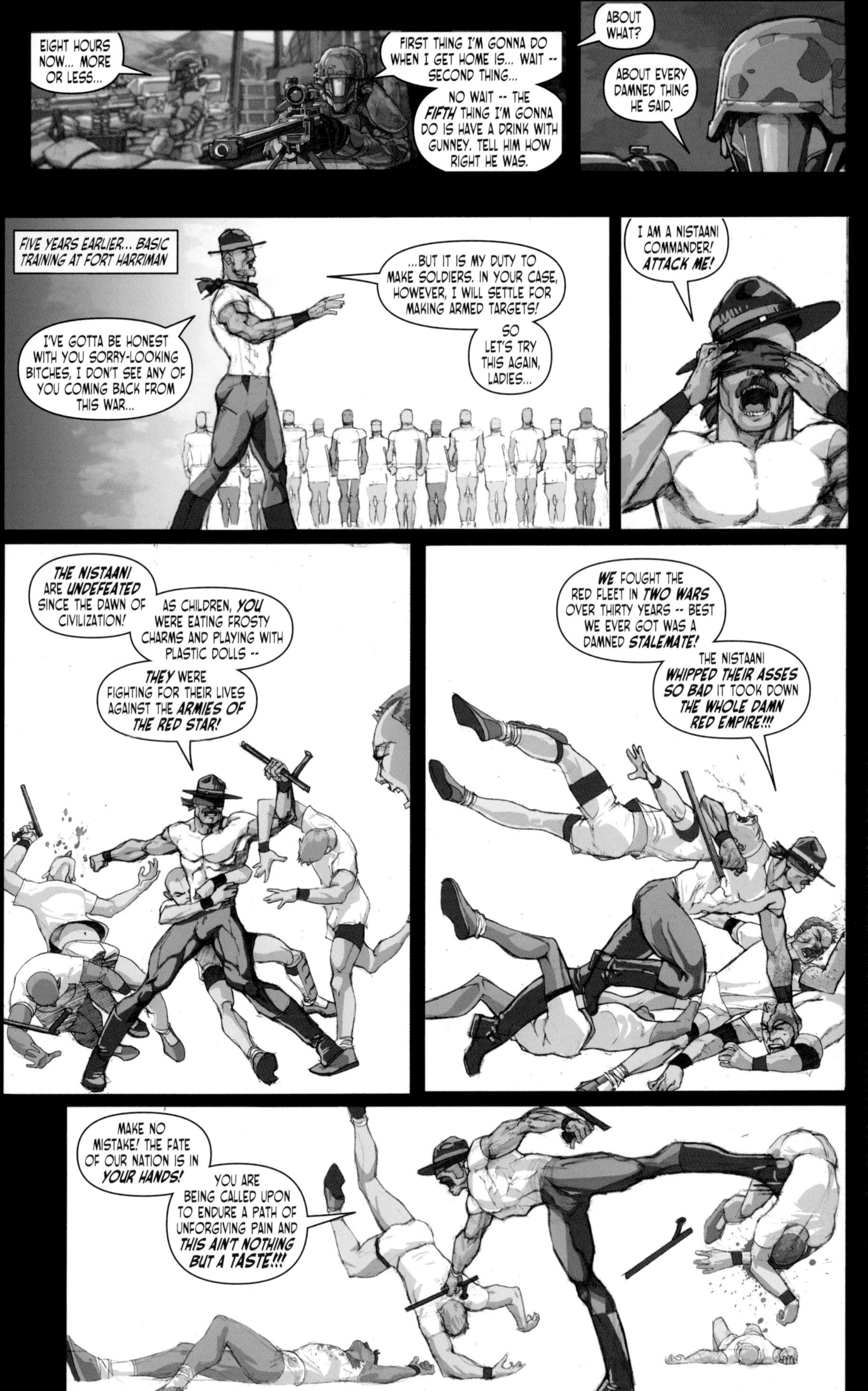

EIGHT HOURS NOW... MORE OR LESS...
FIRST THING I'M GONNA DO WHEN I GET HOME IS... WAIT -- SECOND THING...
NO WAIT -- THE FIFTH THING I'M GONNA DO IS HAVE A DRINK WITH GUNNEY. TELL HIM HOW RIGHT HE WAS.
ABOUT WHAT?
ABOUT EVERY DAMNED THING HE SAID.
FIVE YEARS EARLIER... BASIC TRAINING AT FORT HARRIMAN
I'VE GOTTA BE HONEST WITH YOU SORRY-LOOKING BITCHES, I DON'T SEE ANY OF YOU COMING BACK FROM THIS WAR...
...BUT IT IS MY DUTY TO MAKE SOLDIERS. IN YOUR CASE, HOWEVER, I WILL SETTLE FOR MAKING ARMED TARGETS!
SO LET'S TRY THIS AGAIN, LADIES...
I AM A NISTAANI COMMANDER! ATTACK ME!
THE NISTAANI ARE UNDEFEATED SINCE THE DAWN OF CIVILIZATION!
AS CHILDREN, YOU WERE EATING FROSTY CHARMS AND PLAYING WITH PLASTIC DOLLS --
THEY WERE FIGHTING FOR THEIR LIVES AGAINST THE ARMIES OF THE RED STAR!
WE FOUGHT THE RED FLEET IN TWO WARS OVER THIRTY YEARS -- BEST WE EVER GOT WAS A DAMNED STALEMATE!
THE NISTAANI WHIPPED THEIR ASSES SO BAD IT TOOK DOWN THE WHOLE DAMN RED EMPIRE!!!
MAKE NO MISTAKE! THE FATE OF OUR NATION IS IN YOUR HANDS!
YOU ARE BEING CALLED UPON TO ENDURE A PATH OF UNFORGIVING PAIN AND THIS AIN'T NOTHING BUT A TASTE!!!

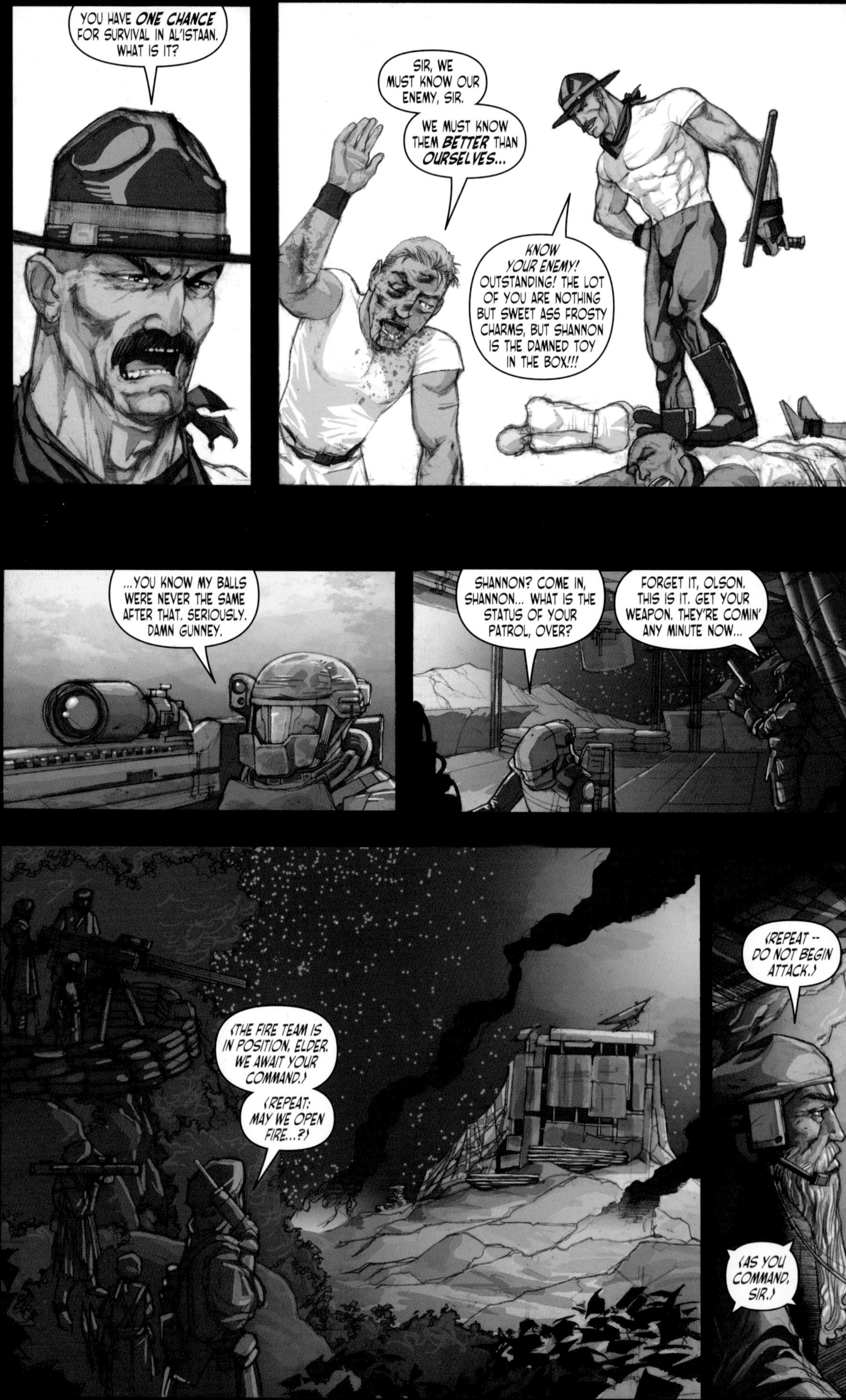
YOU HAVE ONE CHANCE FOR SURVIVAL IN AL'ISTAAN. WHAT IS IT?
SIR, WE MUST KNOW OUR ENEMY, SIR.
WE MUST KNOW THEM BETTER THAN OURSELVES...
KNOW YOUR ENEMY! OUTSTANDING! THE LOT OF YOU ARE NOTHING BUT SWEET ASS FROSTY CHARMS, BUT SHANNON IS THE DAMNED TOY IN THE BOX!!!
...YOU KNOW MY BALLS WERE NEVER THE SAME AFTER THAT. SERIOUSLY. DAMN GUNNEY.
SHANNON? COME IN, SHANNON... WHAT IS THE STATUS OF YOUR PATROL, OVER?
FORGET IT, OLSON. THIS IS IT. GET YOUR WEAPON. THEY'RE COMIN' ANY MINUTE NOW...
‹THE FIRE TEAM IS IN POSITION, ELDER. WE AWAIT YOUR COMMAND.›
‹REPEAT: MAY WE OPEN FIRE...?›
‹REPEAT -- DO NOT BEGIN ATTACK.›
‹AS YOU COMMAND, SIR.›

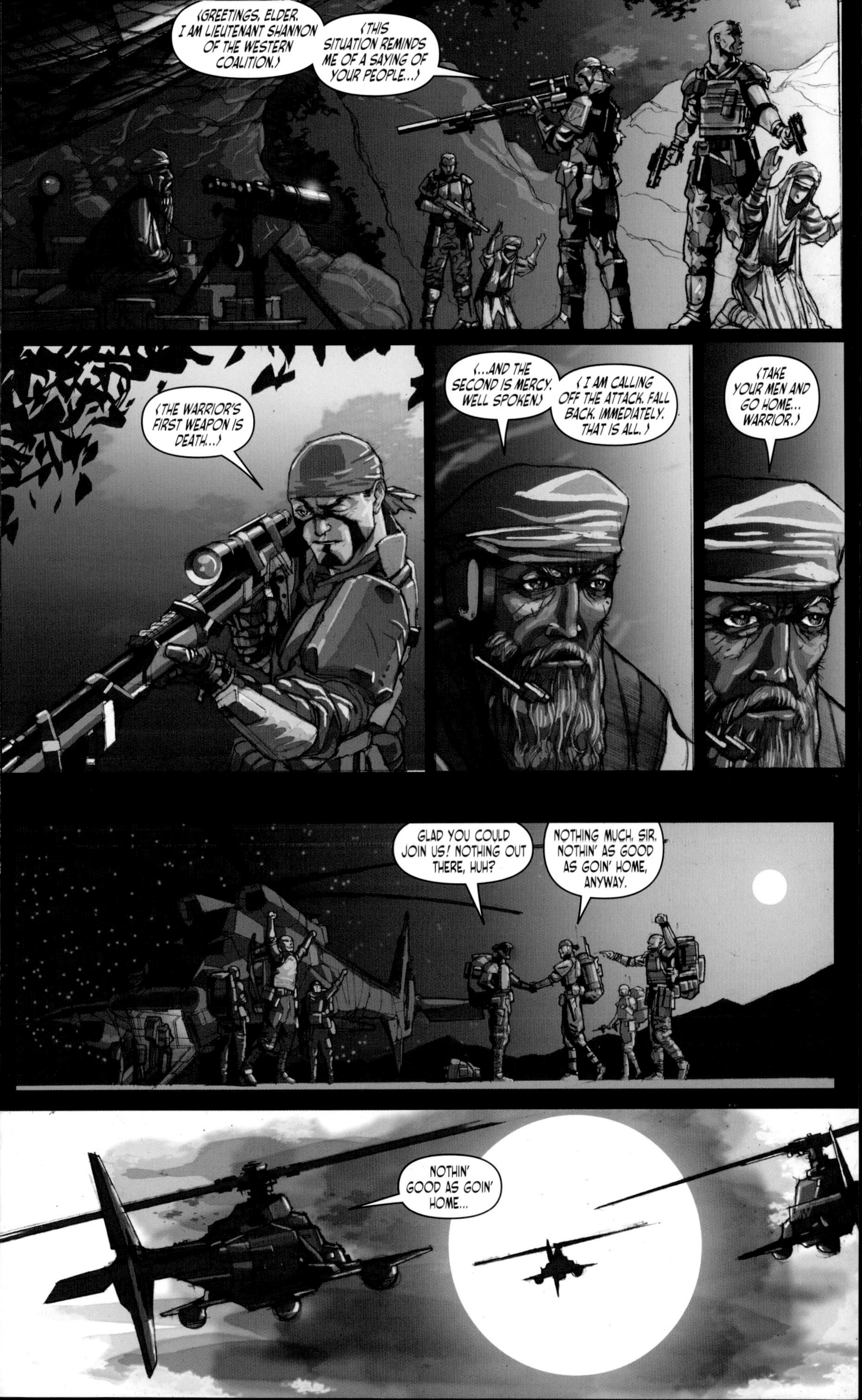
‹GREETINGS, ELDER. I AM LIEUTENANT SHANNON OF THE WESTERN COALITION.›
‹THIS SITUATION REMINDS ME OF A SAYING OF YOUR PEOPLE...›
‹THE WARRIOR'S FIRST WEAPON IS DEATH...›
‹...AND THE SECOND IS MERCY. WELL SPOKEN.›
‹I AM CALLING OFF THE ATTACK. FALL BACK. IMMEDIATELY. THAT IS ALL.›
‹TAKE YOUR MEN AND GO HOME... WARRIOR.›
GLAD YOU COULD JOIN US! NOTHING OUT THERE, HUH?
NOTHING MUCH, SIR. NOTHIN' AS GOOD AS GOIN' HOME, ANYWAY.
NOTHIN' GOOD AS GOIN' HOME...

ELEPHANTMEN

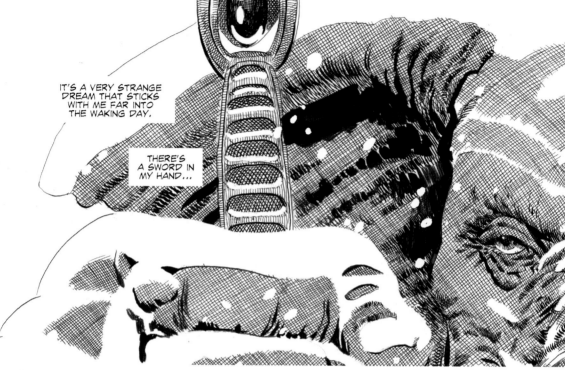

IT'S A VERY STRANGE DREAM THAT STICKS WITH ME FAR INTO THE WAKING DAY.

THERE'S A SWORD IN MY HAND...

EBONY DREAMS

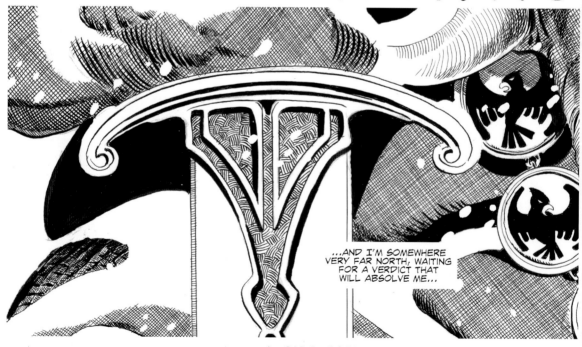

...AND I'M SOMEWHERE VERY FAR NORTH, WAITING FOR A VERDICT THAT WILL ABSOLVE ME...

BY DAVE SIM WITH RICHARD STARKINGS

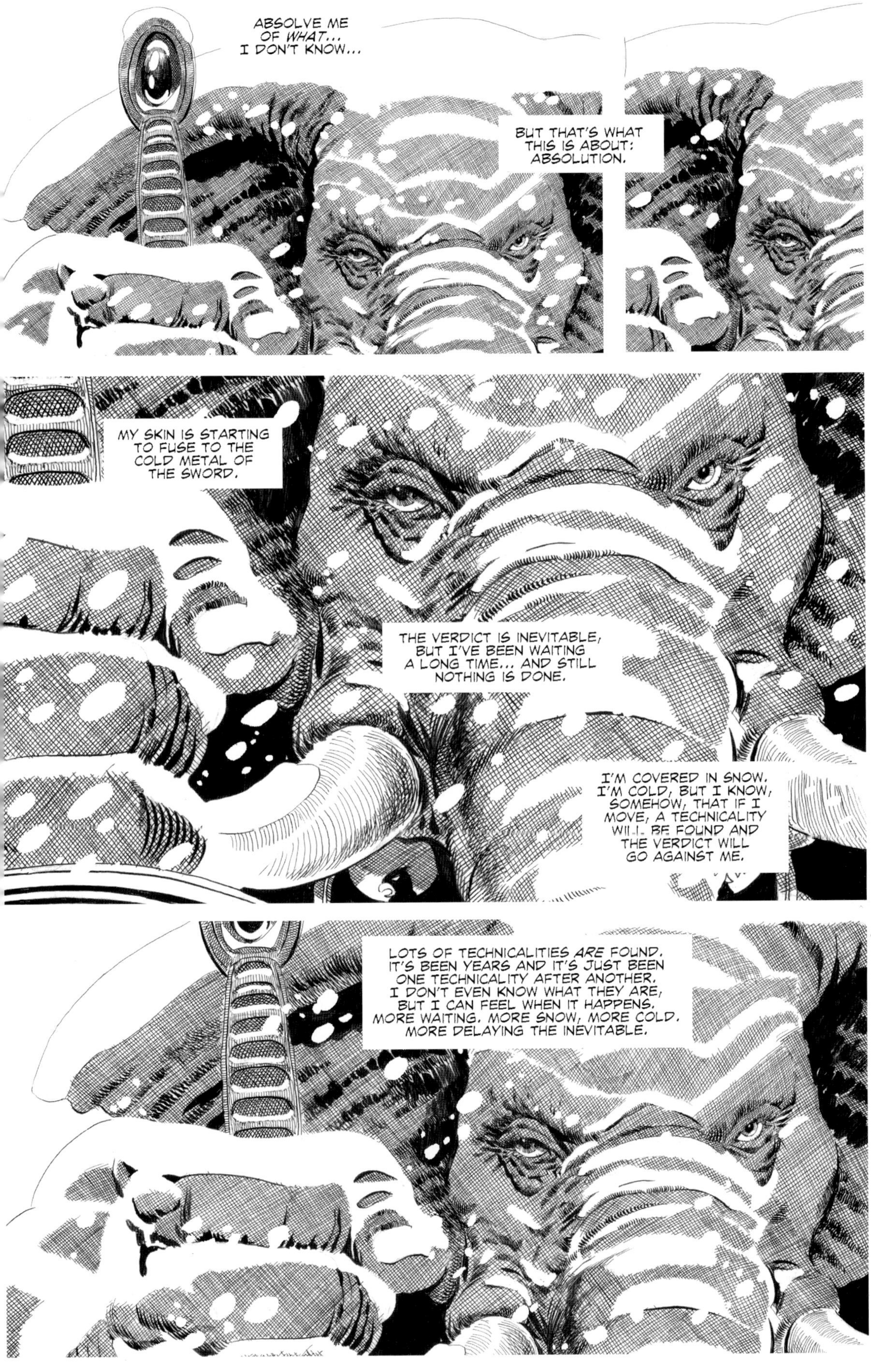
ABSOLVE ME OF WHAT... I DON'T KNOW...
BUT THAT'S WHAT THIS IS ABOUT: ABSOLUTION.
MY SKIN IS STARTING TO FUSE TO THE COLD METAL OF THE SWORD.
THE VERDICT IS INEVITABLE, BUT I'VE BEEN WAITING A LONG TIME... AND STILL NOTHING IS DONE.
I'M COVERED IN SNOW. I'M COLD, BUT I KNOW, SOMEHOW, THAT IF I MOVE, A TECHNICALITY WILL BE FOUND AND THE VERDICT WILL GO AGAINST ME.
LOTS OF TECHNICALITIES ARE FOUND. IT'S BEEN YEARS AND IT'S JUST BEEN ONE TECHNICALITY AFTER ANOTHER. I DON'T EVEN KNOW WHAT THEY ARE, BUT I CAN FEEL WHEN IT HAPPENS. MORE WAITING, MORE SNOW, MORE COLD. MORE DELAYING THE INEVITABLE.

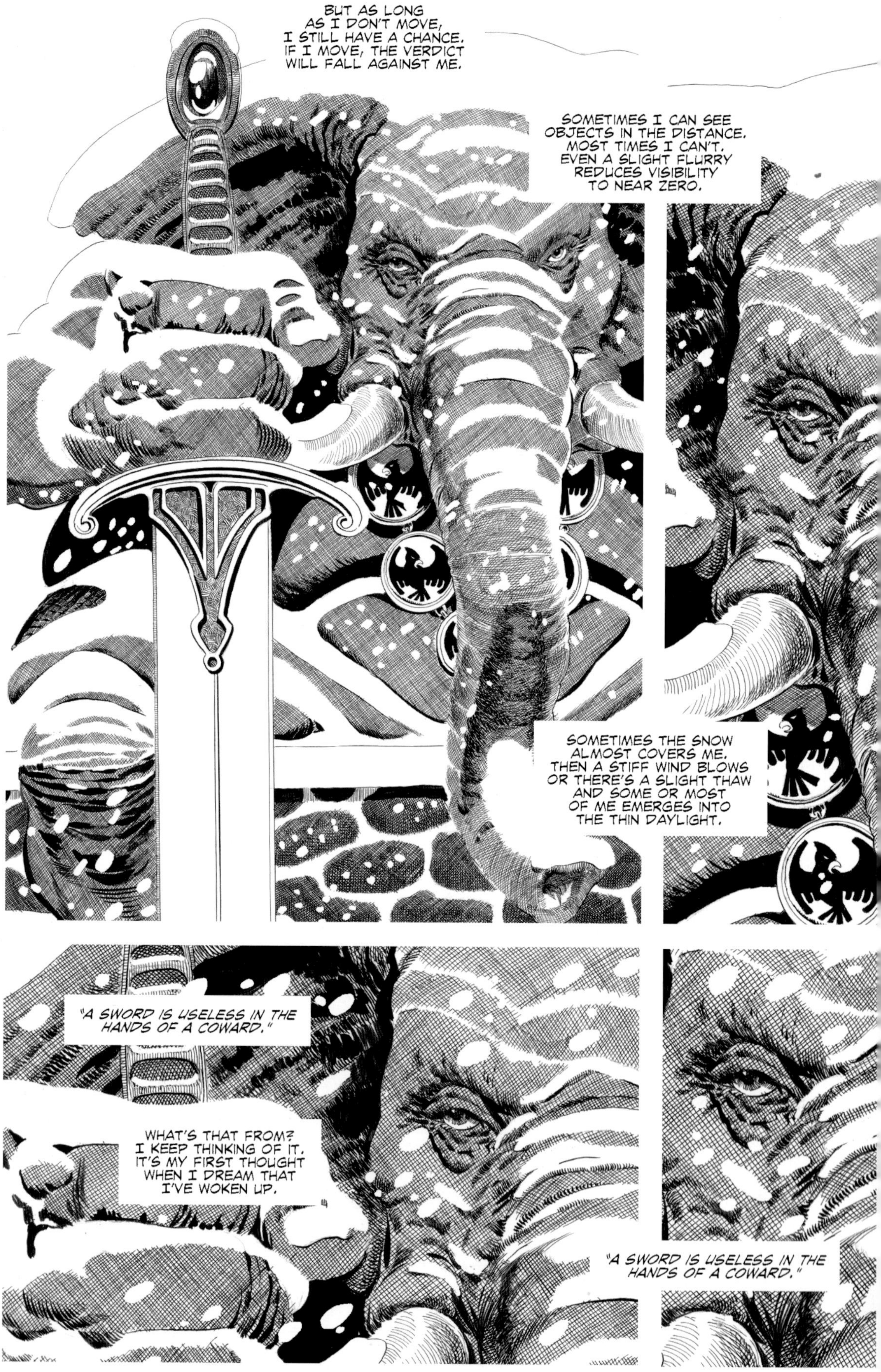
BUT AS LONG AS I DON'T MOVE, I STILL HAVE A CHANCE. IF I MOVE, THE VERDICT WILL FALL AGAINST ME.
SOMETIMES I CAN SEE OBJECTS IN THE DISTANCE. MOST TIMES I CAN'T. EVEN A SLIGHT FLURRY REDUCES VISIBILITY TO NEAR ZERO.
SOMETIMES THE SNOW ALMOST COVERS ME. THEN A STIFF WIND BLOWS OR THERE'S A SLIGHT THAW AND SOME OR MOST OF ME EMERGES INTO THE THIN DAYLIGHT.
"A SWORD IS USELESS IN THE HANDS OF A COWARD."
WHAT'S THAT FROM? I KEEP THINKING OF IT. IT'S MY FIRST THOUGHT WHEN I DREAM THAT I'VE WOKEN UP.
"A SWORD IS USELESS IN THE HANDS OF A COWARD."

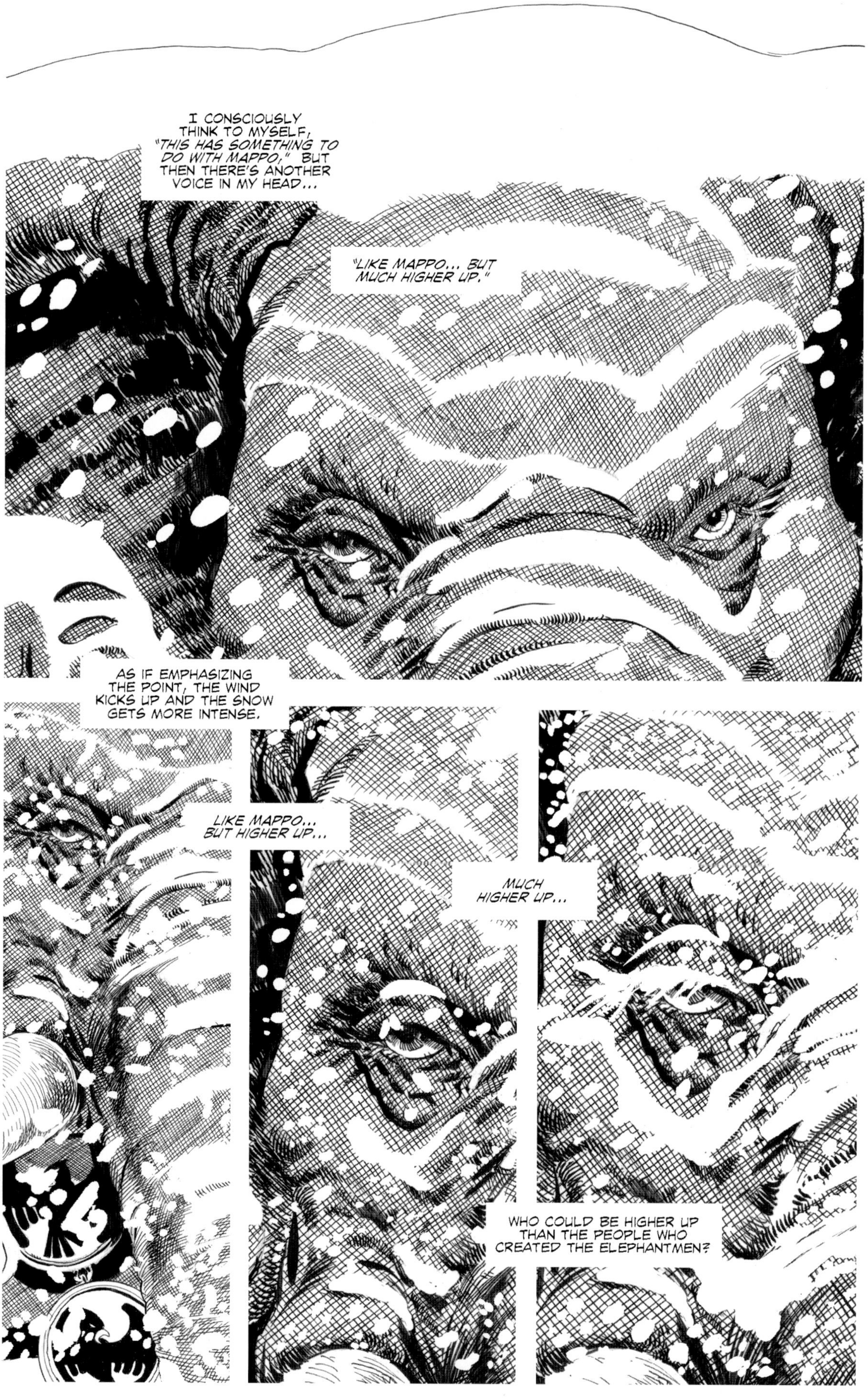
I CONSCIOUSLY THINK TO MYSELF, "THIS HAS SOMETHING TO DO WITH MAPPO," BUT THEN THERE'S ANOTHER VOICE IN MY HEAD...
"LIKE MAPPO... BUT MUCH HIGHER UP."
AS IF EMPHASIZING THE POINT, THE WIND KICKS UP AND THE SNOW GETS MORE INTENSE.
LIKE MAPPO... BUT HIGHER UP...
MUCH HIGHER UP...
WHO COULD BE HIGHER UP THAN THE PEOPLE WHO CREATED THE ELEPHANTMEN?

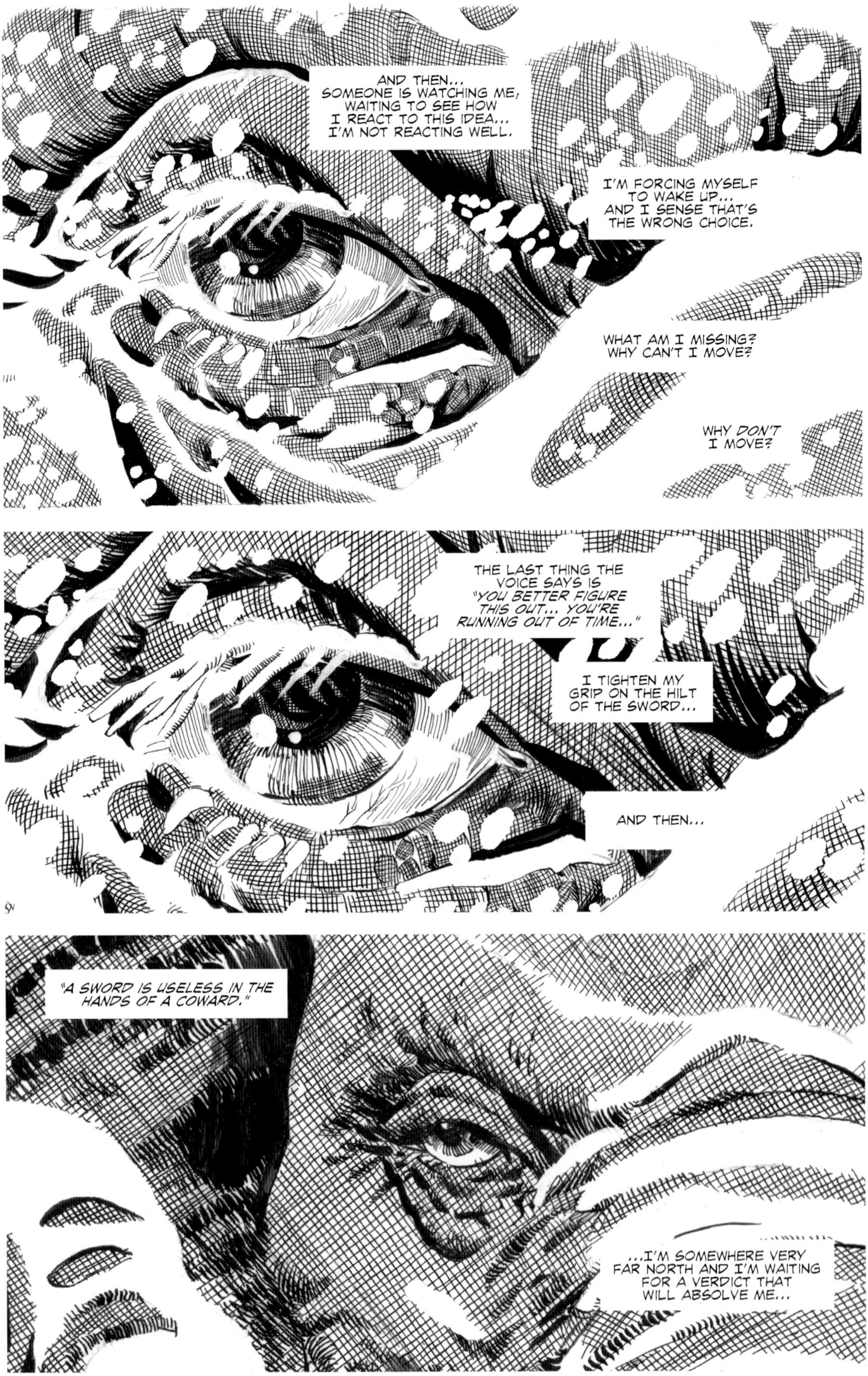
AND THEN... SOMEONE IS WATCHING ME, WAITING TO SEE HOW I REACT TO THIS IDEA... I'M NOT REACTING WELL.
I'M FORCING MYSELF TO WAKE UP... AND I SENSE THAT'S THE WRONG CHOICE.
WHAT AM I MISSING? WHY CAN'T I MOVE?
WHY *DON'T* I MOVE?
THE LAST THING THE VOICE SAYS IS *"YOU BETTER FIGURE THIS OUT... YOU'RE RUNNING OUT OF TIME..."*
I TIGHTEN MY GRIP ON THE HILT OF THE SWORD...
AND THEN...
"A SWORD IS USELESS IN THE HANDS OF A COWARD."
...I'M SOMEWHERE VERY FAR NORTH AND I'M WAITING FOR A VERDICT THAT WILL ABSOLVE ME...

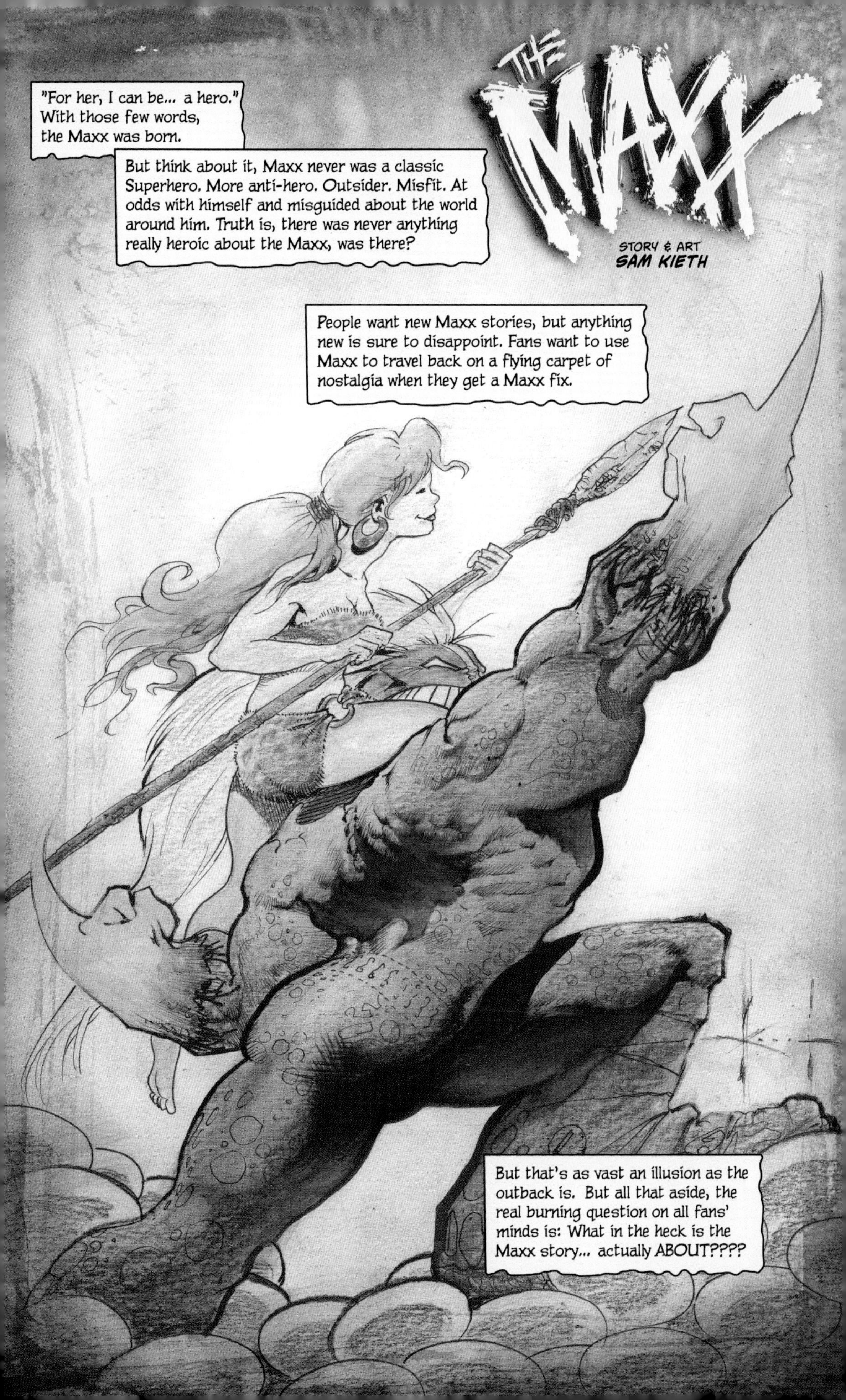

THE MAXX
STORY & ART
SAM KIETH
"For her, I can be... a hero." With those few words, the Maxx was born.
But think about it, Maxx never was a classic Superhero. More anti-hero. Outsider. Misfit. At odds with himself and misguided about the world around him. Truth is, there was never anything really heroic about the Maxx, was there?
People want new Maxx stories, but anything new is sure to disappoint. Fans want to use Maxx to travel back on a flying carpet of nostalgia when they get a Maxx fix.
But that's as vast an illusion as the outback is. But all that aside, the real burning question on all fans' minds is: What in the heck is the Maxx story... actually ABOUT????

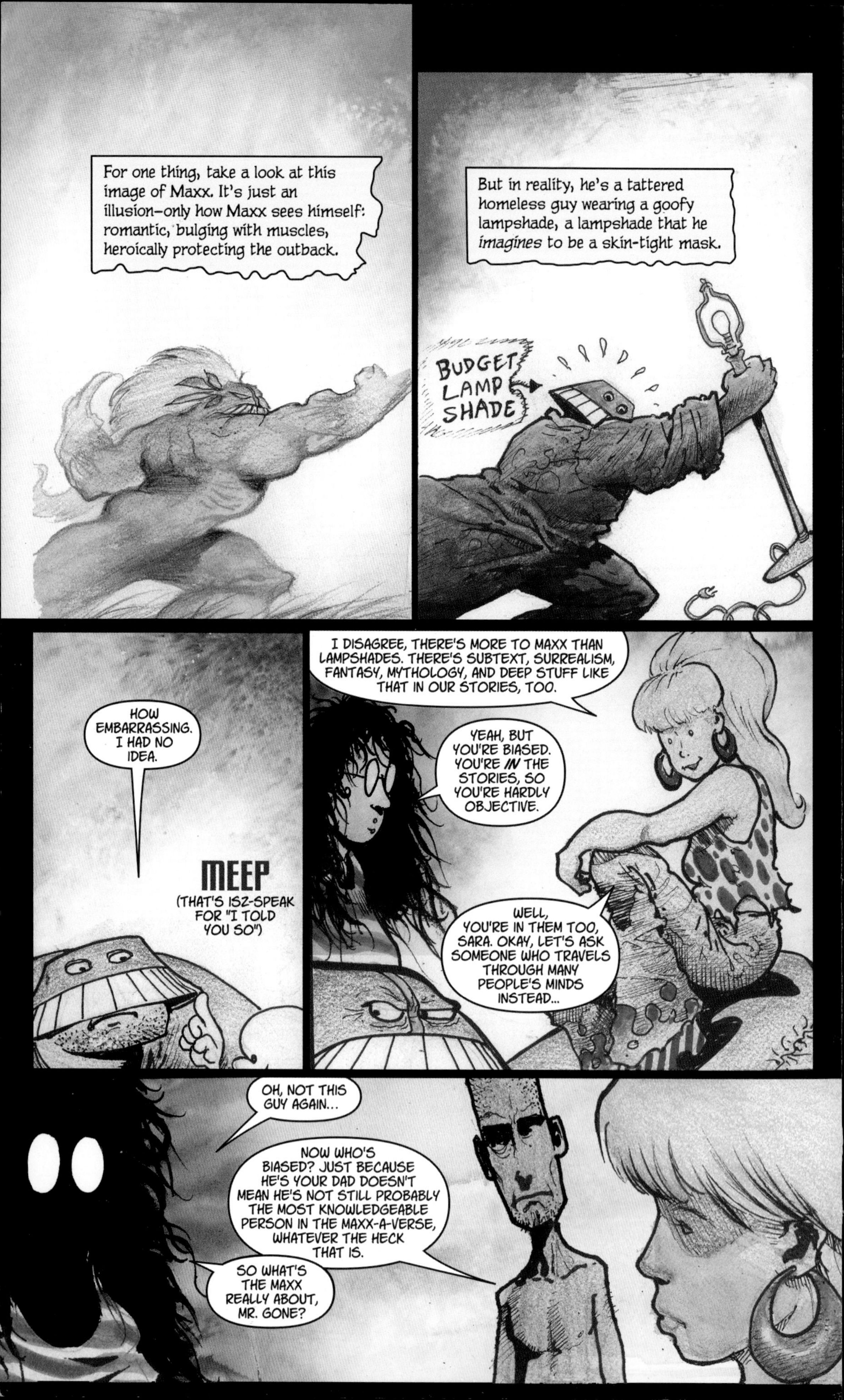
For one thing, take a look at this image of Maxx. It's just an illusion–only how Maxx sees himself: romantic, bulging with muscles, heroically protecting the outback.
But in reality, he's a tattered homeless guy wearing a goofy lampshade, a lampshade that he *imagines* to be a skin-tight mask.
BUDGET LAMP SHADE
HOW EMBARRASSING. I HAD NO IDEA.
MEEP
(THAT'S ISZ-SPEAK FOR "I TOLD YOU SO")
I DISAGREE, THERE'S MORE TO MAXX THAN LAMPSHADES. THERE'S SUBTEXT, SURREALISM, FANTASY, MYTHOLOGY, AND DEEP STUFF LIKE THAT IN OUR STORIES, TOO.
YEAH, BUT YOU'RE BIASED. YOU'RE *IN* THE STORIES, SO YOU'RE HARDLY OBJECTIVE.
WELL, YOU'RE IN THEM TOO, SARA. OKAY, LET'S ASK SOMEONE WHO TRAVELS THROUGH MANY PEOPLE'S MINDS INSTEAD...
OH, NOT THIS GUY AGAIN...
NOW WHO'S BIASED? JUST BECAUSE HE'S YOUR DAD DOESN'T MEAN HE'S NOT STILL PROBABLY THE MOST KNOWLEDGEABLE PERSON IN THE MAXX-A-VERSE, WHATEVER THE HECK THAT IS.
SO WHAT'S THE MAXX REALLY ABOUT, MR. GONE?

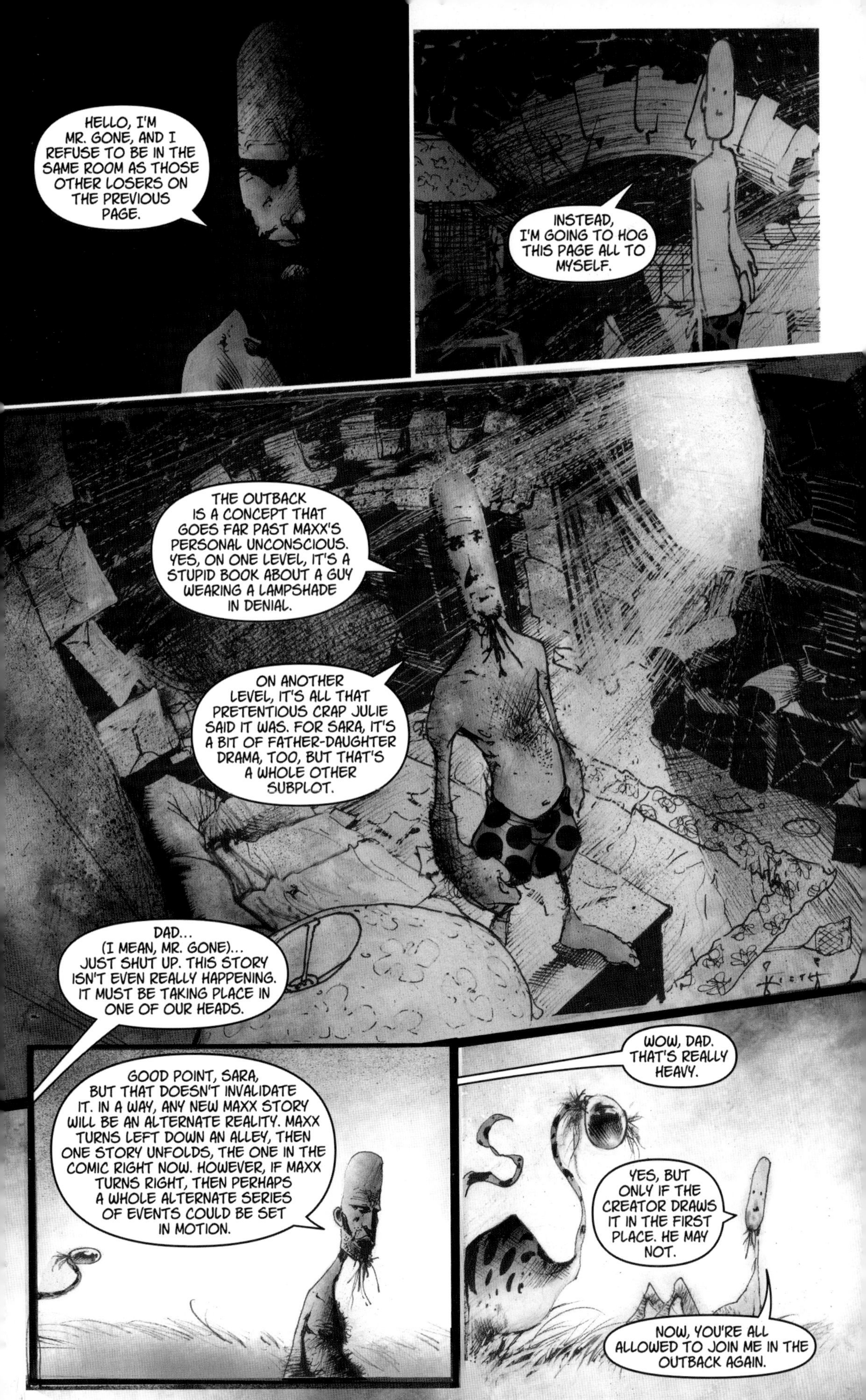
HELLO, I'M MR. GONE, AND I REFUSE TO BE IN THE SAME ROOM AS THOSE OTHER LOSERS ON THE PREVIOUS PAGE.
INSTEAD, I'M GOING TO HOG THIS PAGE ALL TO MYSELF.
THE OUTBACK IS A CONCEPT THAT GOES FAR PAST MAXX'S PERSONAL UNCONSCIOUS. YES, ON ONE LEVEL, IT'S A STUPID BOOK ABOUT A GUY WEARING A LAMPSHADE IN DENIAL.
ON ANOTHER LEVEL, IT'S ALL THAT PRETENTIOUS CRAP JULIE SAID IT WAS. FOR SARA, IT'S A BIT OF FATHER-DAUGHTER DRAMA, TOO, BUT THAT'S A WHOLE OTHER SUBPLOT.
DAD... (I MEAN, MR. GONE)... JUST SHUT UP. THIS STORY ISN'T EVEN REALLY HAPPENING. IT MUST BE TAKING PLACE IN ONE OF OUR HEADS.
GOOD POINT, SARA, BUT THAT DOESN'T INVALIDATE IT. IN A WAY, ANY NEW MAXX STORY WILL BE AN ALTERNATE REALITY. MAXX TURNS LEFT DOWN AN ALLEY, THEN ONE STORY UNFOLDS, THE ONE IN THE COMIC RIGHT NOW. HOWEVER, IF MAXX TURNS RIGHT, THEN PERHAPS A WHOLE ALTERNATE SERIES OF EVENTS COULD BE SET IN MOTION.
WOW, DAD. THAT'S REALLY HEAVY.
YES, BUT ONLY IF THE CREATOR DRAWS IT IN THE FIRST PLACE. HE MAY NOT.
NOW, YOU'RE ALL ALLOWED TO JOIN ME IN THE OUTBACK AGAIN.

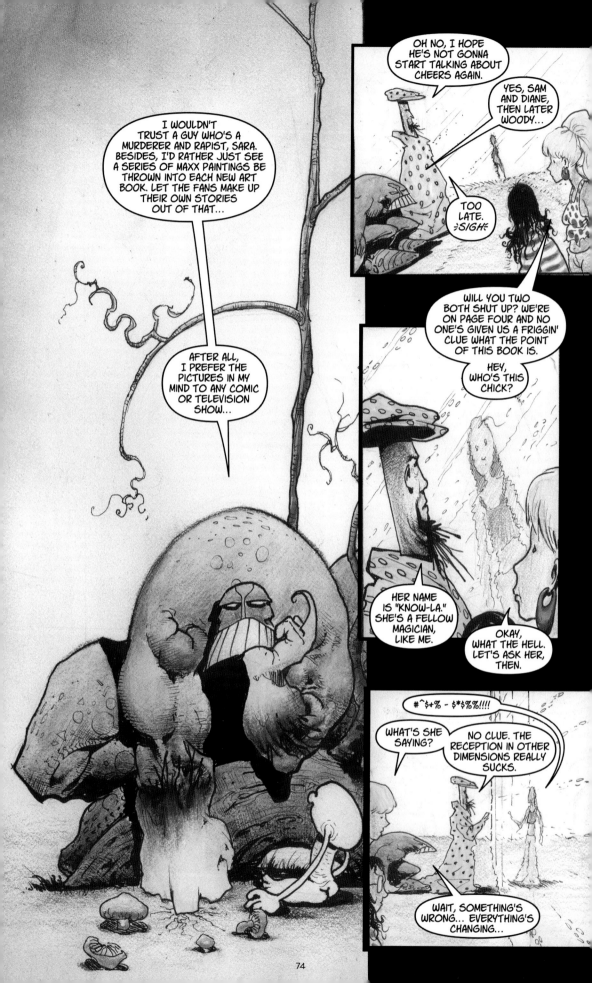

OH NO, I HOPE HE'S NOT GONNA START TALKING ABOUT CHEERS AGAIN.

YES, SAM AND DIANE, THEN LATER WOODY...

TOO LATE. ⊰SIGH⊱

I WOULDN'T TRUST A GUY WHO'S A MURDERER AND RAPIST, SARA. BESIDES, I'D RATHER JUST SEE A SERIES OF MAXX PAINTINGS BE THROWN INTO EACH NEW ART BOOK. LET THE FANS MAKE UP THEIR OWN STORIES OUT OF THAT...

AFTER ALL, I PREFER THE PICTURES IN MY MIND TO ANY COMIC OR TELEVISION SHOW...

WILL YOU TWO BOTH SHUT UP? WE'RE ON PAGE FOUR AND NO ONE'S GIVEN US A FRIGGIN' CLUE WHAT THE POINT OF THIS BOOK IS.

HEY, WHO'S THIS CHICK?

HER NAME IS "KNOW-LA." SHE'S A FELLOW MAGICIAN, LIKE ME.

OKAY, WHAT THE HELL. LET'S ASK HER, THEN.

#^$+% - $*$%%!!!!

WHAT'S SHE SAYING?

NO CLUE. THE RECEPTION IN OTHER DIMENSIONS REALLY SUCKS.

WAIT, SOMETHING'S WRONG... EVERYTHING'S CHANGING...

74

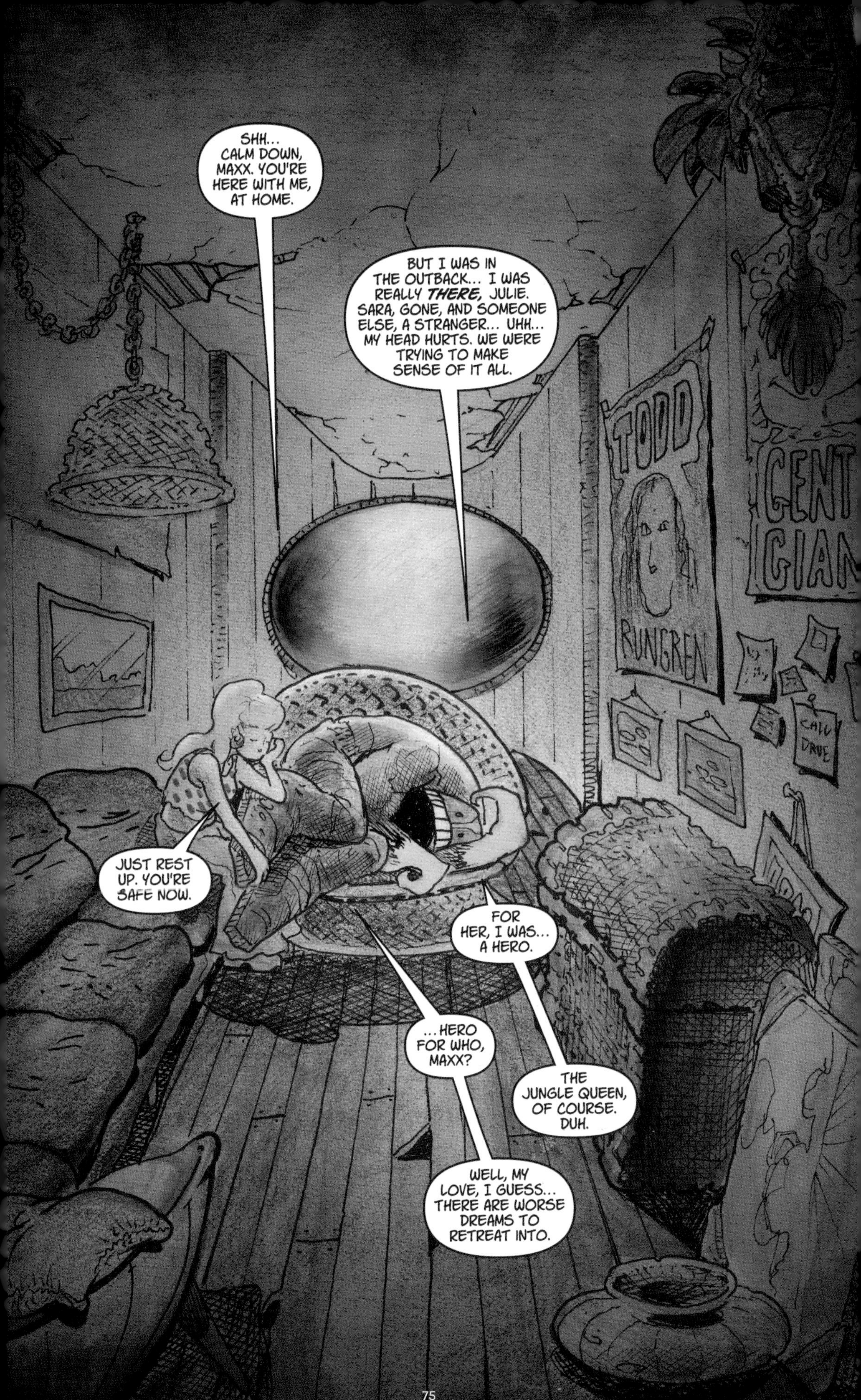
SHH... CALM DOWN, MAXX. YOU'RE HERE WITH ME, AT HOME.
BUT I WAS IN THE OUTBACK... I WAS REALLY THERE, JULIE. SARA, GONE, AND SOMEONE ELSE, A STRANGER... UHH... MY HEAD HURTS. WE WERE TRYING TO MAKE SENSE OF IT ALL.
TODD
RUNGREN
CALL DAVE
JUST REST UP. YOU'RE SAFE NOW.
FOR HER, I WAS... A HERO.
...HERO FOR WHO, MAXX?
THE JUNGLE QUEEN, OF COURSE. DUH.
WELL, MY LOVE, I GUESS... THERE ARE WORSE DREAMS TO RETREAT INTO.

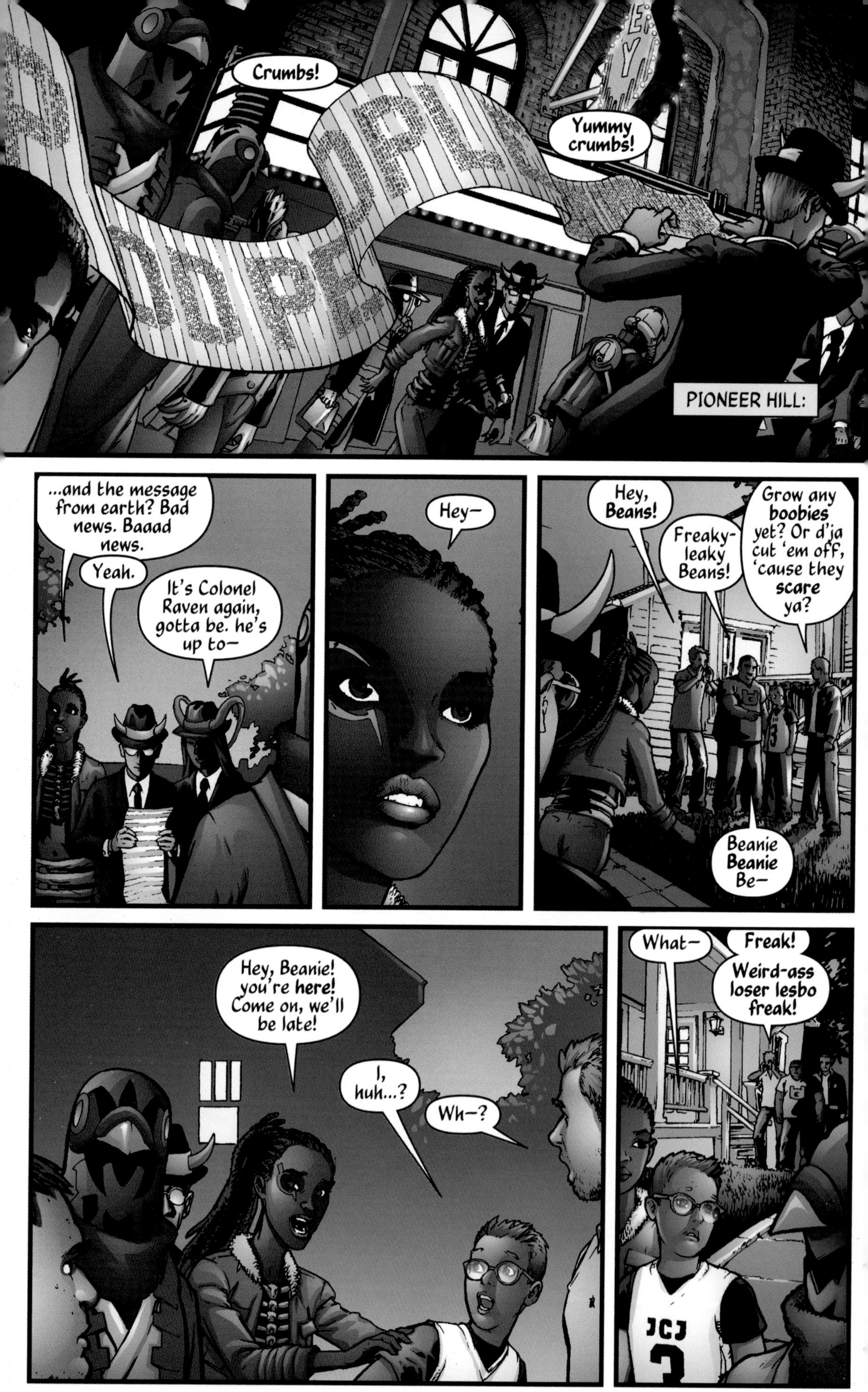
Crumbs!
Yummy crumbs!
PIONEER HILL:
...and the message from earth? Bad news. Baaad news.
Yeah.
It's Colonel Raven again, gotta be. he's up to—
Hey—
Hey, Beans!
Freaky-leaky Beans!
Grow any boobies yet? Or d'ja cut 'em off, 'cause they scare ya?
Beanie Beanie Be—
Hey, Beanie! you're here! Come on, we'll be late!
I, huh...?
Wh–?
What—
Freak! Weird-ass loser lesbo freak!
JCJ
3

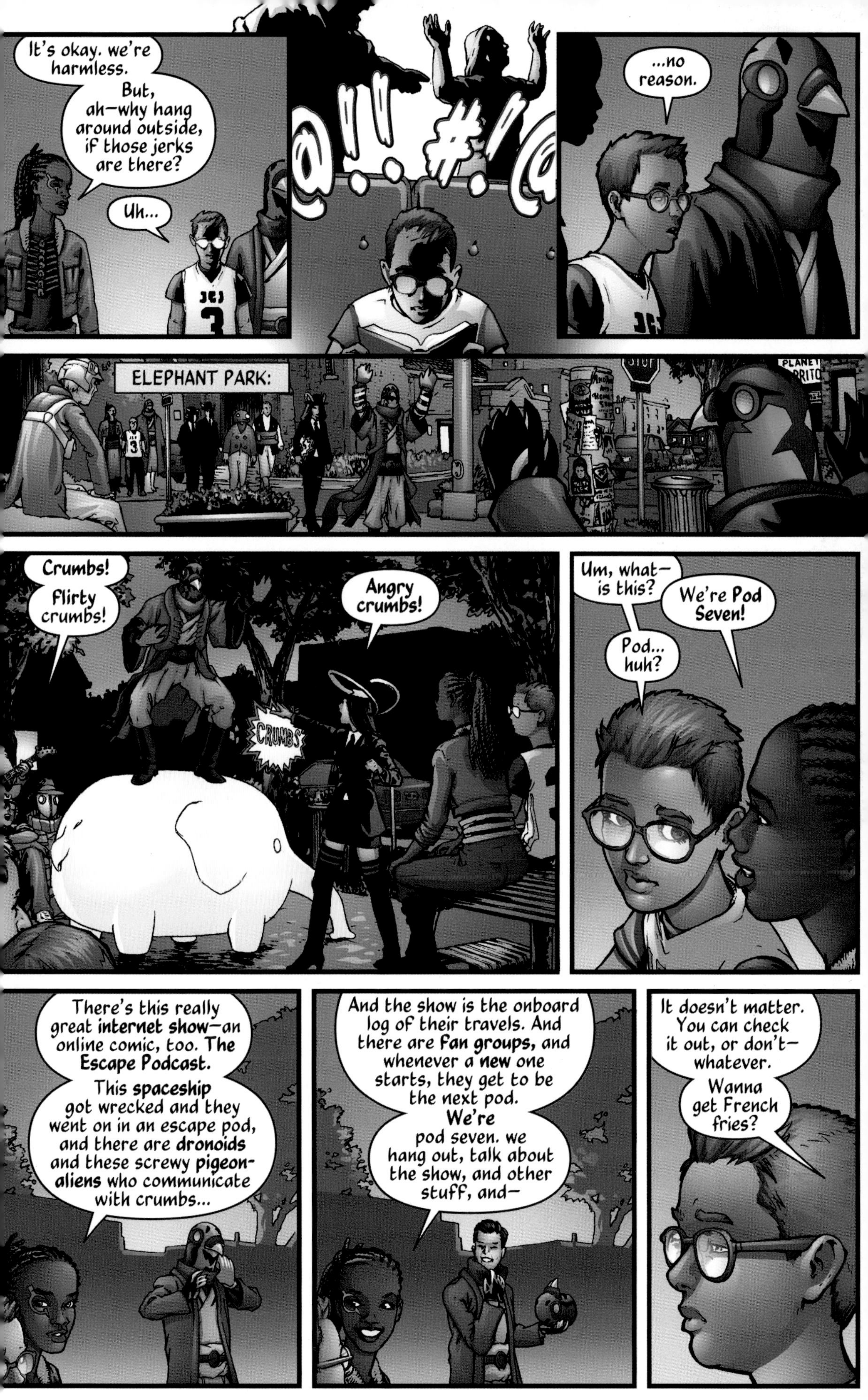
It's okay. we're harmless.
But, ah—why hang around outside, if those jerks are there?
Uh...
@!!#!@
...no reason.
ELEPHANT PARK:
Crumbs! Flirty crumbs!
Angry crumbs!
CRUMBS
Um, what—is this?
We're Pod Seven!
Pod... huh?
There's this really great internet show—an online comic, too. The Escape Podcast.
This spaceship got wrecked and they went on in an escape pod, and there are dronoids and these screwy pigeon-aliens who communicate with crumbs...
And the show is the onboard log of their travels. And there are fan groups, and whenever a new one starts, they get to be the next pod.
We're pod seven. we hang out, talk about the show, and other stuff, and—
It doesn't matter. You can check it out, or don't—whatever.
Wanna get French fries?

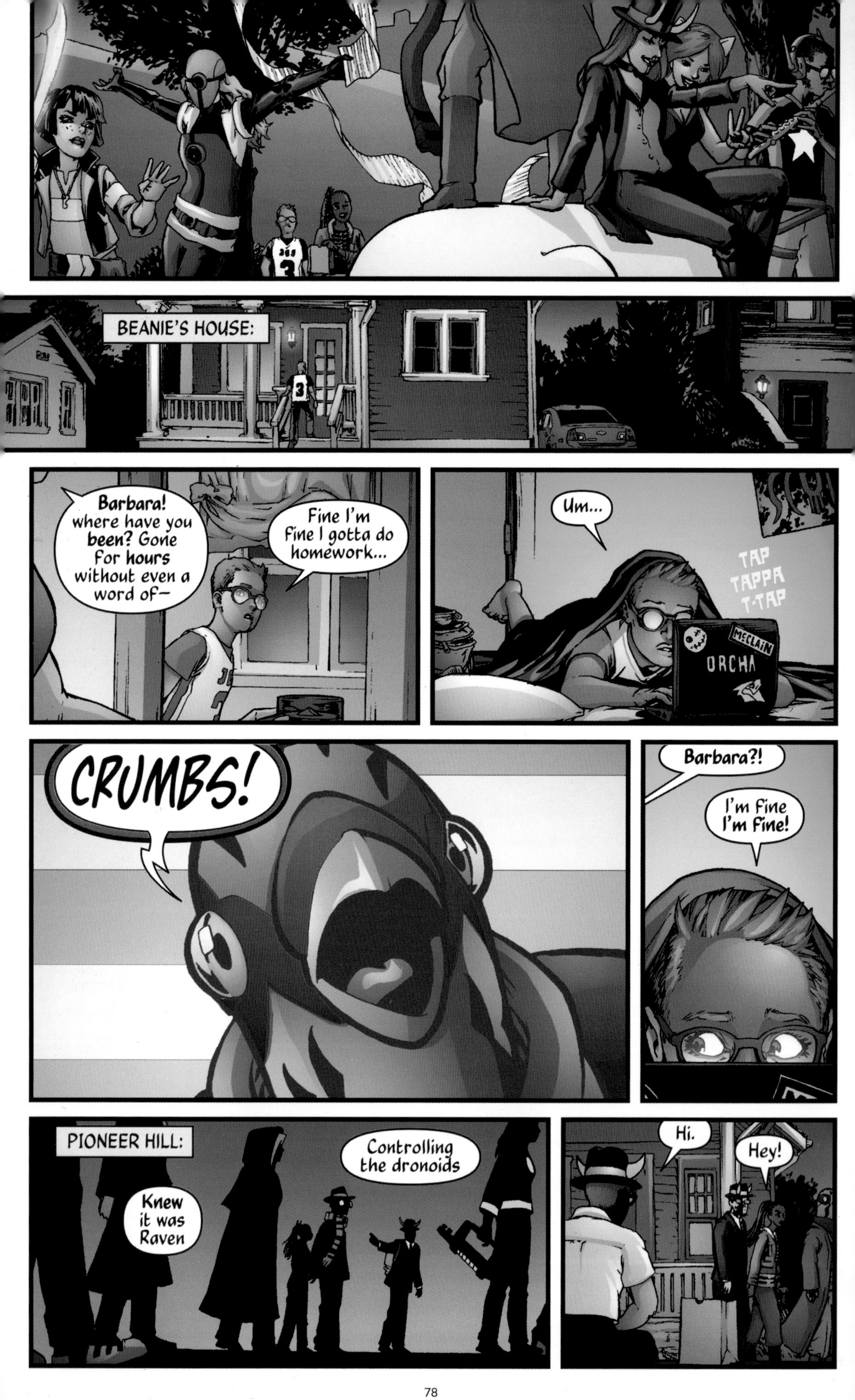

BEANIE'S HOUSE:
Barbara! where have you been? Gone for hours without even a word of—
Fine I'm fine I gotta do homework...
Um...
TAP TAPPA T-TAP
McCLAIN
ORCHA
CRUMBS!
Barbara?!
I'm fine I'm fine!
PIONEER HILL:
Controlling the dronoids
Knew it was Raven
Hi.
Hey!

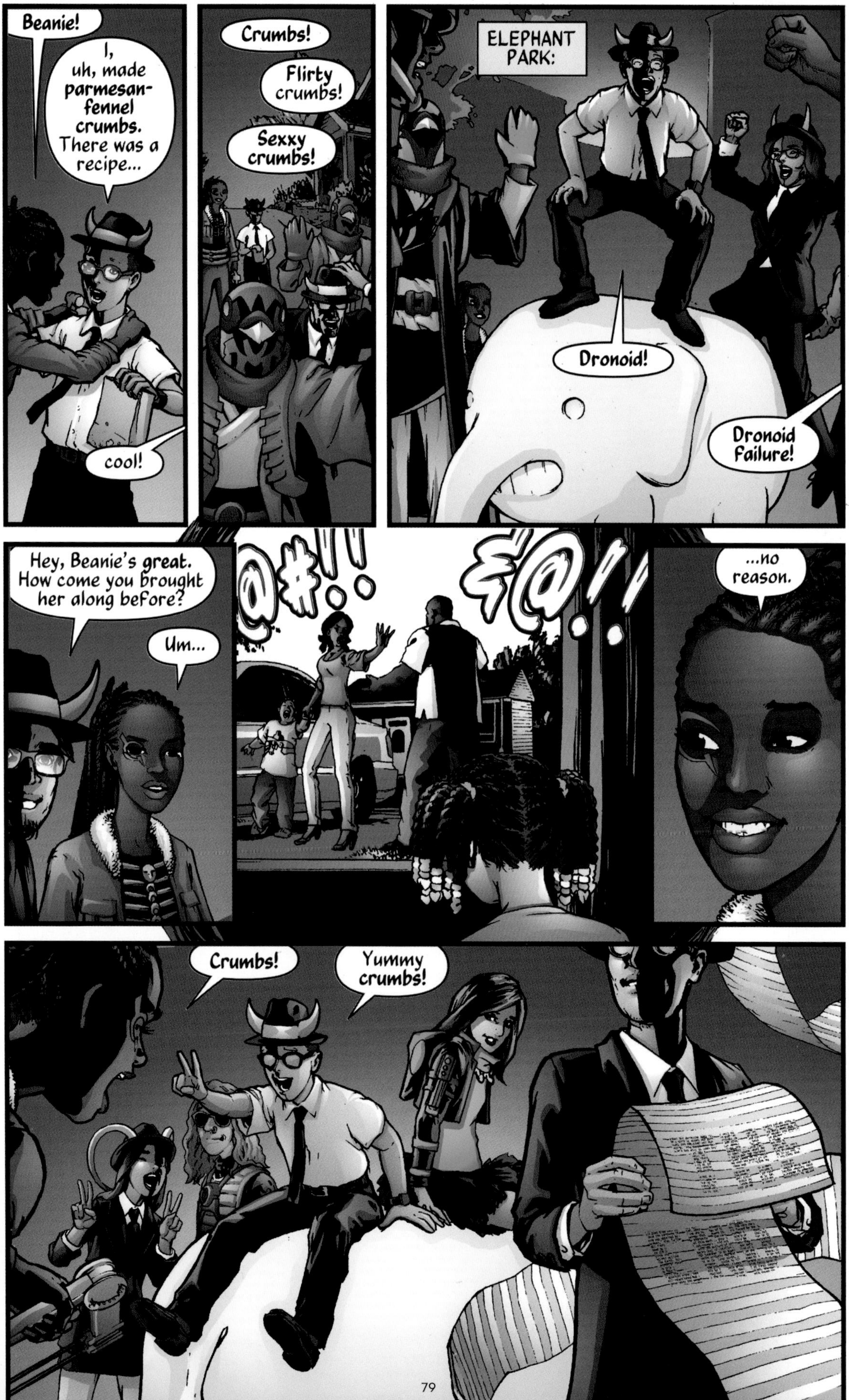
Beanie!
I, uh, made parmesan-fennel crumbs. There was a recipe...
cool!
Crumbs!
Flirty crumbs!
Sexxy crumbs!
ELEPHANT PARK:
Dronoid!
Dronoid failure!
Hey, Beanie's great. How come you brought her along before?
Um...
@#!!
&@!!
...no reason.
Crumbs!
Yummy crumbs!

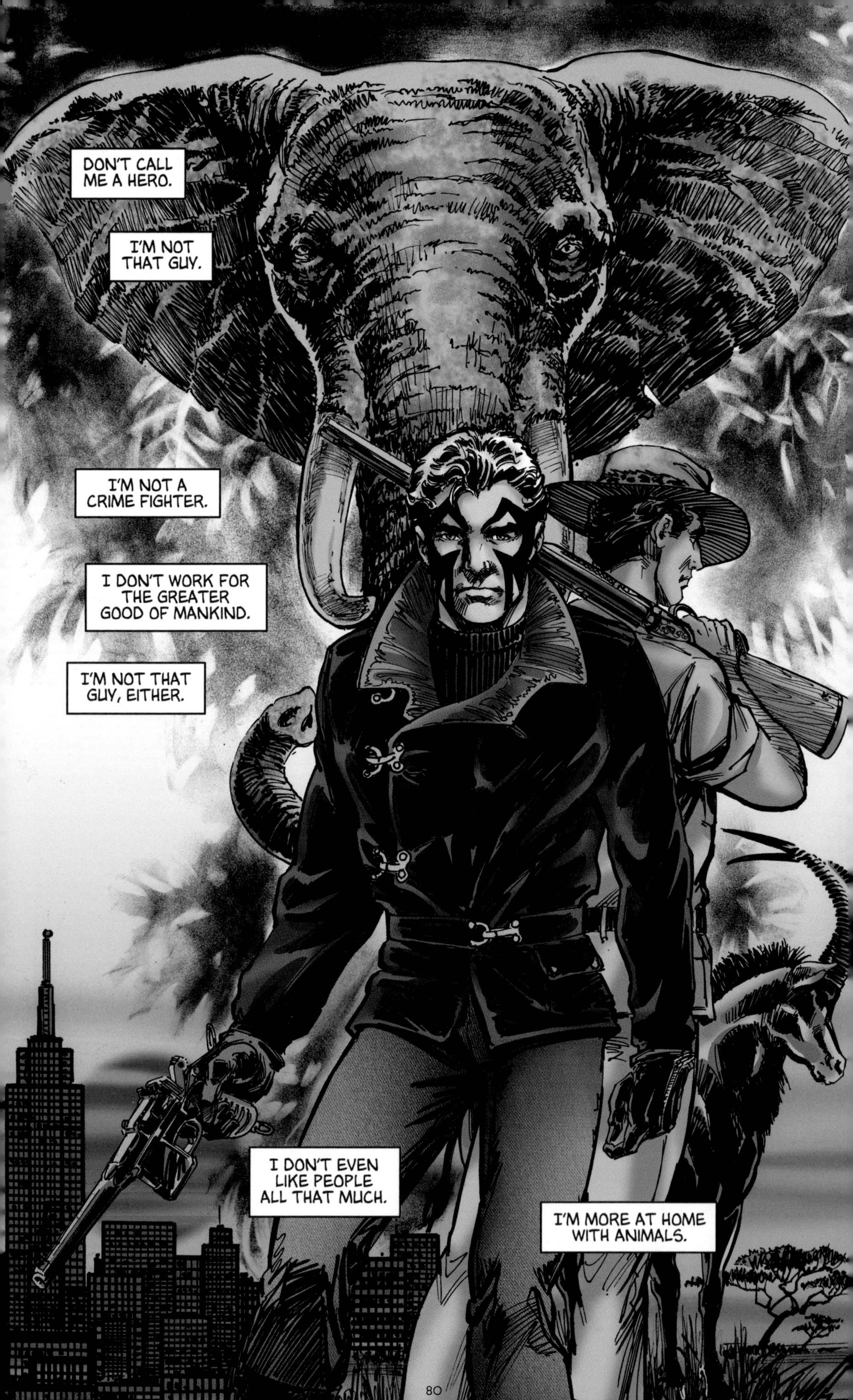
DON'T CALL ME A HERO.
I'M NOT THAT GUY.
I'M NOT A CRIME FIGHTER.
I DON'T WORK FOR THE GREATER GOOD OF MANKIND.
I'M NOT THAT GUY, EITHER.
I DON'T EVEN LIKE PEOPLE ALL THAT MUCH.
I'M MORE AT HOME WITH ANIMALS.

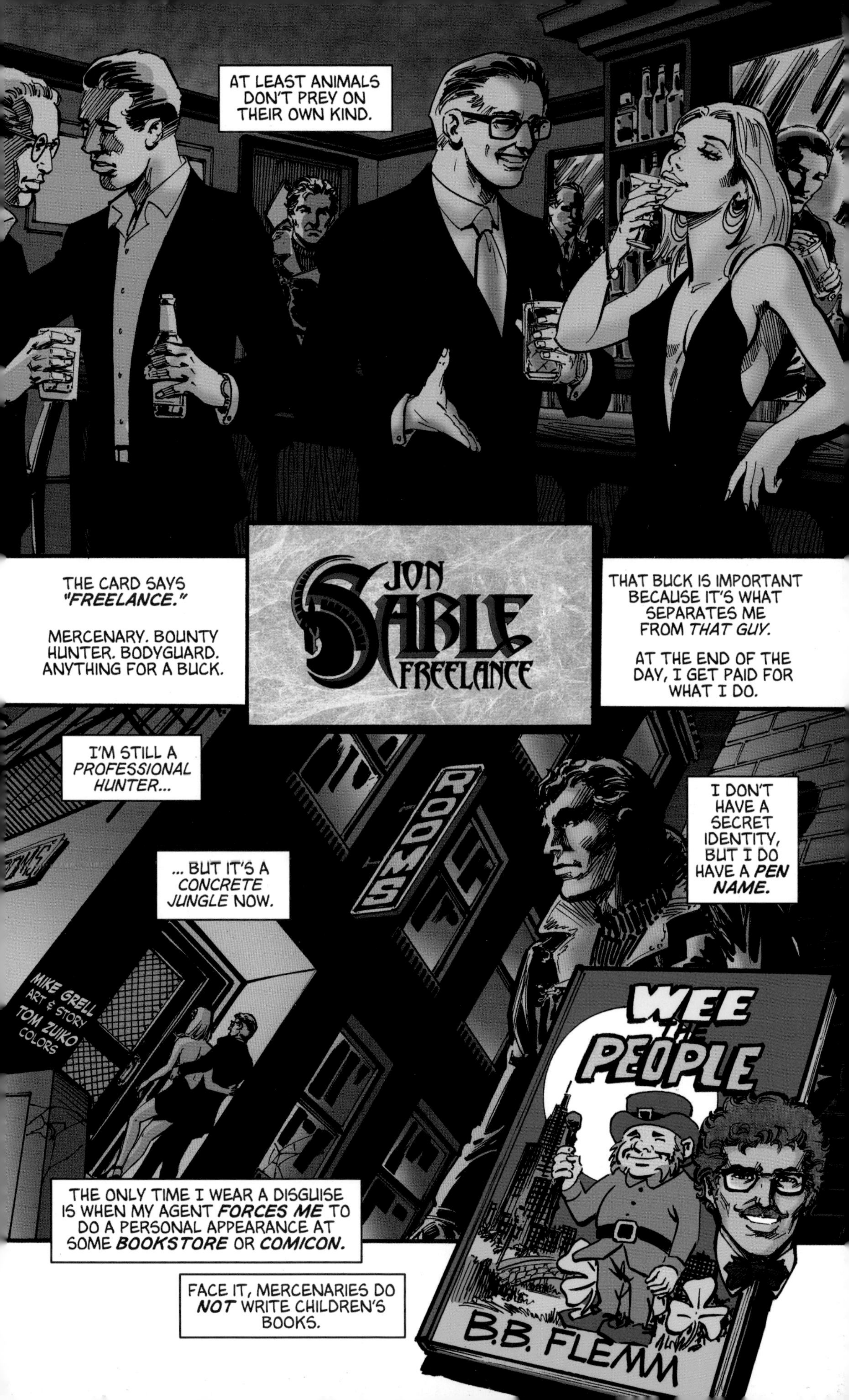
AT LEAST ANIMALS DON'T PREY ON THEIR OWN KIND.
THE CARD SAYS "FREELANCE."
MERCENARY. BOUNTY HUNTER. BODYGUARD. ANYTHING FOR A BUCK.
JON SABLE FREELANCE
THAT BUCK IS IMPORTANT BECAUSE IT'S WHAT SEPARATES ME FROM THAT GUY.
AT THE END OF THE DAY, I GET PAID FOR WHAT I DO.
I'M STILL A PROFESSIONAL HUNTER...
... BUT IT'S A CONCRETE JUNGLE NOW.
ROOMS
I DON'T HAVE A SECRET IDENTITY, BUT I DO HAVE A PEN NAME.
MIKE GRELL ART & STORY
TOM ZUIKO COLORS
WEE THE PEOPLE
THE ONLY TIME I WEAR A DISGUISE IS WHEN MY AGENT FORCES ME TO DO A PERSONAL APPEARANCE AT SOME BOOKSTORE OR COMICON.
FACE IT, MERCENARIES DO NOT WRITE CHILDREN'S BOOKS.
B.B. FLEMM

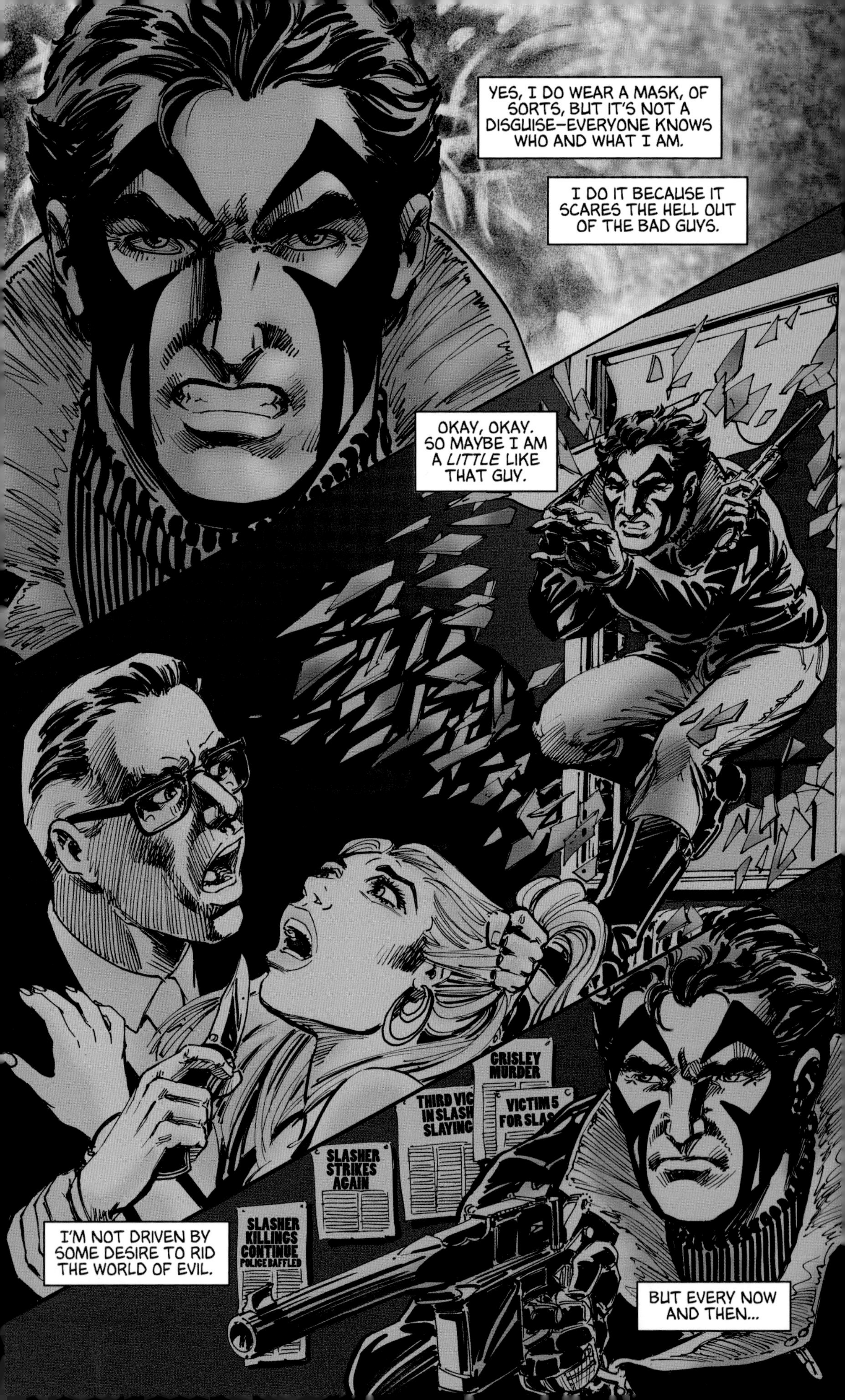
YES, I DO WEAR A MASK, OF SORTS, BUT IT'S NOT A DISGUISE—EVERYONE KNOWS WHO AND WHAT I AM.
I DO IT BECAUSE IT SCARES THE HELL OUT OF THE BAD GUYS.
OKAY, OKAY. SO MAYBE I AM A *LITTLE* LIKE THAT GUY.
GRISLEY MURDER
THIRD VIC IN SLASH SLAYING
VICTIM 5 FOR SLAS
SLASHER STRIKES AGAIN
SLASHER KILLINGS CONTINUE POLICE BAFFLED
I'M NOT DRIVEN BY SOME DESIRE TO RID THE WORLD OF EVIL.
BUT EVERY NOW AND THEN...

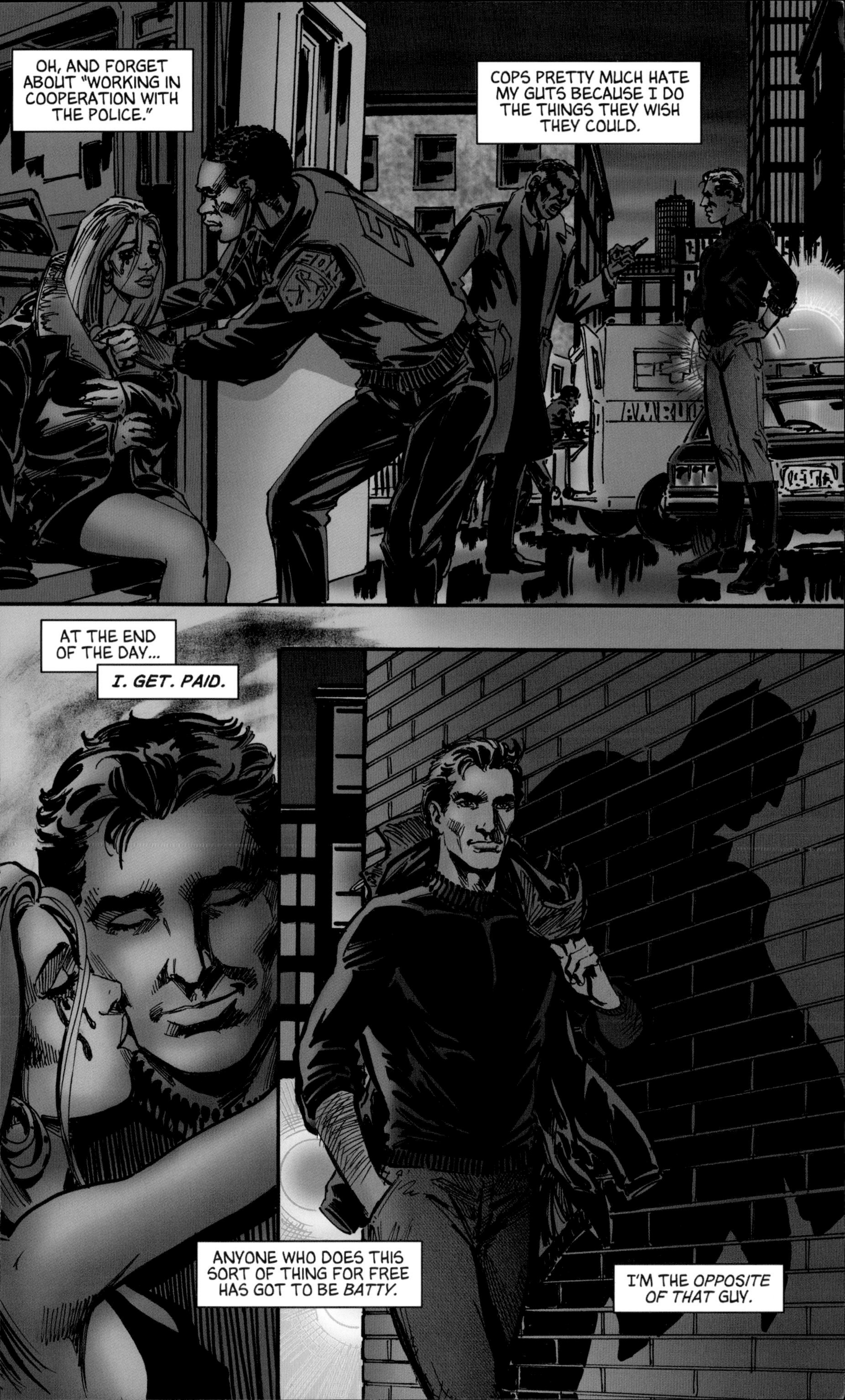
OH, AND FORGET ABOUT "WORKING IN COOPERATION WITH THE POLICE."
COPS PRETTY MUCH HATE MY GUTS BECAUSE I DO THE THINGS THEY WISH THEY COULD.
AT THE END OF THE DAY...
I. GET. PAID.
ANYONE WHO DOES THIS SORT OF THING FOR FREE HAS GOT TO BE *BATTY.*
I'M THE *OPPOSITE OF THAT* GUY.

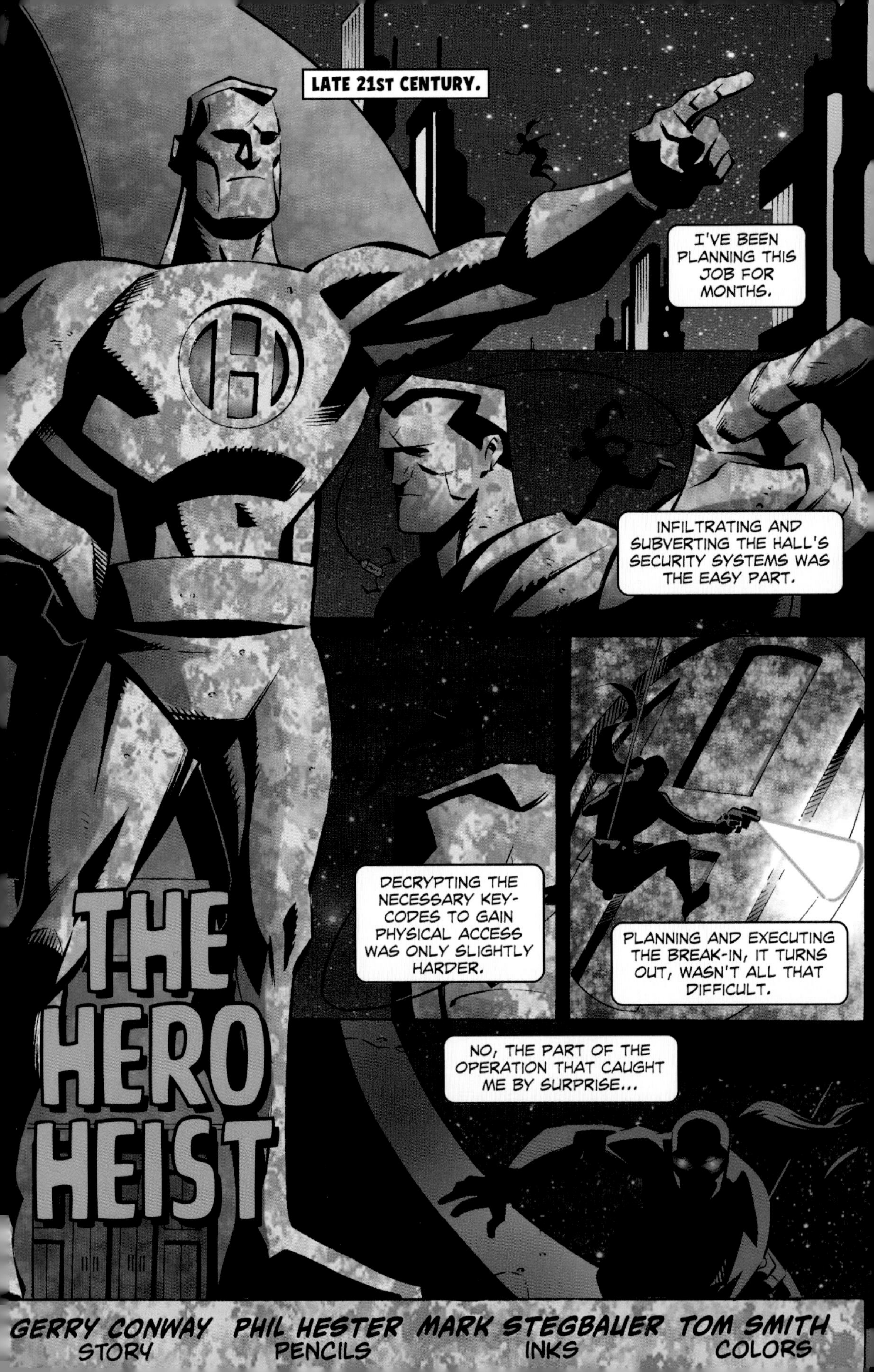
LATE 21ST CENTURY.
I'VE BEEN PLANNING THIS JOB FOR MONTHS.
INFILTRATING AND SUBVERTING THE HALL'S SECURITY SYSTEMS WAS THE EASY PART.
DECRYPTING THE NECESSARY KEY-CODES TO GAIN PHYSICAL ACCESS WAS ONLY SLIGHTLY HARDER.
PLANNING AND EXECUTING THE BREAK-IN, IT TURNS OUT, WASN'T ALL THAT DIFFICULT.
NO, THE PART OF THE OPERATION THAT CAUGHT ME BY SURPRISE...
THE HERO HEIST
GERRY CONWAY STORY
PHIL HESTER PENCILS
MARK STEGBAUER INKS
TOM SMITH COLORS

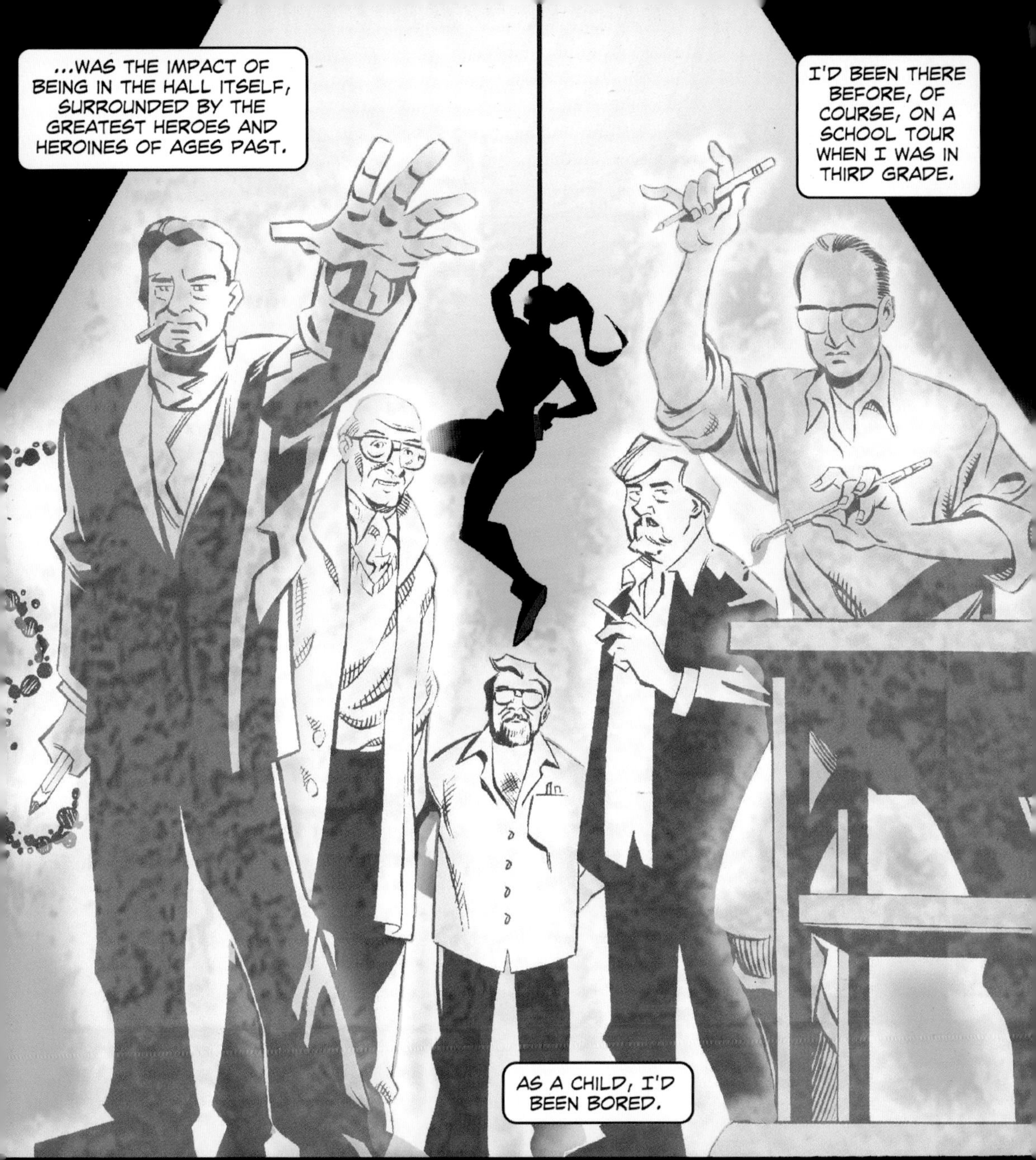
...WAS THE IMPACT OF BEING IN THE HALL ITSELF, SURROUNDED BY THE GREATEST HEROES AND HEROINES OF AGES PAST.
I'D BEEN THERE BEFORE, OF COURSE, ON A SCHOOL TOUR WHEN I WAS IN THIRD GRADE.
AS A CHILD, I'D BEEN BORED.
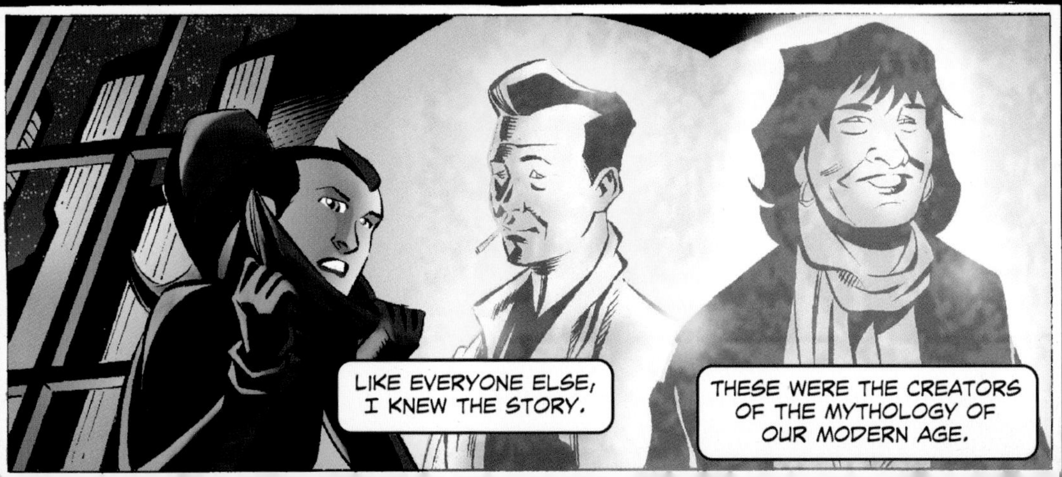
LIKE EVERYONE ELSE, I KNEW THE STORY.
THESE WERE THE CREATORS OF THE MYTHOLOGY OF OUR MODERN AGE.

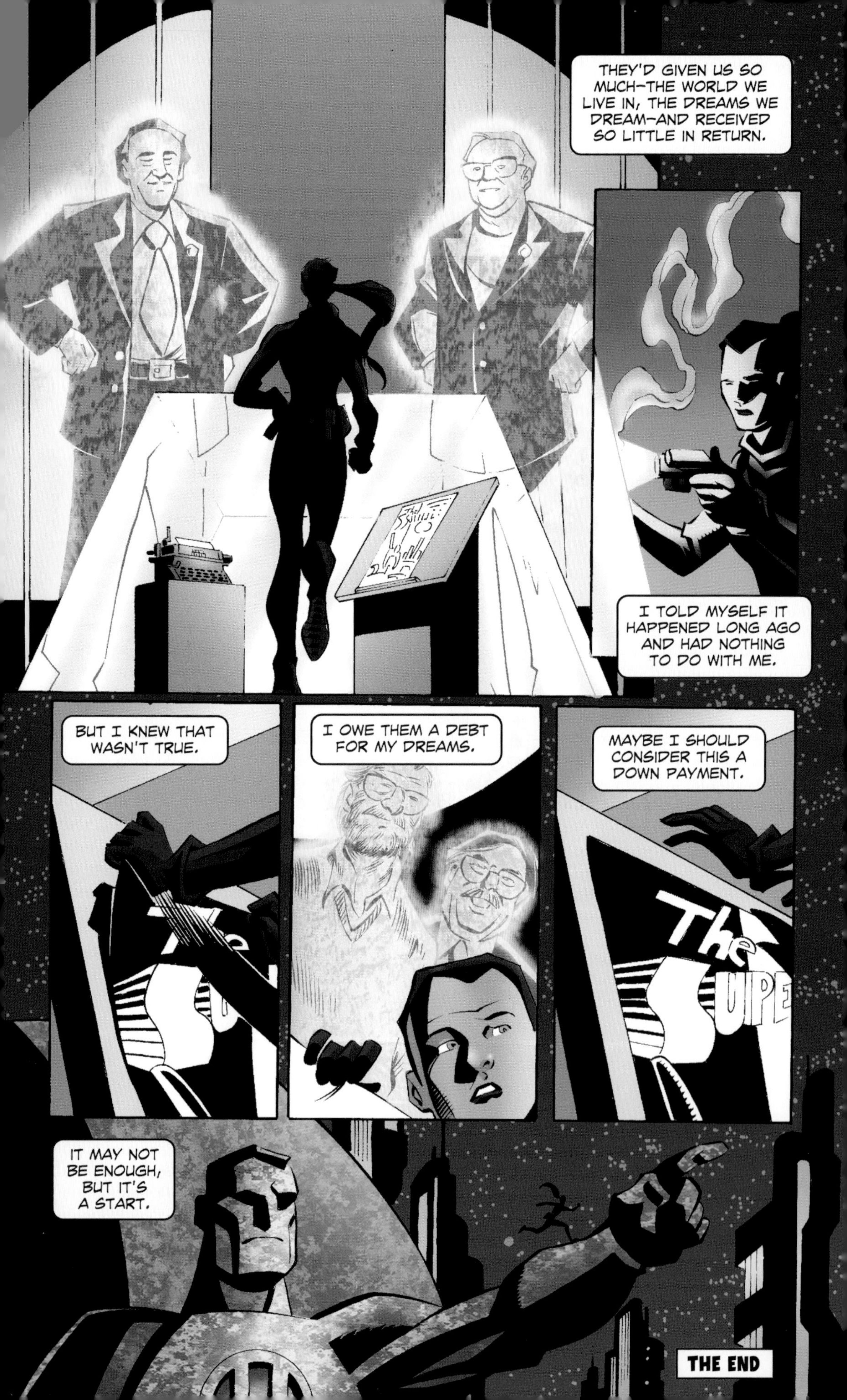
THEY'D GIVEN US SO MUCH—THE WORLD WE LIVE IN, THE DREAMS WE DREAM—AND RECEIVED SO LITTLE IN RETURN.
I TOLD MYSELF IT HAPPENED LONG AGO AND HAD NOTHING TO DO WITH ME.
BUT I KNEW THAT WASN'T TRUE.
I OWE THEM A DEBT FOR MY DREAMS.
MAYBE I SHOULD CONSIDER THIS A DOWN PAYMENT.
IT MAY NOT BE ENOUGH, BUT IT'S A START.
THE END

PART TWO HERO IN ACTION

ALL LETTERING BY **COMICRAFT**
UNLESS OTHERWISE NOTED.

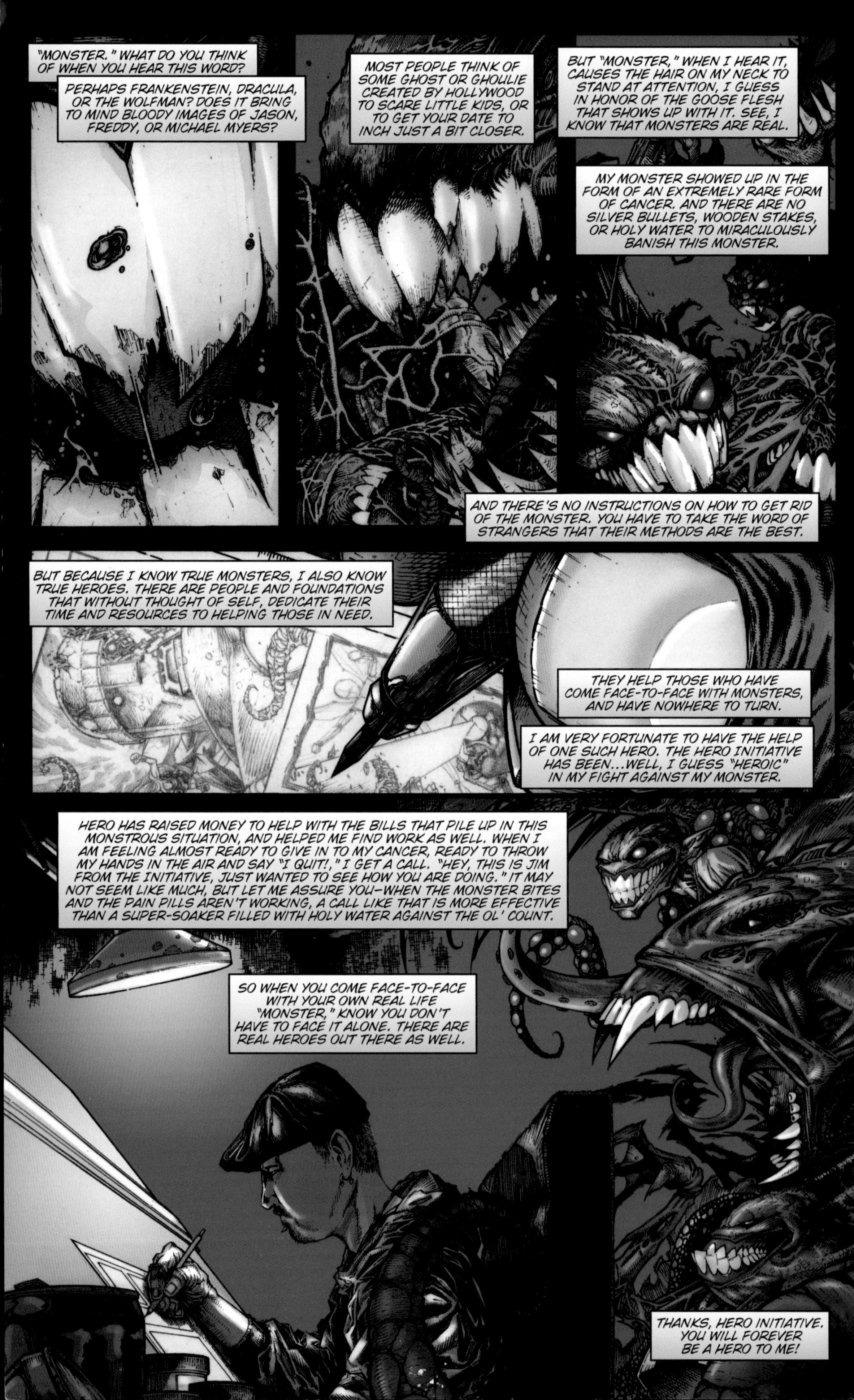
"MONSTER." WHAT DO YOU THINK OF WHEN YOU HEAR THIS WORD?
PERHAPS FRANKENSTEIN, DRACULA, OR THE WOLFMAN? DOES IT BRING TO MIND BLOODY IMAGES OF JASON, FREDDY, OR MICHAEL MYERS?
MOST PEOPLE THINK OF SOME GHOST OR GHOULIE CREATED BY HOLLYWOOD TO SCARE LITTLE KIDS, OR TO GET YOUR DATE TO INCH JUST A BIT CLOSER.
BUT "MONSTER," WHEN I HEAR IT, CAUSES THE HAIR ON MY NECK TO STAND AT ATTENTION, I GUESS IN HONOR OF THE GOOSE FLESH THAT SHOWS UP WITH IT. SEE, I KNOW THAT MONSTERS ARE REAL.
MY MONSTER SHOWED UP IN THE FORM OF AN EXTREMELY RARE FORM OF CANCER. AND THERE ARE NO SILVER BULLETS, WOODEN STAKES, OR HOLY WATER TO MIRACULOUSLY BANISH THIS MONSTER.
AND THERE'S NO INSTRUCTIONS ON HOW TO GET RID OF THE MONSTER. YOU HAVE TO TAKE THE WORD OF STRANGERS THAT THEIR METHODS ARE THE BEST.
BUT BECAUSE I KNOW TRUE MONSTERS, I ALSO KNOW TRUE HEROES. THERE ARE PEOPLE AND FOUNDATIONS THAT WITHOUT THOUGHT OF SELF, DEDICATE THEIR TIME AND RESOURCES TO HELPING THOSE IN NEED.
THEY HELP THOSE WHO HAVE COME FACE-TO-FACE WITH MONSTERS, AND HAVE NOWHERE TO TURN.
I AM VERY FORTUNATE TO HAVE THE HELP OF ONE SUCH HERO. THE HERO INITIATIVE HAS BEEN...WELL, I GUESS "HEROIC" IN MY FIGHT AGAINST MY MONSTER.
HERO HAS RAISED MONEY TO HELP WITH THE BILLS THAT PILE UP IN THIS MONSTROUS SITUATION, AND HELPED ME FIND WORK AS WELL. WHEN I AM FEELING ALMOST READY TO GIVE IN TO MY CANCER, READY TO THROW MY HANDS IN THE AIR AND SAY "I QUIT!," I GET A CALL. "HEY, THIS IS JIM FROM THE INITIATIVE, JUST WANTED TO SEE HOW YOU ARE DOING." IT MAY NOT SEEM LIKE MUCH, BUT LET ME ASSURE YOU–WHEN THE MONSTER BITES AND THE PAIN PILLS AREN'T WORKING, A CALL LIKE THAT IS MORE EFFECTIVE THAN A SUPER-SOAKER FILLED WITH HOLY WATER AGAINST THE OL' COUNT.
SO WHEN YOU COME FACE-TO-FACE WITH YOUR OWN REAL LIFE "MONSTER," KNOW YOU DON'T HAVE TO FACE IT ALONE. THERE ARE REAL HEROES OUT THERE AS WELL.
THANKS, HERO INITIATIVE. YOU WILL FOREVER BE A HERO TO ME!

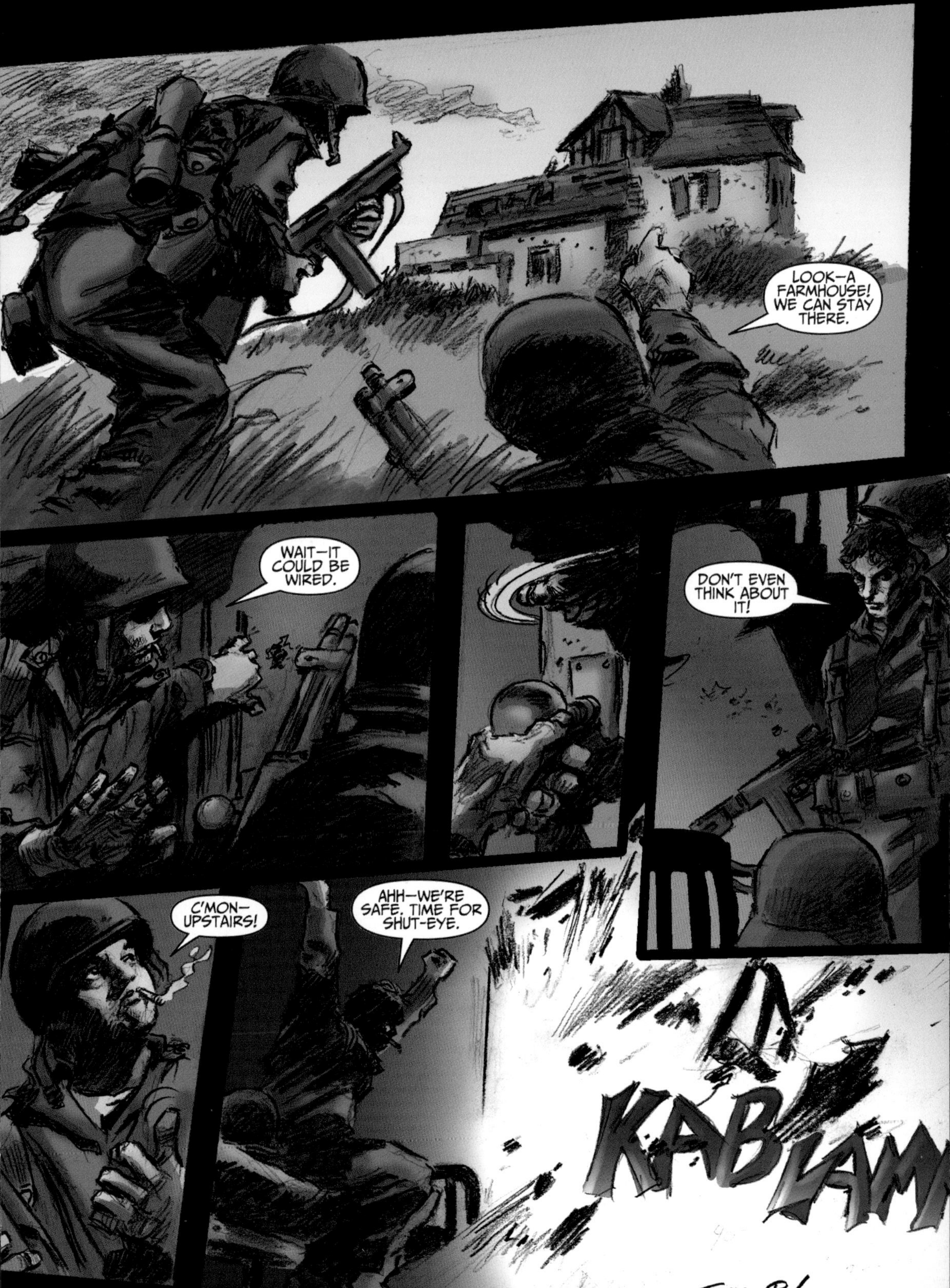
LOOK—A FARMHOUSE! WE CAN STAY THERE.
WAIT—IT COULD BE WIRED.
DON'T EVEN THINK ABOUT IT!
C'MON— UPSTAIRS!
AHH—WE'RE SAFE. TIME FOR SHUT-EYE.
KABLAM
Gene Colan

SOMETIMES, WE ALL NEED A SAFE HAVEN. THANKS, HERO INITIATIVE. —GENE COLAN

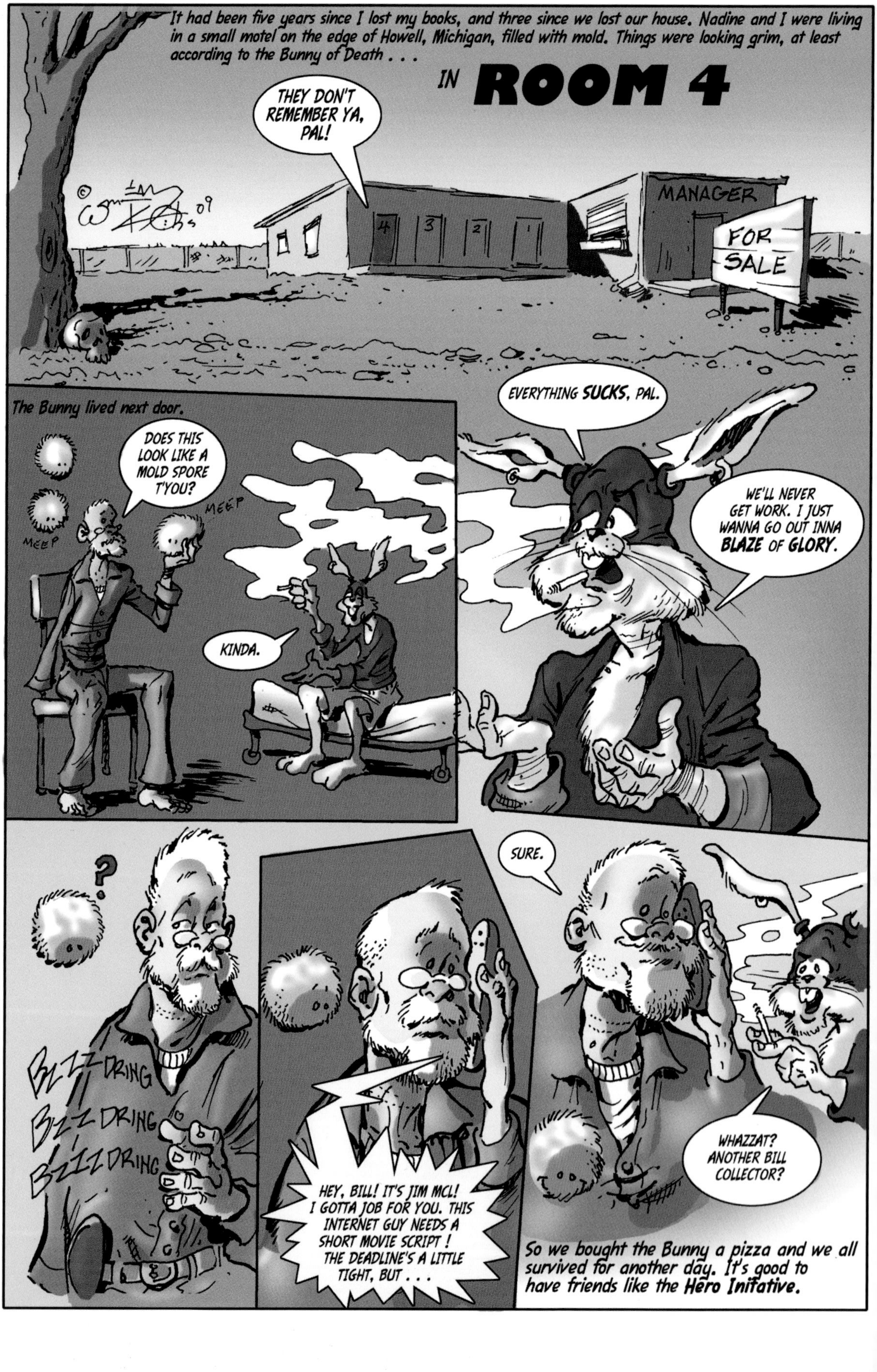
It had been five years since I lost my books, and three since we lost our house. Nadine and I were living in a small motel on the edge of Howell, Michigan, filled with mold. Things were looking grim, at least according to the Bunny of Death . . .
IN ROOM 4
THEY DON'T REMEMBER YA, PAL!
MANAGER
4
3
2
1
FOR SALE
The Bunny lived next door.
DOES THIS LOOK LIKE A MOLD SPORE T'YOU?
MEEP
MEEP
KINDA.
EVERYTHING SUCKS, PAL.
WE'LL NEVER GET WORK. I JUST WANNA GO OUT INNA BLAZE OF GLORY.
?
BZZ DRING
BZZ DRING
BZZZ DRING
HEY, BILL! IT'S JIM MCL! I GOTTA JOB FOR YOU. THIS INTERNET GUY NEEDS A SHORT MOVIE SCRIPT ! THE DEADLINE'S A LITTLE TIGHT, BUT . . .
SURE.
WHAZZAT? ANOTHER BILL COLLECTOR?
So we bought the Bunny a pizza and we all survived for another day. It's good to have friends like the Hero Initative.

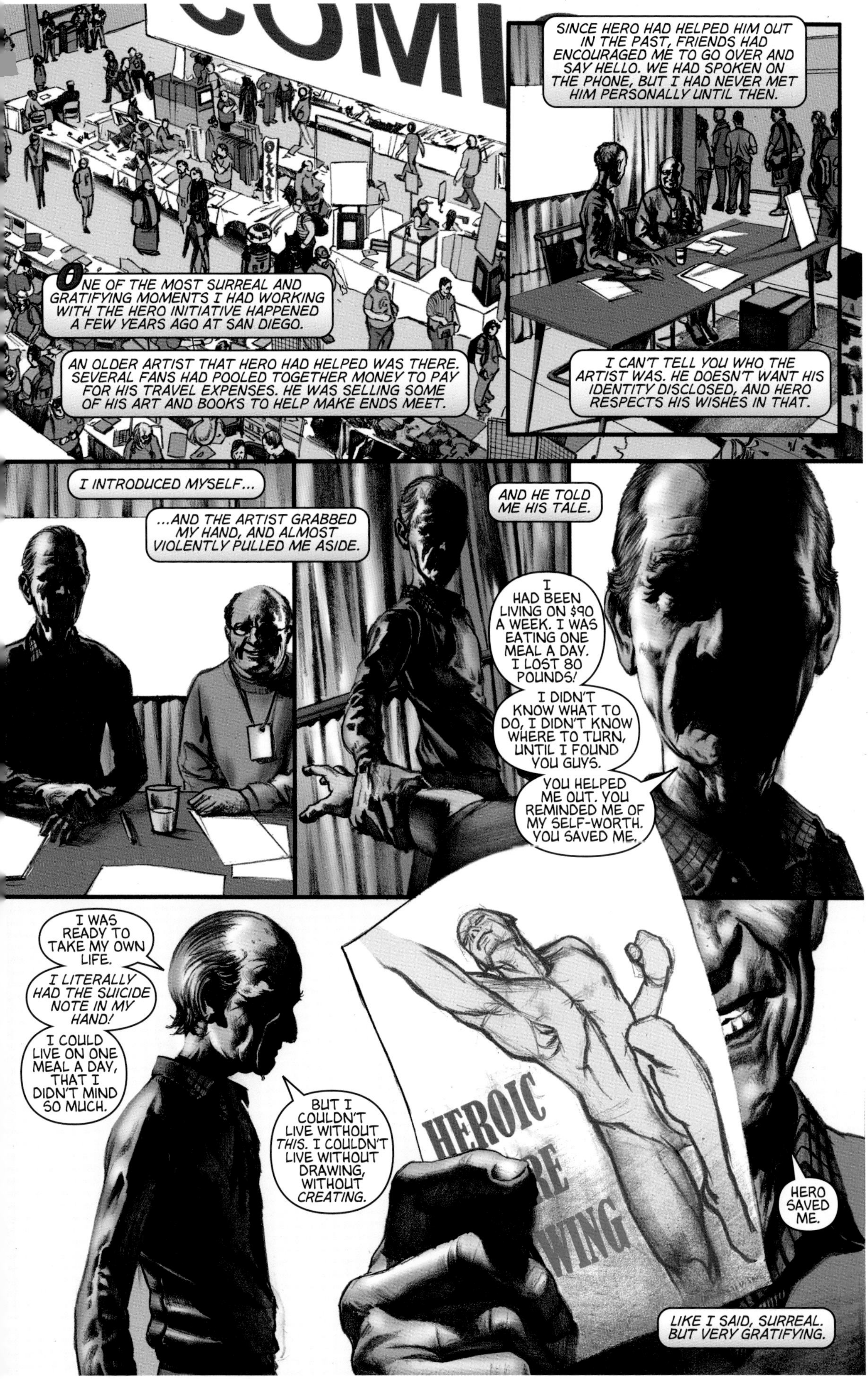

ONE OF THE MOST SURREAL AND GRATIFYING MOMENTS I HAD WORKING WITH THE HERO INITIATIVE HAPPENED A FEW YEARS AGO AT SAN DIEGO.
AN OLDER ARTIST THAT HERO HAD HELPED WAS THERE. SEVERAL FANS HAD POOLED TOGETHER MONEY TO PAY FOR HIS TRAVEL EXPENSES. HE WAS SELLING SOME OF HIS ART AND BOOKS TO HELP MAKE ENDS MEET.
SINCE HERO HAD HELPED HIM OUT IN THE PAST, FRIENDS HAD ENCOURAGED ME TO GO OVER AND SAY HELLO. WE HAD SPOKEN ON THE PHONE, BUT I HAD NEVER MET HIM PERSONALLY UNTIL THEN.
I CAN'T TELL YOU WHO THE ARTIST WAS. HE DOESN'T WANT HIS IDENTITY DISCLOSED, AND HERO RESPECTS HIS WISHES IN THAT.
I INTRODUCED MYSELF...
...AND THE ARTIST GRABBED MY HAND, AND ALMOST VIOLENTLY PULLED ME ASIDE.
AND HE TOLD ME HIS TALE.
I HAD BEEN LIVING ON $90 A WEEK. I WAS EATING ONE MEAL A DAY. I LOST 80 POUNDS!
I DIDN'T KNOW WHAT TO DO, I DIDN'T KNOW WHERE TO TURN, UNTIL I FOUND YOU GUYS.
YOU HELPED ME OUT. YOU REMINDED ME OF MY SELF-WORTH. YOU SAVED ME.
I WAS READY TO TAKE MY OWN LIFE.
I LITERALLY HAD THE SUICIDE NOTE IN MY HAND!
I COULD LIVE ON ONE MEAL A DAY, THAT I DIDN'T MIND SO MUCH.
BUT I COULDN'T LIVE WITHOUT THIS. I COULDN'T LIVE WITHOUT DRAWING, WITHOUT CREATING.
HEROIC
HERO SAVED ME.
LIKE I SAID, SURREAL. BUT VERY GRATIFYING.

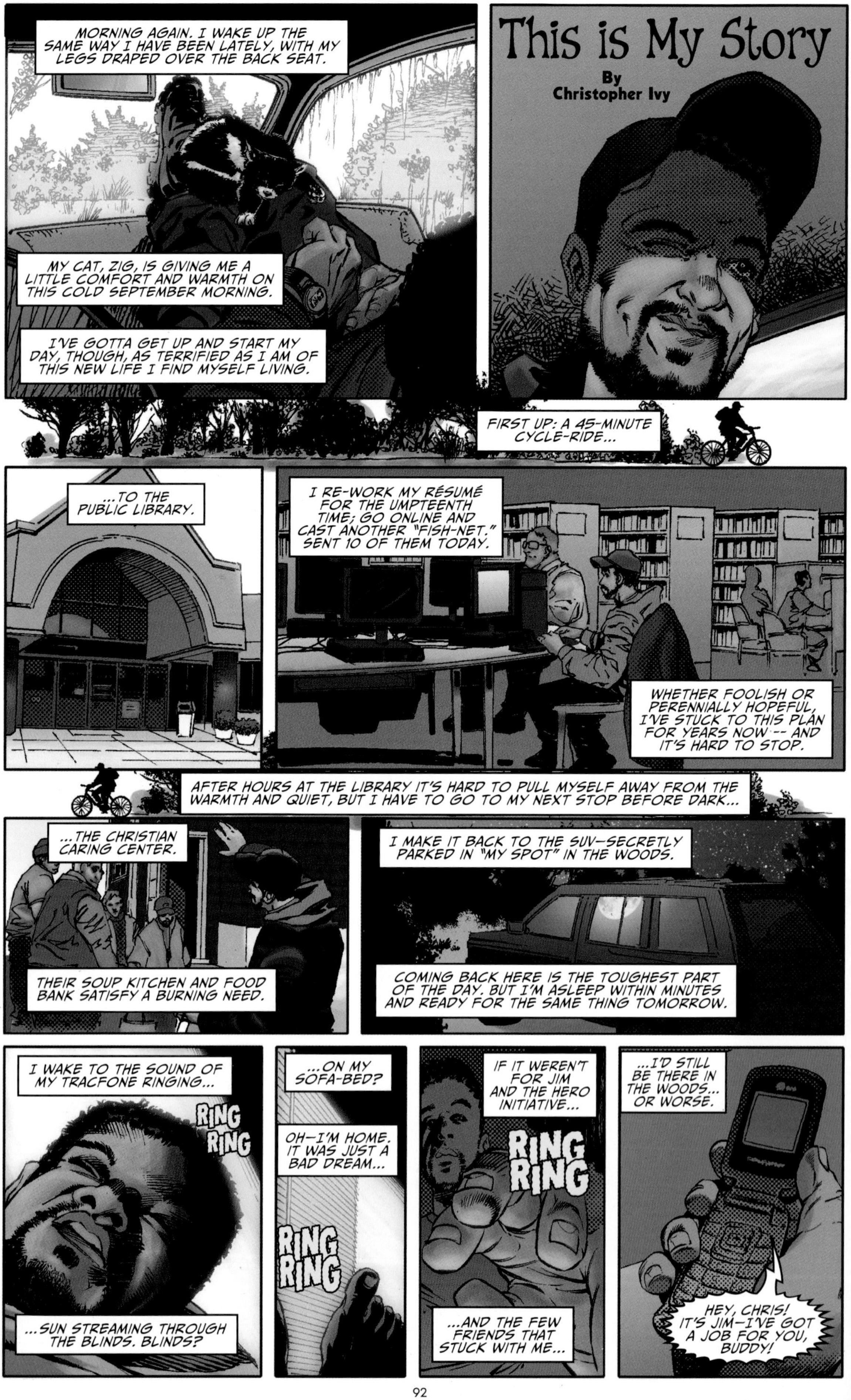
MORNING AGAIN. I WAKE UP THE SAME WAY I HAVE BEEN LATELY, WITH MY LEGS DRAPED OVER THE BACK SEAT.
MY CAT, ZIG, IS GIVING ME A LITTLE COMFORT AND WARMTH ON THIS COLD SEPTEMBER MORNING.
I'VE GOTTA GET UP AND START MY DAY, THOUGH, AS TERRIFIED AS I AM OF THIS NEW LIFE I FIND MYSELF LIVING.
This is My Story
By
Christopher Ivy
FIRST UP: A 45-MINUTE CYCLE-RIDE...
...TO THE PUBLIC LIBRARY.
I RE-WORK MY RÉSUMÉ FOR THE UMPTEENTH TIME; GO ONLINE AND CAST ANOTHER "FISH-NET." SENT 10 OF THEM TODAY.
WHETHER FOOLISH OR PERENNIALLY HOPEFUL, I'VE STUCK TO THIS PLAN FOR YEARS NOW -- AND IT'S HARD TO STOP.
AFTER HOURS AT THE LIBRARY IT'S HARD TO PULL MYSELF AWAY FROM THE WARMTH AND QUIET, BUT I HAVE TO GO TO MY NEXT STOP BEFORE DARK...
...THE CHRISTIAN CARING CENTER.
THEIR SOUP KITCHEN AND FOOD BANK SATISFY A BURNING NEED.
I MAKE IT BACK TO THE SUV—SECRETLY PARKED IN "MY SPOT" IN THE WOODS.
COMING BACK HERE IS THE TOUGHEST PART OF THE DAY. BUT I'M ASLEEP WITHIN MINUTES AND READY FOR THE SAME THING TOMORROW.
I WAKE TO THE SOUND OF MY TRACFONE RINGING...
RING RING
...SUN STREAMING THROUGH THE BLINDS. BLINDS?
...ON MY SOFA-BED?
OH—I'M HOME. IT WAS JUST A BAD DREAM...
RING RING
IF IT WEREN'T FOR JIM AND THE HERO INITIATIVE...
RING RING
...AND THE FEW FRIENDS THAT STUCK WITH ME...
...I'D STILL BE THERE IN THE WOODS... OR WORSE.
HEY, CHRIS! IT'S JIM—I'VE GOT A JOB FOR YOU, BUDDY!

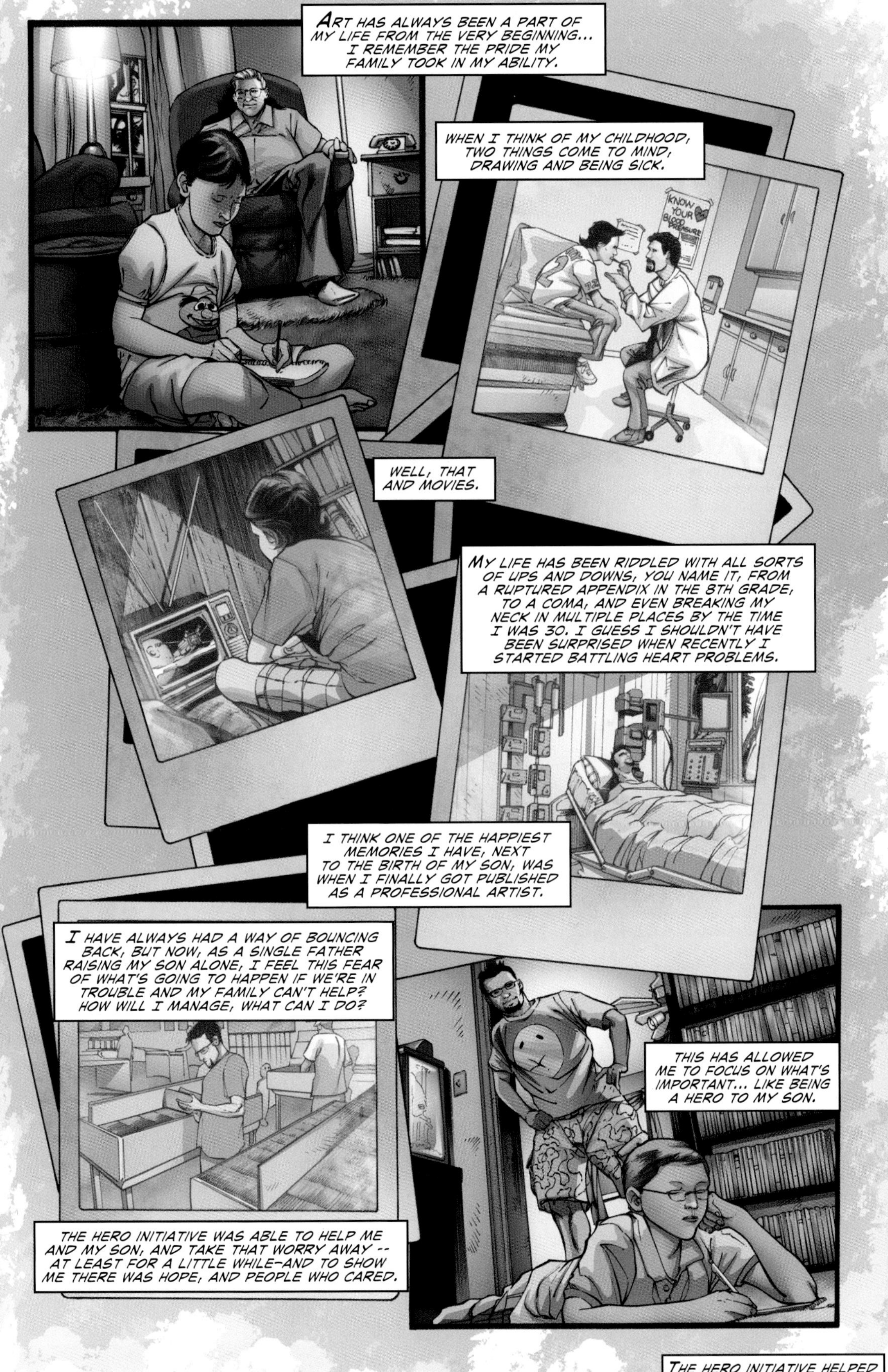
ART HAS ALWAYS BEEN A PART OF MY LIFE FROM THE VERY BEGINNING... I REMEMBER THE PRIDE MY FAMILY TOOK IN MY ABILITY.
WHEN I THINK OF MY CHILDHOOD, TWO THINGS COME TO MIND; DRAWING AND BEING SICK.
WELL, THAT AND MOVIES.
MY LIFE HAS BEEN RIDDLED WITH ALL SORTS OF UPS AND DOWNS, YOU NAME IT, FROM A RUPTURED APPENDIX IN THE 8TH GRADE, TO A COMA, AND EVEN BREAKING MY NECK IN MULTIPLE PLACES BY THE TIME I WAS 30. I GUESS I SHOULDN'T HAVE BEEN SURPRISED WHEN RECENTLY I STARTED BATTLING HEART PROBLEMS.
I THINK ONE OF THE HAPPIEST MEMORIES I HAVE, NEXT TO THE BIRTH OF MY SON, WAS WHEN I FINALLY GOT PUBLISHED AS A PROFESSIONAL ARTIST.
I HAVE ALWAYS HAD A WAY OF BOUNCING BACK, BUT NOW, AS A SINGLE FATHER RAISING MY SON ALONE, I FEEL THIS FEAR OF WHAT'S GOING TO HAPPEN IF WE'RE IN TROUBLE AND MY FAMILY CAN'T HELP? HOW WILL I MANAGE, WHAT CAN I DO?
THE HERO INITIATIVE WAS ABLE TO HELP ME AND MY SON, AND TAKE THAT WORRY AWAY -- AT LEAST FOR A LITTLE WHILE--AND TO SHOW ME THERE WAS HOPE, AND PEOPLE WHO CARED.
THIS HAS ALLOWED ME TO FOCUS ON WHAT'S IMPORTANT... LIKE BEING A HERO TO MY SON.
THE HERO INITIATIVE HELPED MAKE THAT POSSIBLE.

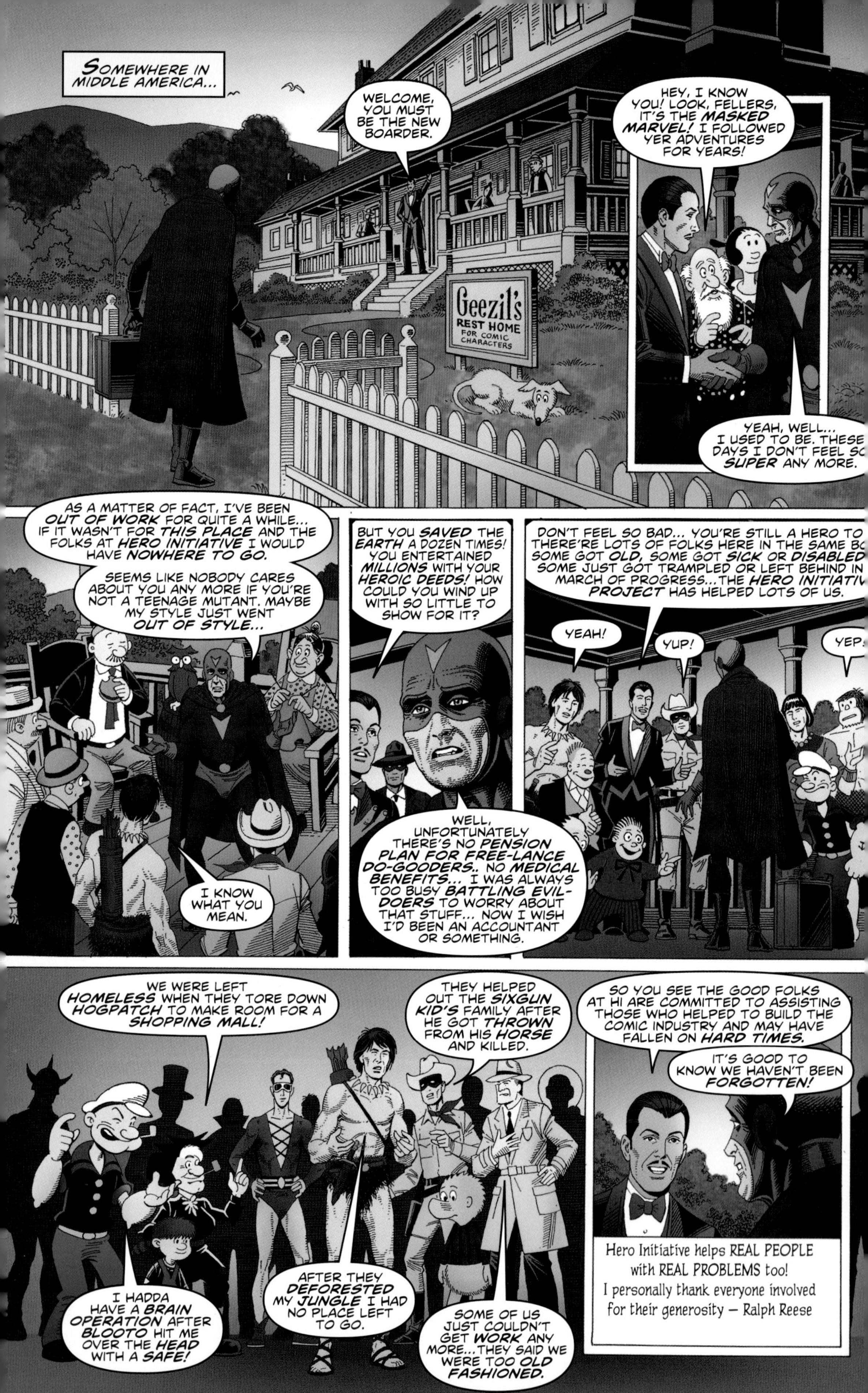
SOMEWHERE IN MIDDLE AMERICA...
WELCOME, YOU MUST BE THE NEW BOARDER.
Geezil's REST HOME FOR COMIC CHARACTERS
HEY, I KNOW YOU! LOOK, FELLERS, IT'S THE MASKED MARVEL! I FOLLOWED YER ADVENTURES FOR YEARS!
YEAH, WELL... I USED TO BE. THESE DAYS I DON'T FEEL SO SUPER ANY MORE.
AS A MATTER OF FACT, I'VE BEEN OUT OF WORK FOR QUITE A WHILE... IF IT WASN'T FOR THIS PLACE AND THE FOLKS AT HERO INITIATIVE I WOULD HAVE NOWHERE TO GO.
SEEMS LIKE NOBODY CARES ABOUT YOU ANY MORE IF YOU'RE NOT A TEENAGE MUTANT. MAYBE MY STYLE JUST WENT OUT OF STYLE...
I KNOW WHAT YOU MEAN.
BUT YOU SAVED THE EARTH A DOZEN TIMES! YOU ENTERTAINED MILLIONS WITH YOUR HEROIC DEEDS! HOW COULD YOU WIND UP WITH SO LITTLE TO SHOW FOR IT?
WELL, UNFORTUNATELY THERE'S NO PENSION PLAN FOR FREE-LANCE DO-GOODERS.. NO MEDICAL BENEFITS... I WAS ALWAYS TOO BUSY BATTLING EVIL-DOERS TO WORRY ABOUT THAT STUFF... NOW I WISH I'D BEEN AN ACCOUNTANT OR SOMETHING.
DON'T FEEL SO BAD... YOU'RE STILL A HERO TO US. THERE'RE LOTS OF FOLKS HERE IN THE SAME BO SOME GOT OLD, SOME GOT SICK OR DISABLED SOME JUST GOT TRAMPLED OR LEFT BEHIND IN MARCH OF PROGRESS...THE HERO INITIATIV PROJECT HAS HELPED LOTS OF US.
YEAH!
YUP!
YEP.
WE WERE LEFT HOMELESS WHEN THEY TORE DOWN HOGPATCH TO MAKE ROOM FOR A SHOPPING MALL!
THEY HELPED OUT THE SIXGUN KID'S FAMILY AFTER HE GOT THROWN FROM HIS HORSE AND KILLED.
SO YOU SEE THE GOOD FOLKS AT HI ARE COMMITTED TO ASSISTING THOSE WHO HELPED TO BUILD THE COMIC INDUSTRY AND MAY HAVE FALLEN ON HARD TIMES.
IT'S GOOD TO KNOW WE HAVEN'T BEEN FORGOTTEN!
I HADDA HAVE A BRAIN OPERATION AFTER BLOOTO HIT ME OVER THE HEAD WITH A SAFE!
AFTER THEY DEFORESTED MY JUNGLE I HAD NO PLACE LEFT TO GO.
SOME OF US JUST COULDN'T GET WORK ANY MORE...THEY SAID WE WERE TOO OLD FASHIONED.
Hero Initiative helps REAL PEOPLE with REAL PROBLEMS too! I personally thank everyone involved for their generosity — Ralph Reese

*I WAS NEVER A BELIEVER! BUT THEN I LEARNED THE TRUTH--ON EARTH, THERE **DO** EXIST-*

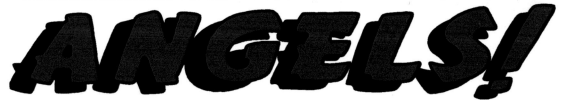

ANGELS!

LAST YEAR WAS BRUTAL. I'D SPENT TWO MONTHS IN THE HOSPITAL BATTLING KIDNEY FAILURE. THIS TIME IT WAS EMERGENCY SURGERY TO SAVE MY COLON. A BLOOD CLOT IN MY LEG WAS THREATNING TO KILL ME. IT SEEMED I HAD MORE IV'S IN MY ARMS THAN VEINS LEFT TO TAP...

I ENCOUNTERED SO MANY NURSES THAT I LOST TRACK OF THEIR NAMES. BUT ONE CONSISTENT THING WAS THEIR PARADE OF UNIFORMS... WHICH NOWADAYS HAD BECOME COLORFUL OUTFITS, FESTOONED WITH ENDLESSLY CHEERFUL AND CHILDISHLY HAPPY MOTIFS...

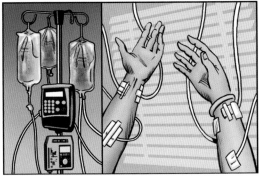

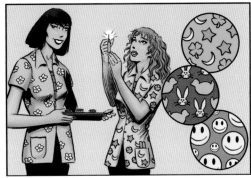

I WAS TAKING MORE PAINKILLERS THAN I THOUGHT WAS HUMANLY POSSIBLE. BEDRIDDEN AND UNABLE TO WALK, THE DAYS TURNED INTO WEEKS AS I SEEMED TO DRIFT IN AND OUT OF REALITY... THEN LATE ONE NIGHT, I HEARD AN ETHEREAL FEMALE VOICE...

FAINT AND QUIET, YET LILTING AND STRANGELY MELODIC AT THE SAME TIME... CLEARLY SHE WAS TALKING ABOUT ME, AND YET I COULDN'T MAKE OUT WHAT SHE WAS SAYING. AND WHO SHE WAS TALKING TO -- NO ONE WAS ANSWERING HER! MY GAZE WAS LOCKED UPON THE DOOR AS IT SLOWLY OPENED...

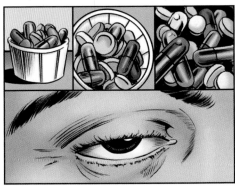

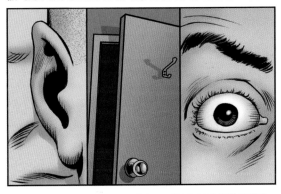

...AND THEN A NURSE - OR WAS IT THE VISION OF A NURSE? DRIFTED INTO THE ROOM, SEEMING TO FLOAT ALONG IN SLOW MOTION. SHE WAS THIN, WITH NEARLY TRANSLUCENT SKIN... BUT THE STRANGEST THING WAS THE WAY SHE WAS DRESSED - LIKE A CLASSIC NURSE FROM OUT OF THE PAST, ALL IN WHITE FROM HEAD TO TOE - WHITE DRESS, WHITE STOCKINGS, WHITE SHOES. SHE TURNED TO ME AND SAID SOMETHING...

...BUT HER VOICE WAS SO QUIET I COULDN'T QUITE MAKE IT OUT. WAS THIS AN ANGEL OF MERCY, SENT FROM HEAVEN TO PROTECT ME? OR WAS THIS IN FACT AN ANGEL OF DEATH, COME TO ESCORT ME OFF TO THE HEREAFTER? THE ANGEL OF DEATH - NOT A SKELETAL FIGURE CLAD IN A BLACK ROBE, CARRYING A SCYTHE TO CUT ME DOWN - BUT RATHER DRESSED ALL IN WHITE?

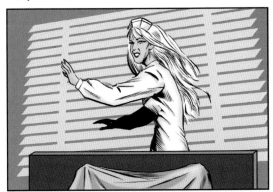

AS QUICKLY AS SHE HAD ENTERED, SHE WAS GONE. I SHOOK MY HEAD IN DISBELIEF AND WAS LEFT WONDERING - WAS SHE REAL? DID SHE EVEN EXIST?? WAS IT JUST A DRUG-FUELED HALLUCINATION???

THE FOLLOWING DAY ALL MY QUESTIONS WERE PUT TO REST. SHE WAS INDEED QUITE REAL - IN FACT, SHE WAS THE HEAD OF NURSING FOR THE ENTIRE HOSPITAL. AN ELEGANT WOMAN IN HER LATE FIFTIES, SHE CONTINUED TO WEAR THE OFFICIAL UNIFORM OF HER YOUTH... CORRECTLY BELIEVING THAT IT LENT HER AN AIR OF AUTHORITY AND RESPECT.

YOU CAN'T BEGIN TO IMAGINE HOW RELIEVED I WAS TO HAVE SOLVED THE MYSTERY OF THE ANGELIC NURSE IN WHITE.

AS I RECUPERATED OVER THE FOLLOWING WEEKS, THIS INCIDENT GAVE ME PAUSE TO REFLECT UPON THE IDEA THAT ANGELS REALLY *DO* EXIST. BECAUSE, JUST AS IN THE AFTERMATH OF MY KIDNEY FAILURE, I KNEW THAT THE *HERO INITIATIVE* WOULD BE THERE TO COME TO MY AID AFTER MY RELEASE FROM THE HOSPITAL.

TO ASSIST ME FINANCIALLY - TO HELP ME PAY THE RENT, AND TO COVER MY BILLS AND LIVING EXPENSES WHILE I WAS HEALING AND UNABLE TO WORK. AND THIS IS WHAT MAKES THE GOOD PEOPLE OF THE HERO INITIATIVE - AND EVERYONE WHO CONTRIBUTES TO THE ORGANIZATION - REAL-LIFE ANGELS, RIGHT HERE ON EARTH.

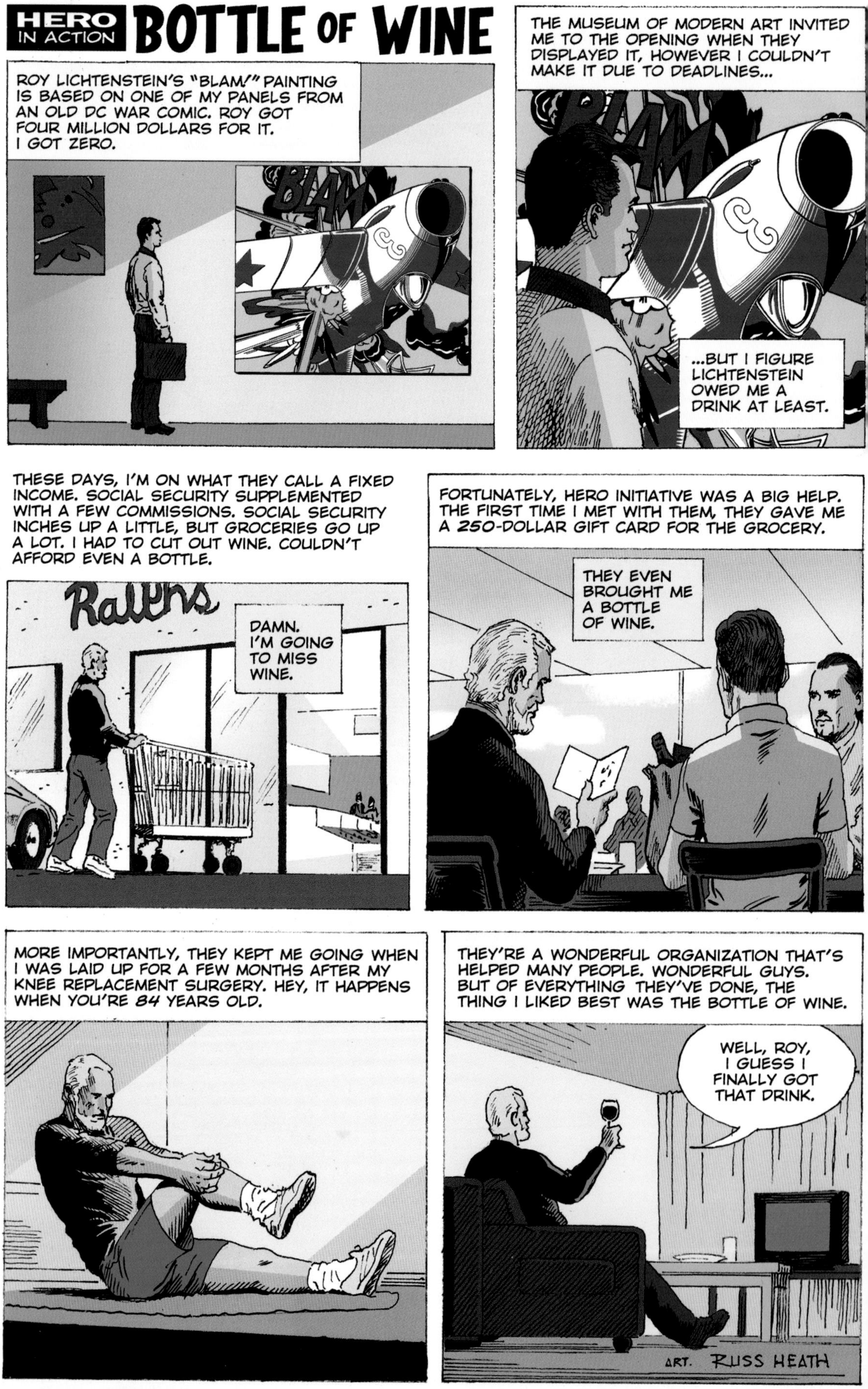
HERO IN ACTION
BOTTLE OF WINE
ROY LICHTENSTEIN'S "BLAM!" PAINTING IS BASED ON ONE OF MY PANELS FROM AN OLD DC WAR COMIC. ROY GOT FOUR MILLION DOLLARS FOR IT. I GOT ZERO.
BLAM
THE MUSEUM OF MODERN ART INVITED ME TO THE OPENING WHEN THEY DISPLAYED IT, HOWEVER I COULDN'T MAKE IT DUE TO DEADLINES...
BLAM
...BUT I FIGURE LICHTENSTEIN OWED ME A DRINK AT LEAST.
THESE DAYS, I'M ON WHAT THEY CALL A FIXED INCOME. SOCIAL SECURITY SUPPLEMENTED WITH A FEW COMMISSIONS. SOCIAL SECURITY INCHES UP A LITTLE, BUT GROCERIES GO UP A LOT. I HAD TO CUT OUT WINE. COULDN'T AFFORD EVEN A BOTTLE.
Ralphs
DAMN. I'M GOING TO MISS WINE.
FORTUNATELY, HERO INITIATIVE WAS A BIG HELP. THE FIRST TIME I MET WITH THEM, THEY GAVE ME A 250-DOLLAR GIFT CARD FOR THE GROCERY.
THEY EVEN BROUGHT ME A BOTTLE OF WINE.
MORE IMPORTANTLY, THEY KEPT ME GOING WHEN I WAS LAID UP FOR A FEW MONTHS AFTER MY KNEE REPLACEMENT SURGERY. HEY, IT HAPPENS WHEN YOU'RE 84 YEARS OLD.
THEY'RE A WONDERFUL ORGANIZATION THAT'S HELPED MANY PEOPLE. WONDERFUL GUYS. BUT OF EVERYTHING THEY'VE DONE, THE THING I LIKED BEST WAS THE BOTTLE OF WINE.
WELL, ROY, I GUESS I FINALLY GOT THAT DRINK.
ART. RUSS HEATH

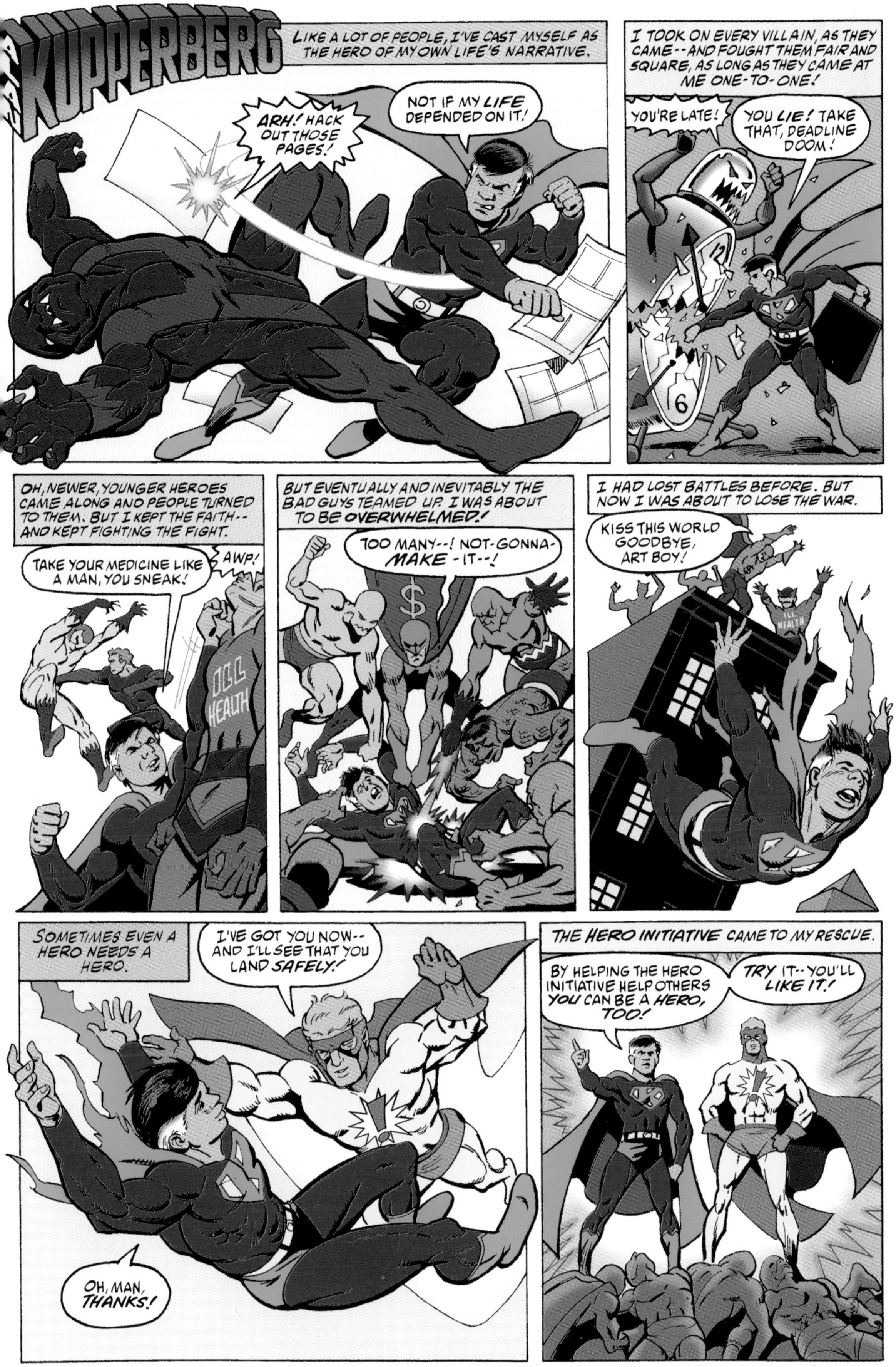

KUPPERBERG
LIKE A LOT OF PEOPLE, I'VE CAST MYSELF AS THE HERO OF MY OWN LIFE'S NARRATIVE.
ARH! HACK OUT THOSE PAGES!
NOT IF MY LIFE DEPENDED ON IT!
I TOOK ON EVERY VILLAIN, AS THEY CAME--AND FOUGHT THEM FAIR AND SQUARE, AS LONG AS THEY CAME AT ME ONE-TO-ONE!
YOU'RE LATE!
YOU LIE! TAKE THAT, DEADLINE DOOM!
OH, NEWER, YOUNGER HEROES CAME ALONG AND PEOPLE TURNED TO THEM. BUT I KEPT THE FAITH--AND KEPT FIGHTING THE FIGHT.
TAKE YOUR MEDICINE LIKE A MAN, YOU SNEAK!
AWP!
ILL HEALTH
BUT EVENTUALLY AND INEVITABLY THE BAD GUYS TEAMED UP. I WAS ABOUT TO BE OVERWHELMED!
TOO MANY--! NOT-GONNA-MAKE-IT--!
I HAD LOST BATTLES BEFORE. BUT NOW I WAS ABOUT TO LOSE THE WAR.
KISS THIS WORLD GOODBYE, ART BOY!
ILL HEALTH
SOMETIMES EVEN A HERO NEEDS A HERO.
I'VE GOT YOU NOW--AND I'LL SEE THAT YOU LAND SAFELY!
OH, MAN, THANKS!
THE HERO INITIATIVE CAME TO MY RESCUE.
BY HELPING THE HERO INITIATIVE HELP OTHERS YOU CAN BE A HERO, TOO!
TRY IT--YOU'LL LIKE IT!

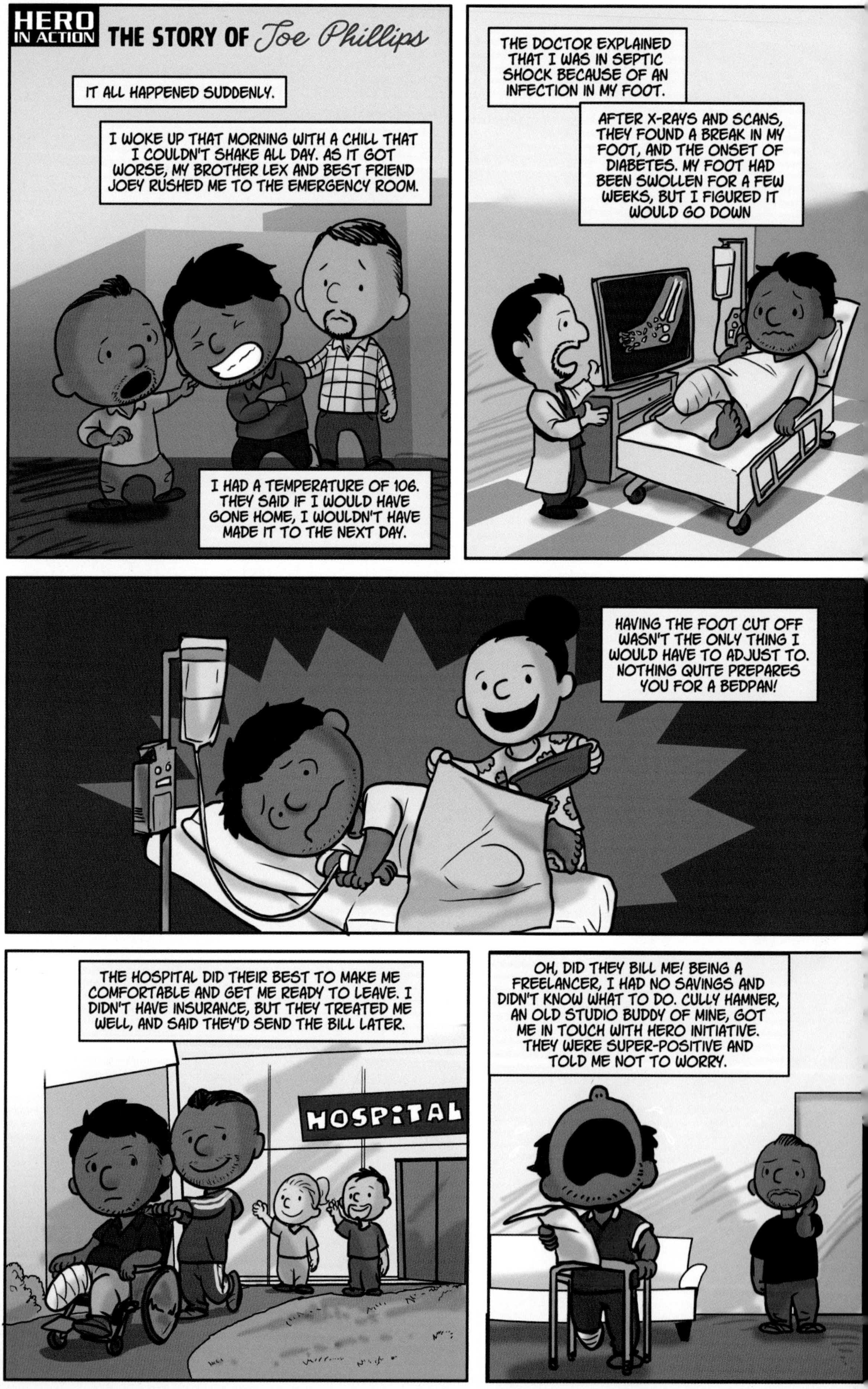
HERO IN ACTION
THE STORY OF Joe Phillips
IT ALL HAPPENED SUDDENLY.
I WOKE UP THAT MORNING WITH A CHILL THAT I COULDN'T SHAKE ALL DAY. AS IT GOT WORSE, MY BROTHER LEX AND BEST FRIEND JOEY RUSHED ME TO THE EMERGENCY ROOM.
I HAD A TEMPERATURE OF 106. THEY SAID IF I WOULD HAVE GONE HOME, I WOULDN'T HAVE MADE IT TO THE NEXT DAY.
THE DOCTOR EXPLAINED THAT I WAS IN SEPTIC SHOCK BECAUSE OF AN INFECTION IN MY FOOT.
AFTER X-RAYS AND SCANS, THEY FOUND A BREAK IN MY FOOT, AND THE ONSET OF DIABETES. MY FOOT HAD BEEN SWOLLEN FOR A FEW WEEKS, BUT I FIGURED IT WOULD GO DOWN
HAVING THE FOOT CUT OFF WASN'T THE ONLY THING I WOULD HAVE TO ADJUST TO. NOTHING QUITE PREPARES YOU FOR A BEDPAN!
THE HOSPITAL DID THEIR BEST TO MAKE ME COMFORTABLE AND GET ME READY TO LEAVE. I DIDN'T HAVE INSURANCE, BUT THEY TREATED ME WELL, AND SAID THEY'D SEND THE BILL LATER.
HOSPITAL
OH, DID THEY BILL ME! BEING A FREELANCER, I HAD NO SAVINGS AND DIDN'T KNOW WHAT TO DO. CULLY HAMNER, AN OLD STUDIO BUDDY OF MINE, GOT ME IN TOUCH WITH HERO INITIATIVE. THEY WERE SUPER-POSITIVE AND TOLD ME NOT TO WORRY.

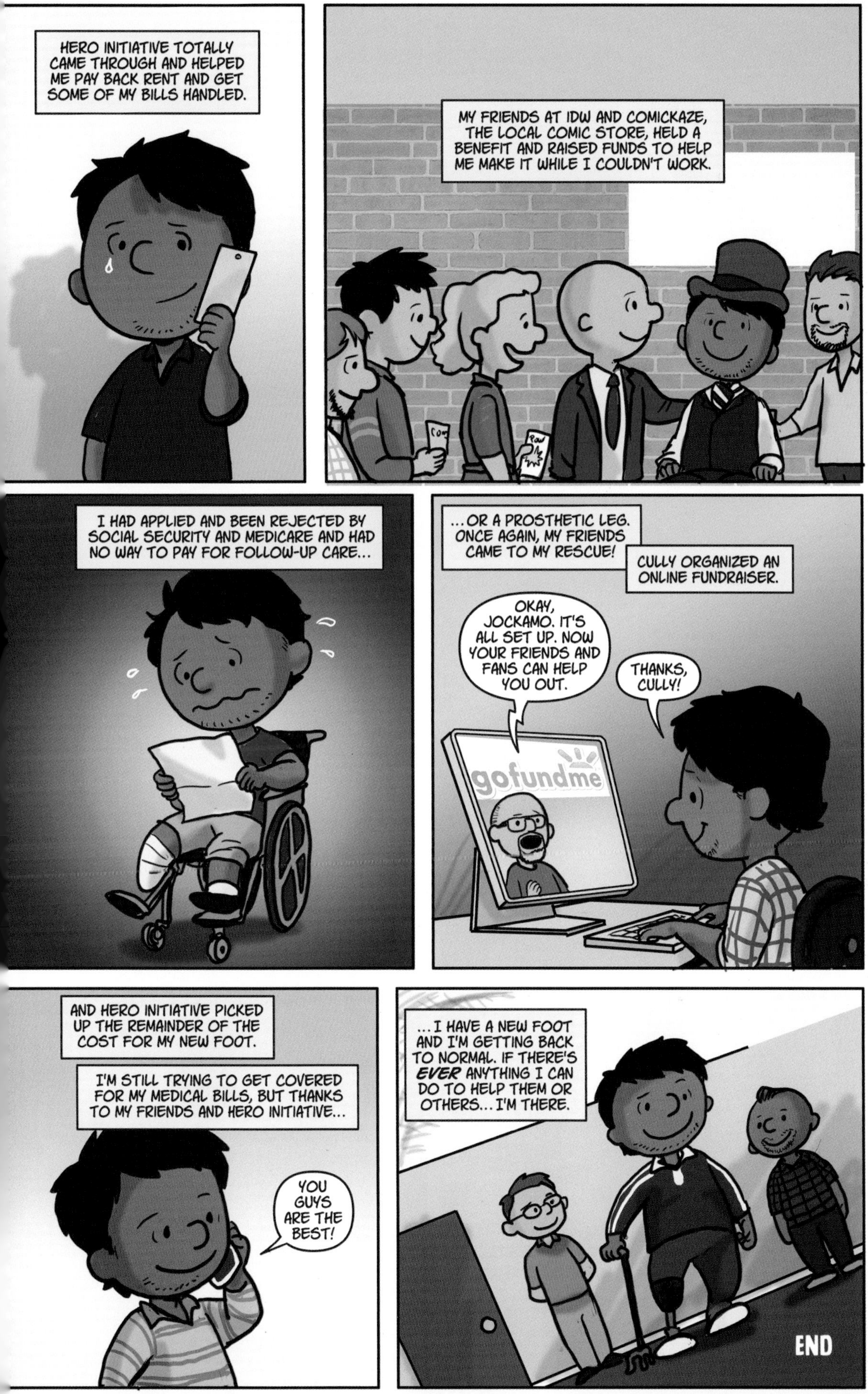
HERO INITIATIVE TOTALLY CAME THROUGH AND HELPED ME PAY BACK RENT AND GET SOME OF MY BILLS HANDLED.
MY FRIENDS AT IDW AND COMICKAZE, THE LOCAL COMIC STORE, HELD A BENEFIT AND RAISED FUNDS TO HELP ME MAKE IT WHILE I COULDN'T WORK.
I HAD APPLIED AND BEEN REJECTED BY SOCIAL SECURITY AND MEDICARE AND HAD NO WAY TO PAY FOR FOLLOW-UP CARE...
...OR A PROSTHETIC LEG. ONCE AGAIN, MY FRIENDS CAME TO MY RESCUE!
CULLY ORGANIZED AN ONLINE FUNDRAISER.
OKAY, JOCKAMO. IT'S ALL SET UP. NOW YOUR FRIENDS AND FANS CAN HELP YOU OUT.
THANKS, CULLY!
gofundme
AND HERO INITIATIVE PICKED UP THE REMAINDER OF THE COST FOR MY NEW FOOT.
I'M STILL TRYING TO GET COVERED FOR MY MEDICAL BILLS, BUT THANKS TO MY FRIENDS AND HERO INITIATIVE...
YOU GUYS ARE THE BEST!
...I HAVE A NEW FOOT AND I'M GETTING BACK TO NORMAL. IF THERE'S *EVER* ANYTHING I CAN DO TO HELP THEM OR OTHERS... I'M THERE.
END

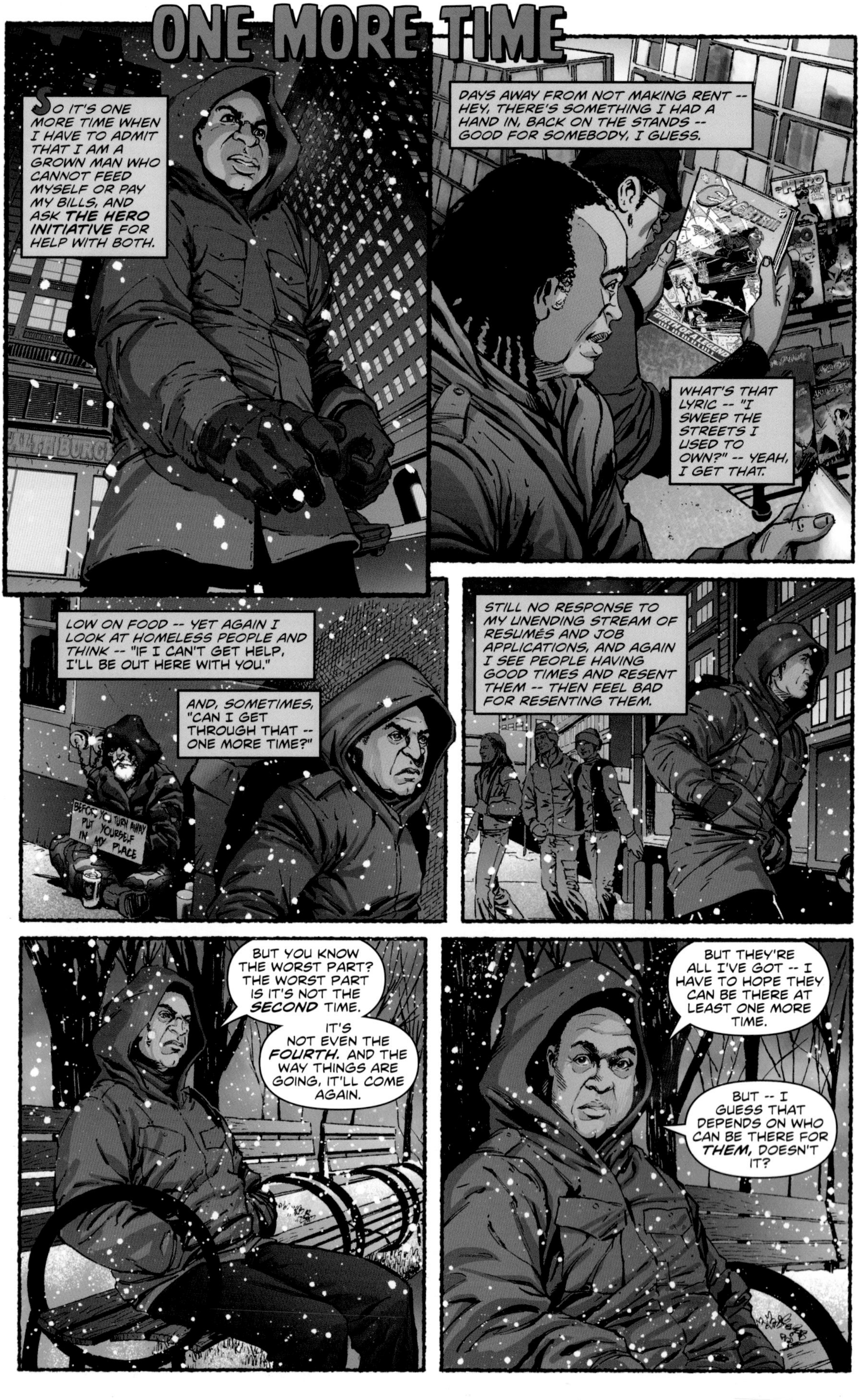
ONE MORE TIME
SO IT'S ONE MORE TIME WHEN I HAVE TO ADMIT THAT I AM A GROWN MAN WHO CANNOT FEED MYSELF OR PAY MY BILLS, AND ASK THE HERO INITIATIVE FOR HELP WITH BOTH.
DAYS AWAY FROM NOT MAKING RENT -- HEY, THERE'S SOMETHING I HAD A HAND IN, BACK ON THE STANDS -- GOOD FOR SOMEBODY, I GUESS.
WHAT'S THAT LYRIC -- "I SWEEP THE STREETS I USED TO OWN?" -- YEAH, I GET THAT.
LOW ON FOOD -- YET AGAIN I LOOK AT HOMELESS PEOPLE AND THINK -- "IF I CAN'T GET HELP, I'LL BE OUT HERE WITH YOU."
AND, SOMETIMES, "CAN I GET THROUGH THAT -- ONE MORE TIME?"
BEFORE YOU TURN AWAY PUT YOURSELF IN MY PLACE
STILL NO RESPONSE TO MY UNENDING STREAM OF RESUMÉS AND JOB APPLICATIONS, AND AGAIN I SEE PEOPLE HAVING GOOD TIMES AND RESENT THEM -- THEN FEEL BAD FOR RESENTING THEM.
BUT YOU KNOW THE WORST PART? THE WORST PART IS IT'S NOT THE SECOND TIME.
IT'S NOT EVEN THE FOURTH. AND THE WAY THINGS ARE GOING, IT'LL COME AGAIN.
BUT THEY'RE ALL I'VE GOT -- I HAVE TO HOPE THEY CAN BE THERE AT LEAST ONE MORE TIME.
BUT -- I GUESS THAT DEPENDS ON WHO CAN BE THERE FOR THEM, DOESN'T IT?

HERO IN ACTION

TANYA AND RICHARD HORIE
ART & STORY

a game of life where truth is stranger than fiction.

In full color ComicBookLand

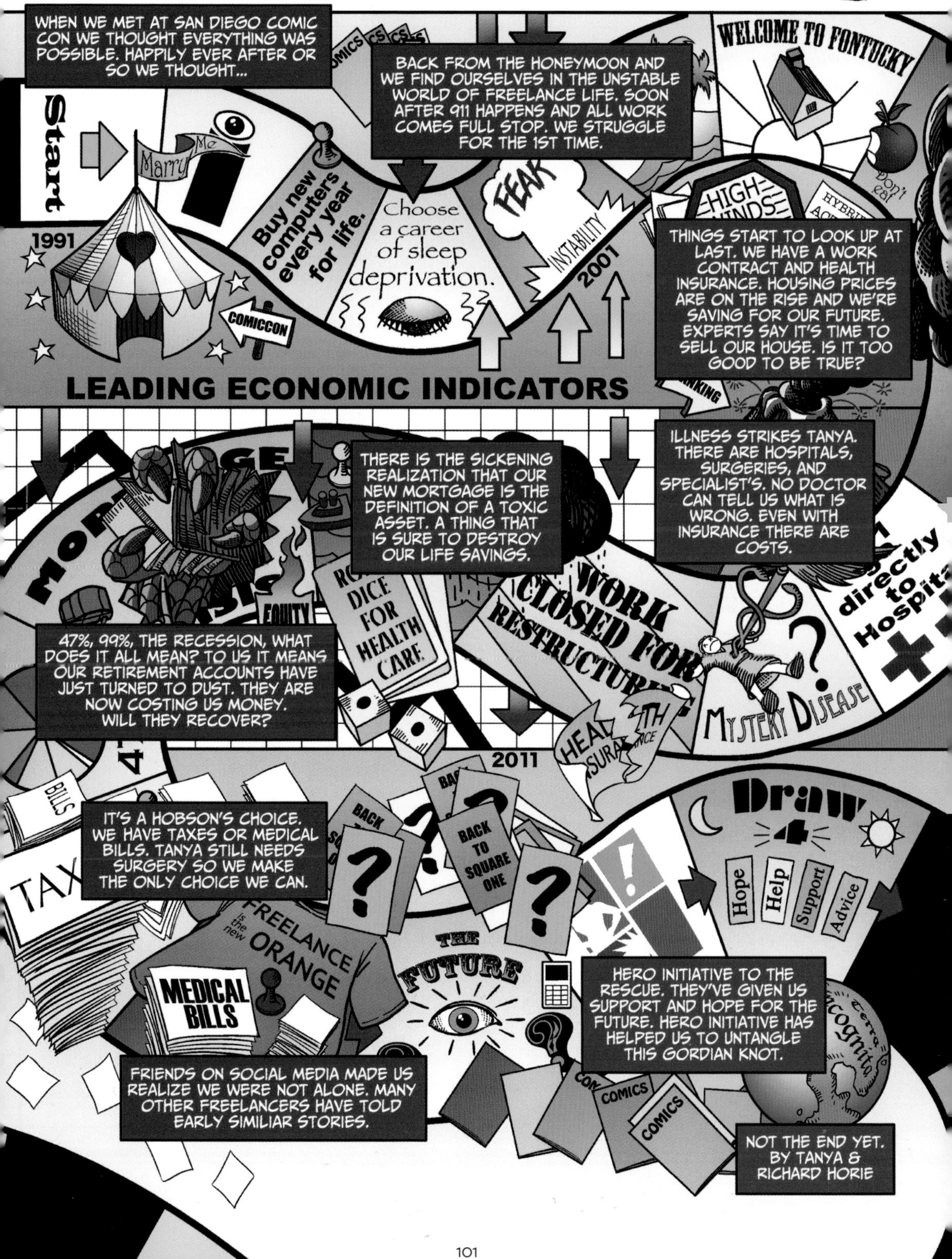

WHEN WE MET AT SAN DIEGO COMIC CON WE THOUGHT EVERYTHING WAS POSSIBLE. HAPPILY EVER AFTER OR SO WE THOUGHT...
Start
Marry Me
1991
COMICCON
Buy new computers every year for life.
BACK FROM THE HONEYMOON AND WE FIND OURSELVES IN THE UNSTABLE WORLD OF FREELANCE LIFE. SOON AFTER 911 HAPPENS AND ALL WORK COMES FULL STOP. WE STRUGGLE FOR THE 1ST TIME.
Choose a career of sleep deprivation.
FEAR
INSTABILITY
2001
WELCOME TO FONTUCKY
Don't eat
THINGS START TO LOOK UP AT LAST. WE HAVE A WORK CONTRACT AND HEALTH INSURANCE. HOUSING PRICES ARE ON THE RISE AND WE'RE SAVING FOR OUR FUTURE. EXPERTS SAY IT'S TIME TO SELL OUR HOUSE. IS IT TOO GOOD TO BE TRUE?
LEADING ECONOMIC INDICATORS
THERE IS THE SICKENING REALIZATION THAT OUR NEW MORTGAGE IS THE DEFINITION OF A TOXIC ASSET. A THING THAT IS SURE TO DESTROY OUR LIFE SAVINGS.
ILLNESS STRIKES TANYA. THERE ARE HOSPITALS, SURGERIES, AND SPECIALIST'S. NO DOCTOR CAN TELL US WHAT IS WRONG. EVEN WITH INSURANCE THERE ARE COSTS.
directly to Hospital
47%, 99%, THE RECESSION, WHAT DOES IT ALL MEAN? TO US IT MEANS OUR RETIREMENT ACCOUNTS HAVE JUST TURNED TO DUST. THEY ARE NOW COSTING US MONEY. WILL THEY RECOVER?
DICE FOR HEALTH CARE
WORK CLOSED FOR RESTRUCTURING
MYSTERY DISEASE
2011
BILLS
TAX
IT'S A HOBSON'S CHOICE. WE HAVE TAXES OR MEDICAL BILLS. TANYA STILL NEEDS SURGERY SO WE MAKE THE ONLY CHOICE WE CAN.
BACK TO SQUARE ONE
Draw 4
Hope
Help
Support
Advice
FREELANCE is the new ORANGE
MEDICAL BILLS
THE FUTURE
HERO INITIATIVE TO THE RESCUE. THEY'VE GIVEN US SUPPORT AND HOPE FOR THE FUTURE. HERO INITIATIVE HAS HELPED US TO UNTANGLE THIS GORDIAN KNOT.
Terra Incognita
FRIENDS ON SOCIAL MEDIA MADE US REALIZE WE WERE NOT ALONE. MANY OTHER FREELANCERS HAVE TOLD EARLY SIMILIAR STORIES.
COMICS
COMICS
NOT THE END YET. BY TANYA & RICHARD HORIE

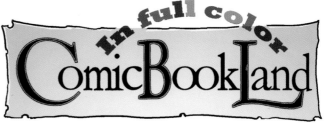

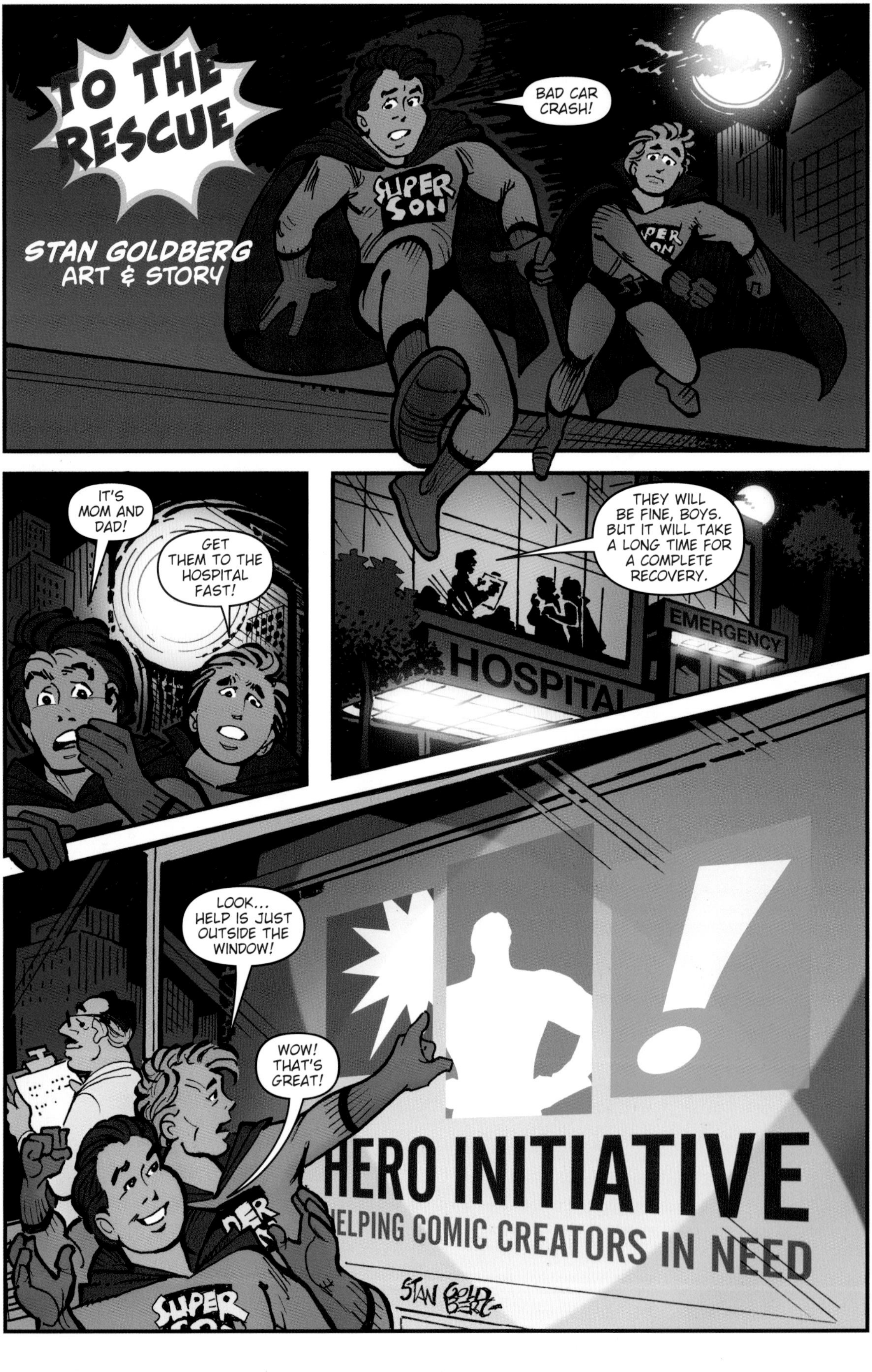
TO THE RESCUE
STAN GOLDBERG
ART & STORY
BAD CAR CRASH!
SUPER SON
IT'S MOM AND DAD!
GET THEM TO THE HOSPITAL FAST!
THEY WILL BE FINE, BOYS. BUT IT WILL TAKE A LONG TIME FOR A COMPLETE RECOVERY.
EMERGENCY
HOSPITAL
LOOK... HELP IS JUST OUTSIDE THE WINDOW!
WOW! THAT'S GREAT!
HERO INITIATIVE
HELPING COMIC CREATORS IN NEED
STAN GOLDBERG
SUPER

HERO IN ACTION — THOSE WHO STAY

CONNIE CARLTON WITH **TROY HICKMAN** - STORY
CHRIS IVY - ART

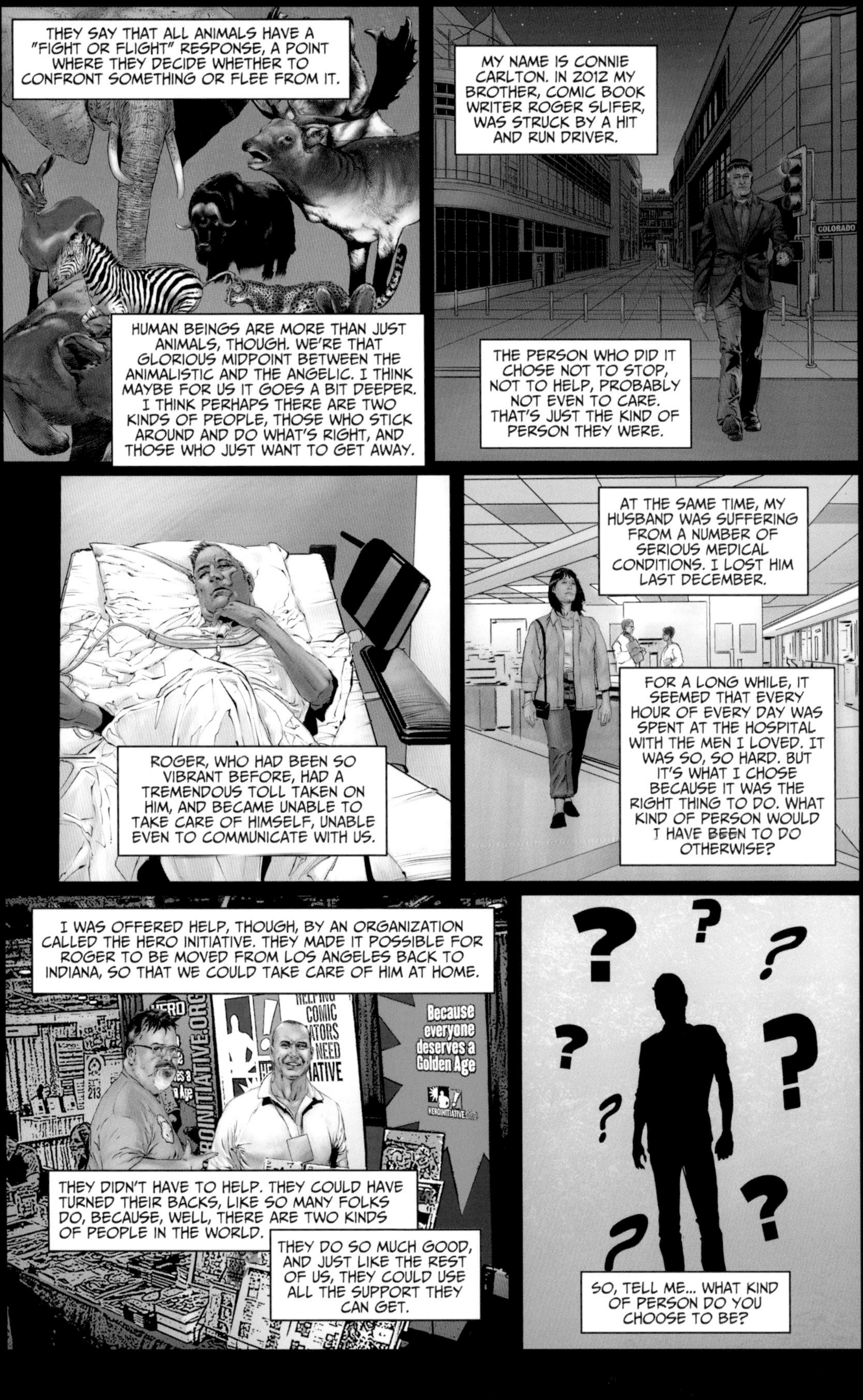
THEY SAY THAT ALL ANIMALS HAVE A "FIGHT OR FLIGHT" RESPONSE, A POINT WHERE THEY DECIDE WHETHER TO CONFRONT SOMETHING OR FLEE FROM IT.
HUMAN BEINGS ARE MORE THAN JUST ANIMALS, THOUGH. WE'RE THAT GLORIOUS MIDPOINT BETWEEN THE ANIMALISTIC AND THE ANGELIC. I THINK MAYBE FOR US IT GOES A BIT DEEPER. I THINK PERHAPS THERE ARE TWO KINDS OF PEOPLE, THOSE WHO STICK AROUND AND DO WHAT'S RIGHT, AND THOSE WHO JUST WANT TO GET AWAY.
MY NAME IS CONNIE CARLTON. IN 2012 MY BROTHER, COMIC BOOK WRITER ROGER SLIFER, WAS STRUCK BY A HIT AND RUN DRIVER.
COLORADO
THE PERSON WHO DID IT CHOSE NOT TO STOP, NOT TO HELP, PROBABLY NOT EVEN TO CARE. THAT'S JUST THE KIND OF PERSON THEY WERE.
ROGER, WHO HAD BEEN SO VIBRANT BEFORE, HAD A TREMENDOUS TOLL TAKEN ON HIM, AND BECAME UNABLE TO TAKE CARE OF HIMSELF, UNABLE EVEN TO COMMUNICATE WITH US.
AT THE SAME TIME, MY HUSBAND WAS SUFFERING FROM A NUMBER OF SERIOUS MEDICAL CONDITIONS. I LOST HIM LAST DECEMBER.
FOR A LONG WHILE, IT SEEMED THAT EVERY HOUR OF EVERY DAY WAS SPENT AT THE HOSPITAL WITH THE MEN I LOVED. IT WAS SO, SO HARD. BUT IT'S WHAT I CHOSE BECAUSE IT WAS THE RIGHT THING TO DO. WHAT KIND OF PERSON WOULD I HAVE BEEN TO DO OTHERWISE?
I WAS OFFERED HELP, THOUGH, BY AN ORGANIZATION CALLED THE HERO INITIATIVE. THEY MADE IT POSSIBLE FOR ROGER TO BE MOVED FROM LOS ANGELES BACK TO INDIANA, SO THAT WE COULD TAKE CARE OF HIM AT HOME.
Because everyone deserves a Golden Age
THEY DIDN'T HAVE TO HELP. THEY COULD HAVE TURNED THEIR BACKS, LIKE SO MANY FOLKS DO, BECAUSE, WELL, THERE ARE TWO KINDS OF PEOPLE IN THE WORLD.
THEY DO SO MUCH GOOD, AND JUST LIKE THE REST OF US, THEY COULD USE ALL THE SUPPORT THEY CAN GET.
?
SO, TELL ME... WHAT KIND OF PERSON DO YOU CHOOSE TO BE?

DAVE
SIMONS

While I never had the opportunity to meet Dave Simons in person, we did become close friends the past few years thanks to the Internet and telephone conversations. As a teenage comics fan in the 1970s I remember seeing Dave's inking in numerous Marvel comics; *Ghost Rider* and *Howard the Duck* immediately spring to mind.

Fast forward several decades, when I finally talked with Dave via Hero Initiative. It was through this contact that I developed a deeper appreciation of Dave's talent—I was able to see his skill as a penciler as well as inker and I had the wonderful privilege to work with Dave on an animated short that really showcased Dave's abilities—he taught me a lot about storyboarding and how the animation industry works.

Along the way, we developed a strong relationship and it was easy to tell, even over the phone, that Dave was a caring and enthusiastic person. We talked about a variety of subjects, including many ideas Dave had for comic properties, as well as pitches for an entire line of comics. Dave's enthusiasm was contagious, and even when he was diagnosed with cancer, he was still upbeat and still had that fire and desire in his conversations.

On June 9, I learned with disbelief and sadness that Dave had passed away. I had just spoken with Dave a few weeks ago, so it wasn't unexpected, but still a shock. I'll miss those long conversations with Dave, but I will remember his willingness to always care for and help others. He was always donating art or his talents to help promote Hero Initiative in any way that he could. In fact, right to the end he thought of helping others. Dave wrote a story that he was in the process of illustrating for this benefit book. No one knows if Dave had started any layouts or inks yet, but we thought it would be a fitting tribute to Dave's love of comics and his unselfish attitude if we ran what we did have, his finished script.

So enjoy the story, because that's what Dave would have wanted!

Charlie Novinskie
Hero Initiative

DEAL WITH THE DEVIL

PANEL 1
We see a dramatic shot of THE DEVIL. My version looks more like a hot-rod devil, the kind of thing Robert Williams would draw.
CAPTION 1
That's usually who it is in those jokes. It's the kind of tale told over the second or third cocktail, the joke about what you want and what you get in your deal with the devil.

PANEL 2
INT. BAR, angle on DAVE, age 18 and wearing U.S. Coast Guard dress uniform of the period, with a drink and a cigarette, looking smug.
CAPTION 2
In these tales, the **letter** of the contract is always granted, but never the **intent**.

PANEL 3
NIGHT, EXT. CITY STREET, on DAVE, now in his early 50s, sitting on a stoop and looking at the cigarette in his hand, dejectedly.
CAPTION 3
Thirty-five years later, and I still did not have lung cancer or gum cancer. What I did have was esophageal cancer (look it up).
CAPTION 4
Thanks to serving my country in my youth, my medical expenses are well-covered. What's not are my living expenses. I'm in the odd position of being able to work, but not being able to work enough to pay my bills.
CAPTION 5
Hero Initiative has been invaluable here. When the wolf is at the door, Hero Initiative has been there to pay the rent. Many times. That wolf, he does get hungry.

PANEL 4
INT. STUDIO, on DAVE hunched over a drafting table and feverishly drawing away in a cramped studio space.
CAPTION 6
For now, I do what I can. Some days are better than others. It's tough to find the time and energy, whenever I can, I draw,
CAPTION 7
I know now I made a deal with the devil. I just didn't know I'd be rescued by angels.

GALLERY PART THREE

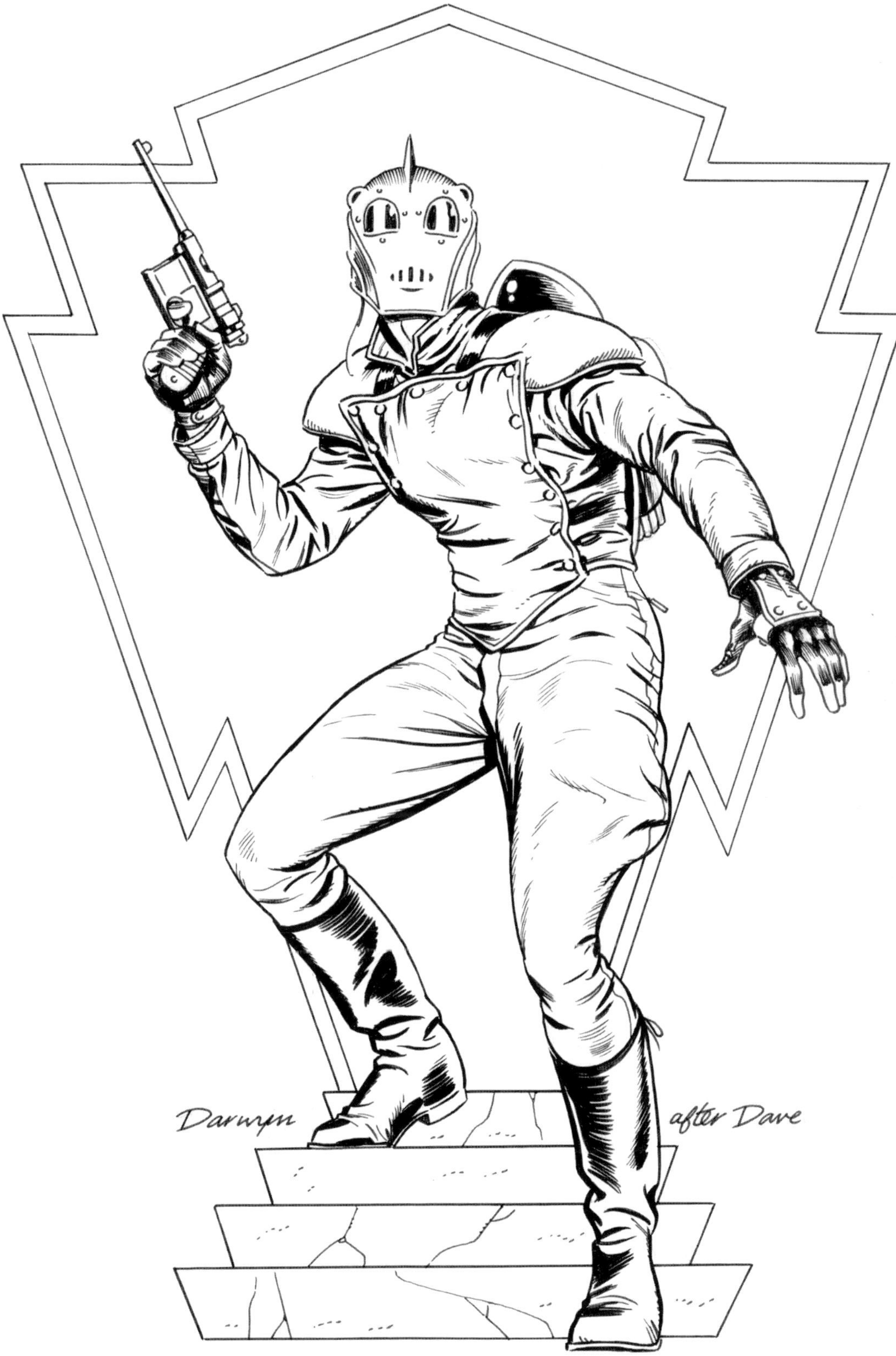
Darwyn
after Dave

ROCKETEER

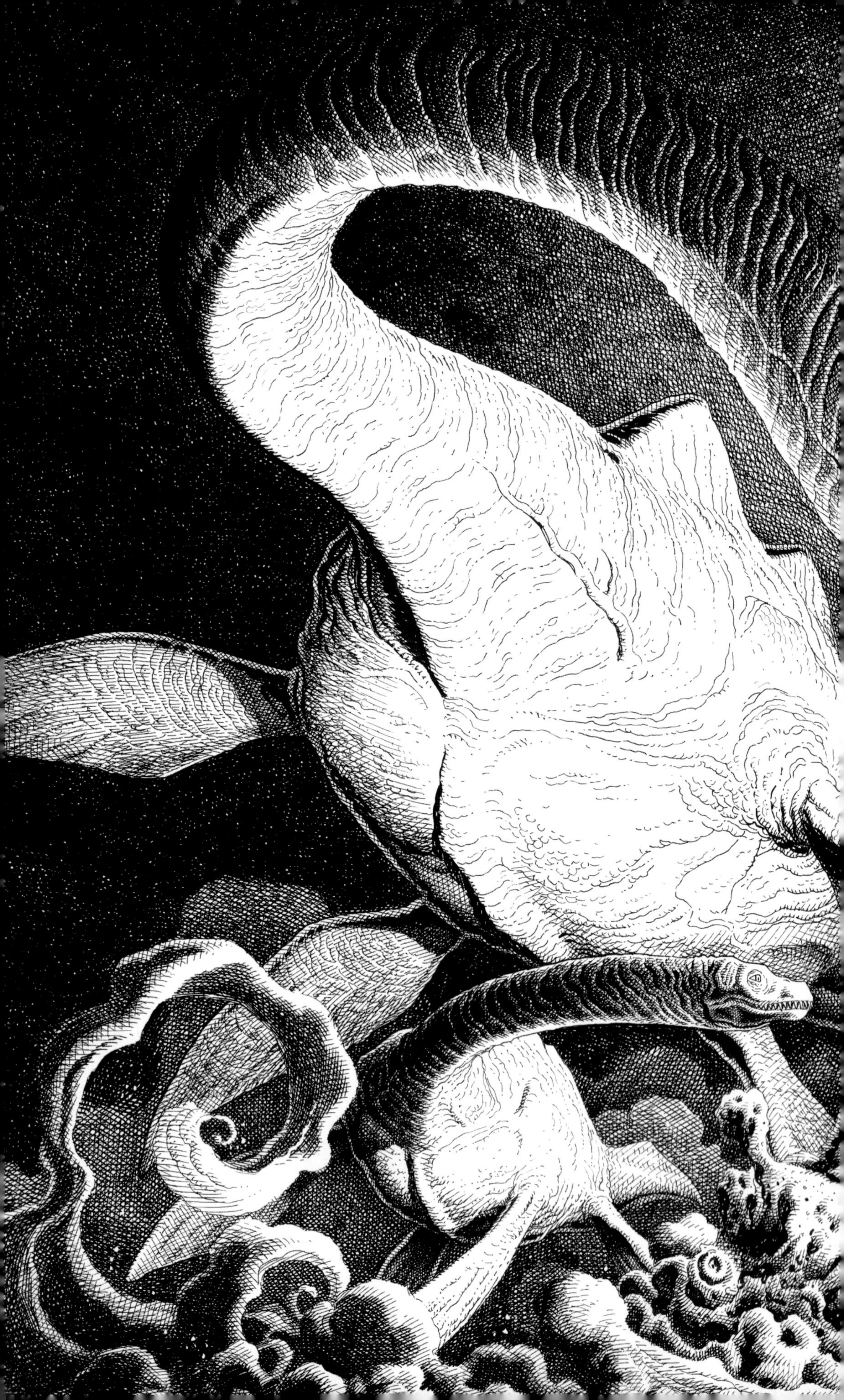

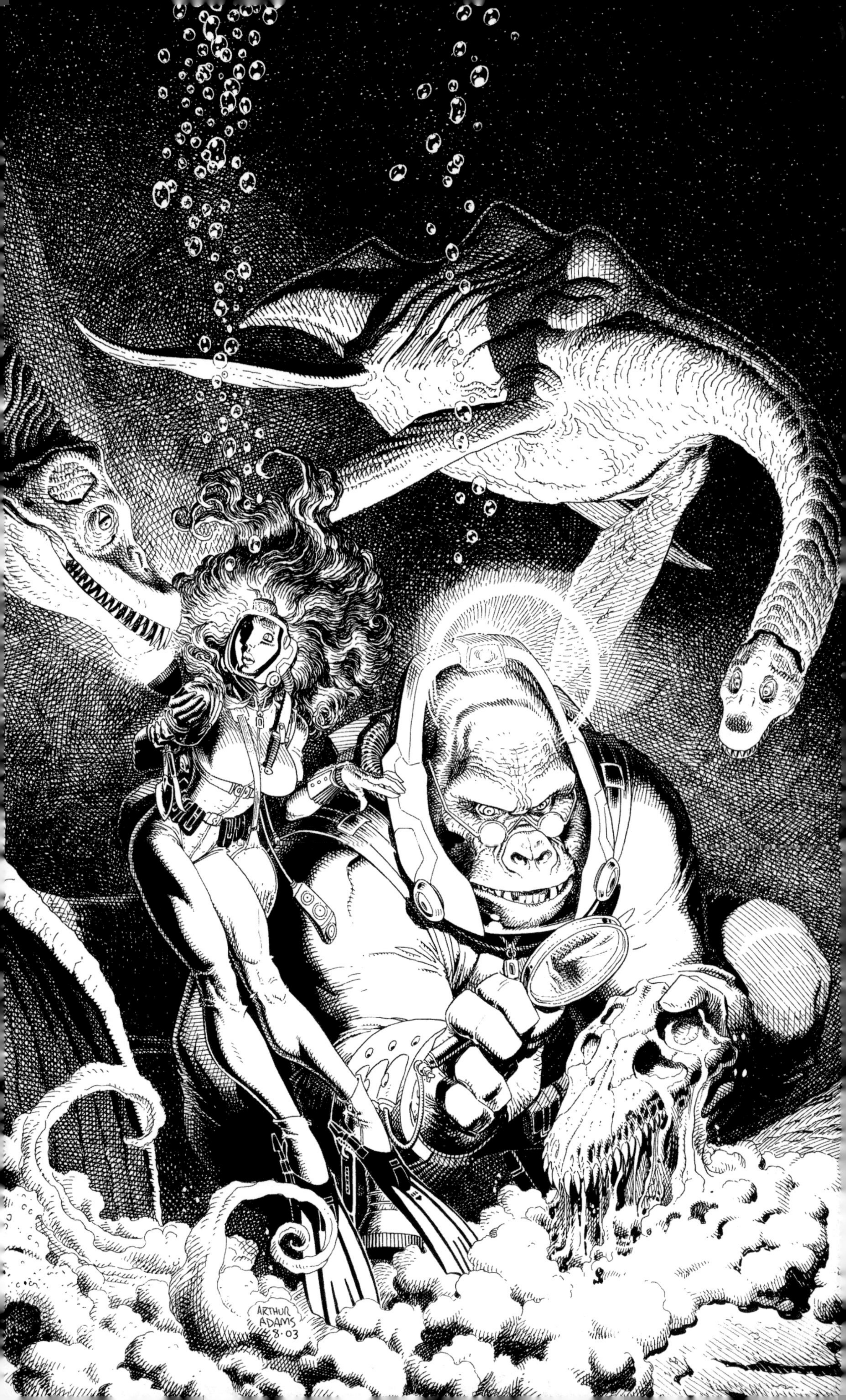
ARTHUR ADAMS 8·03

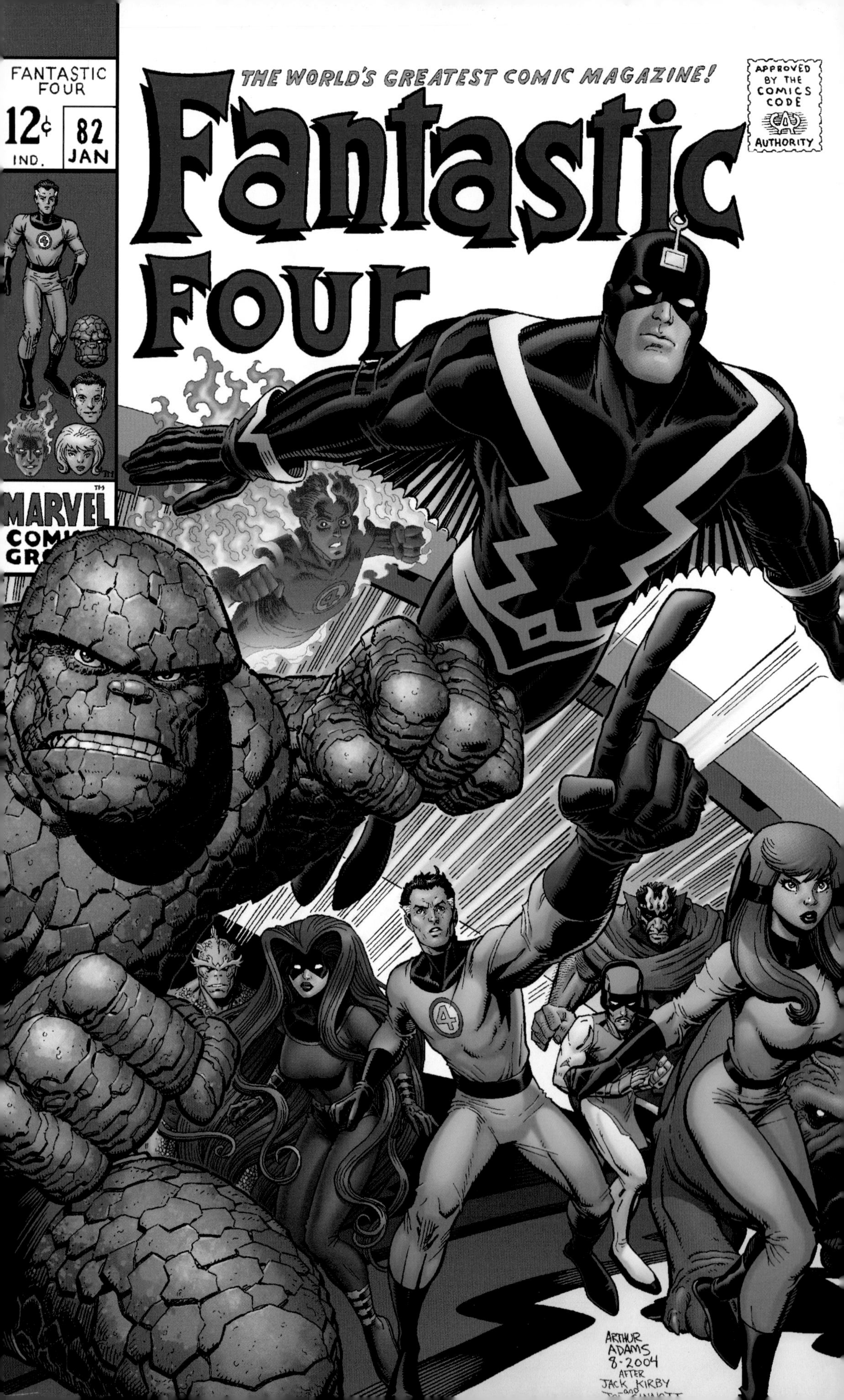
FANTASTIC FOUR
12¢
IND.
82
JAN
THE WORLD'S GREATEST COMIC MAGAZINE!
APPROVED BY THE COMICS CODE AUTHORITY
Fantastic Four
MARVEL
ARTHUR ADAMS 8-2004 AFTER JACK KIRBY and

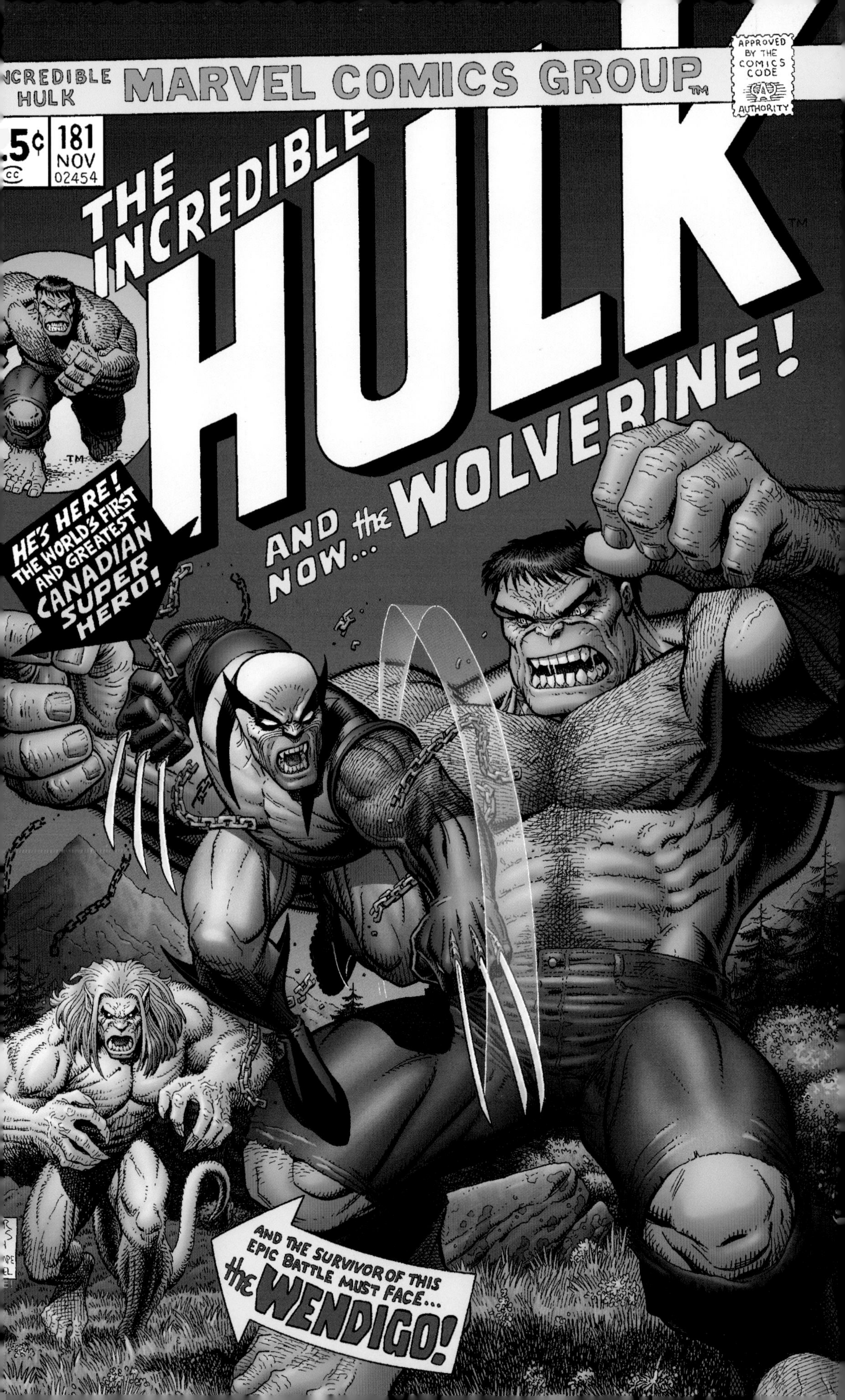

INCREDIBLE HULK
MARVEL COMICS GROUP
APPROVED BY THE COMICS CODE AUTHORITY
15¢ 181 NOV 02454
THE INCREDIBLE HULK
HE'S HERE! THE WORLD'S FIRST AND GREATEST CANADIAN SUPER HERO!
AND NOW... THE WOLVERINE!
AND THE SURVIVOR OF THIS EPIC BATTLE MUST FACE... THE WENDIGO!

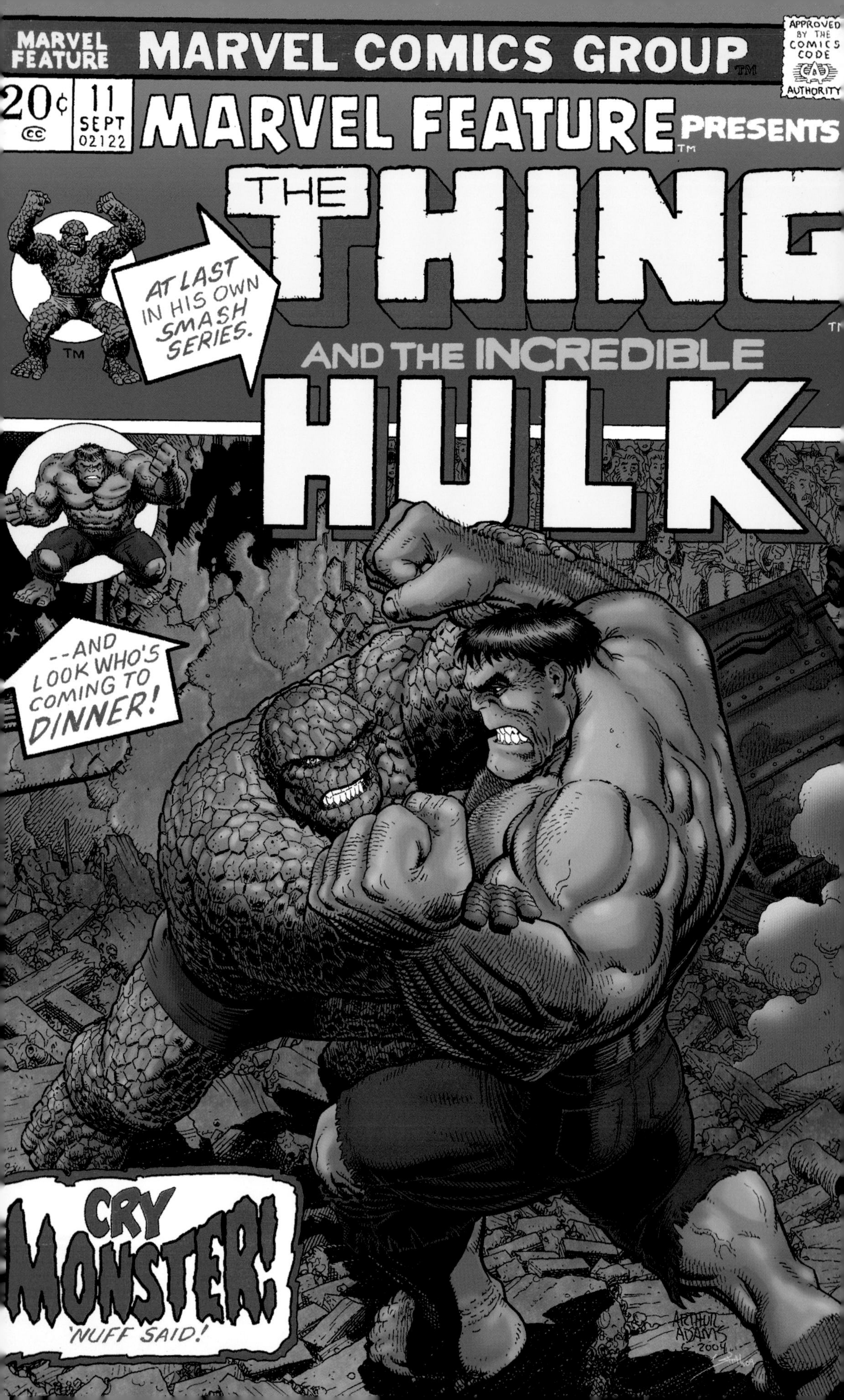
MARVEL FEATURE
MARVEL COMICS GROUP
APPROVED BY THE COMICS CODE AUTHORITY
20¢
11 SEPT 02122
MARVEL FEATURE PRESENTS
THE THING
AT LAST IN HIS OWN SMASH SERIES.
AND THE INCREDIBLE HULK
--AND LOOK WHO'S COMING TO DINNER!
CRY MONSTER!
'NUFF SAID!
ARTHUR ADAMS 6. 2009

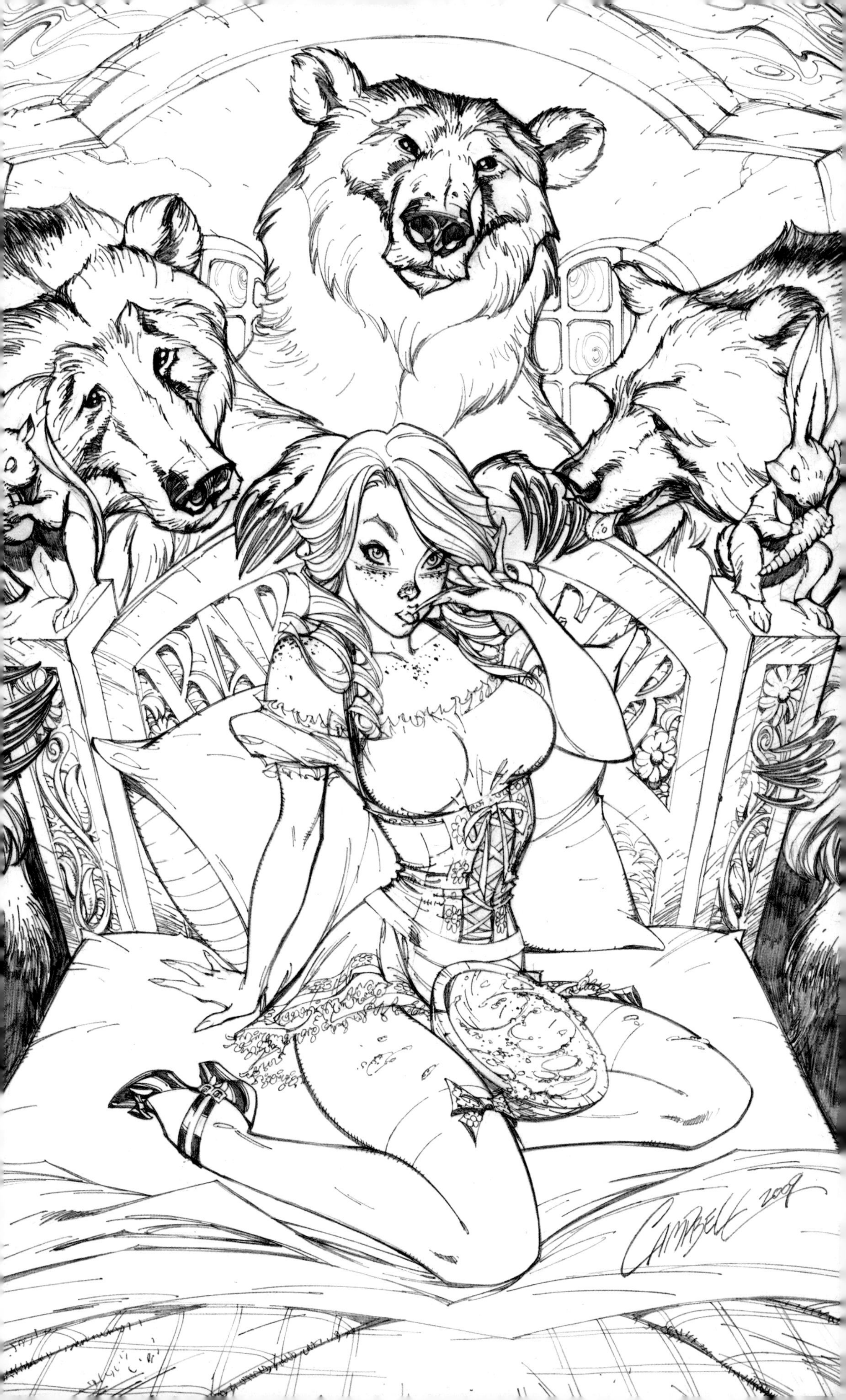
CAMPBELL 2009

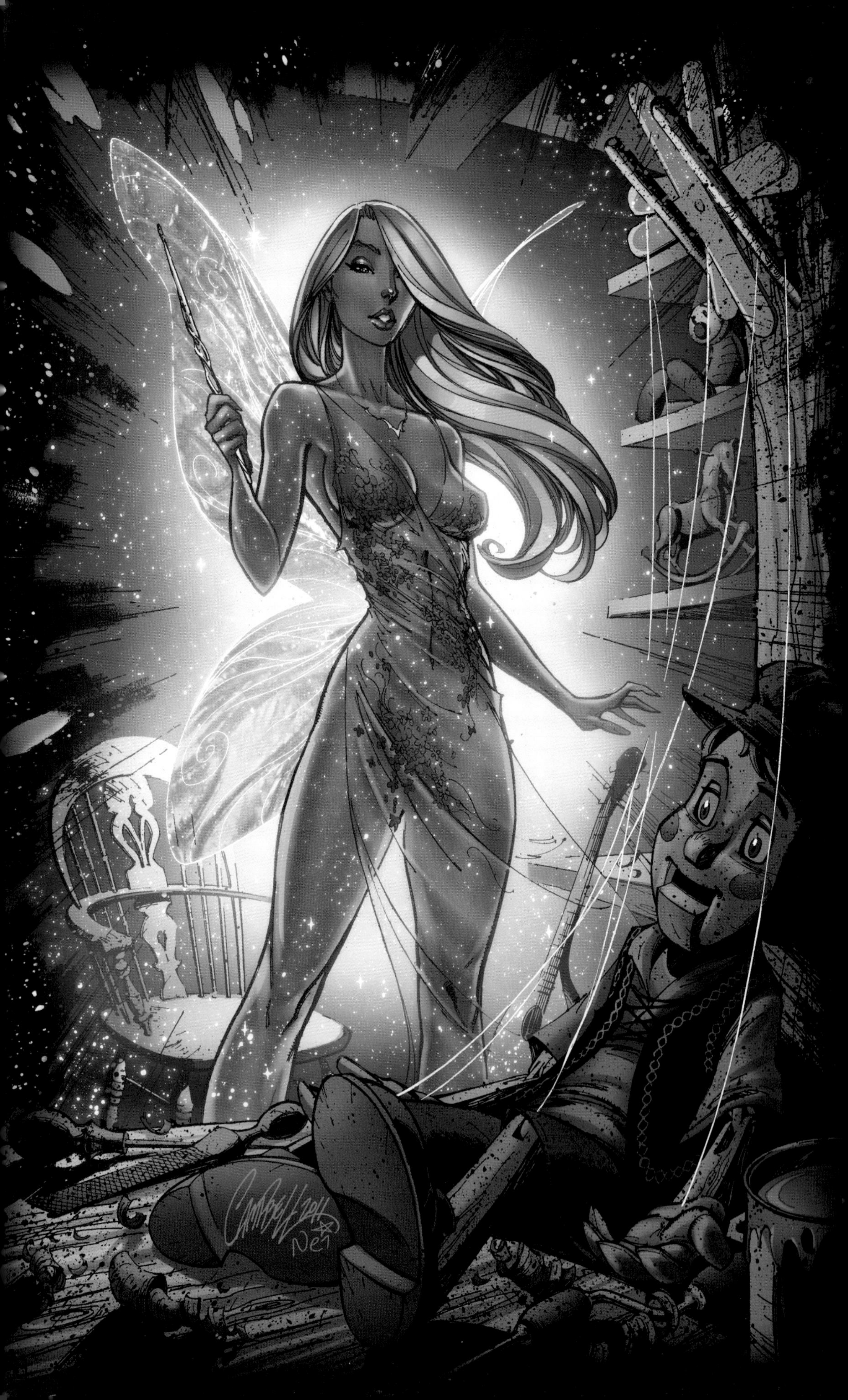

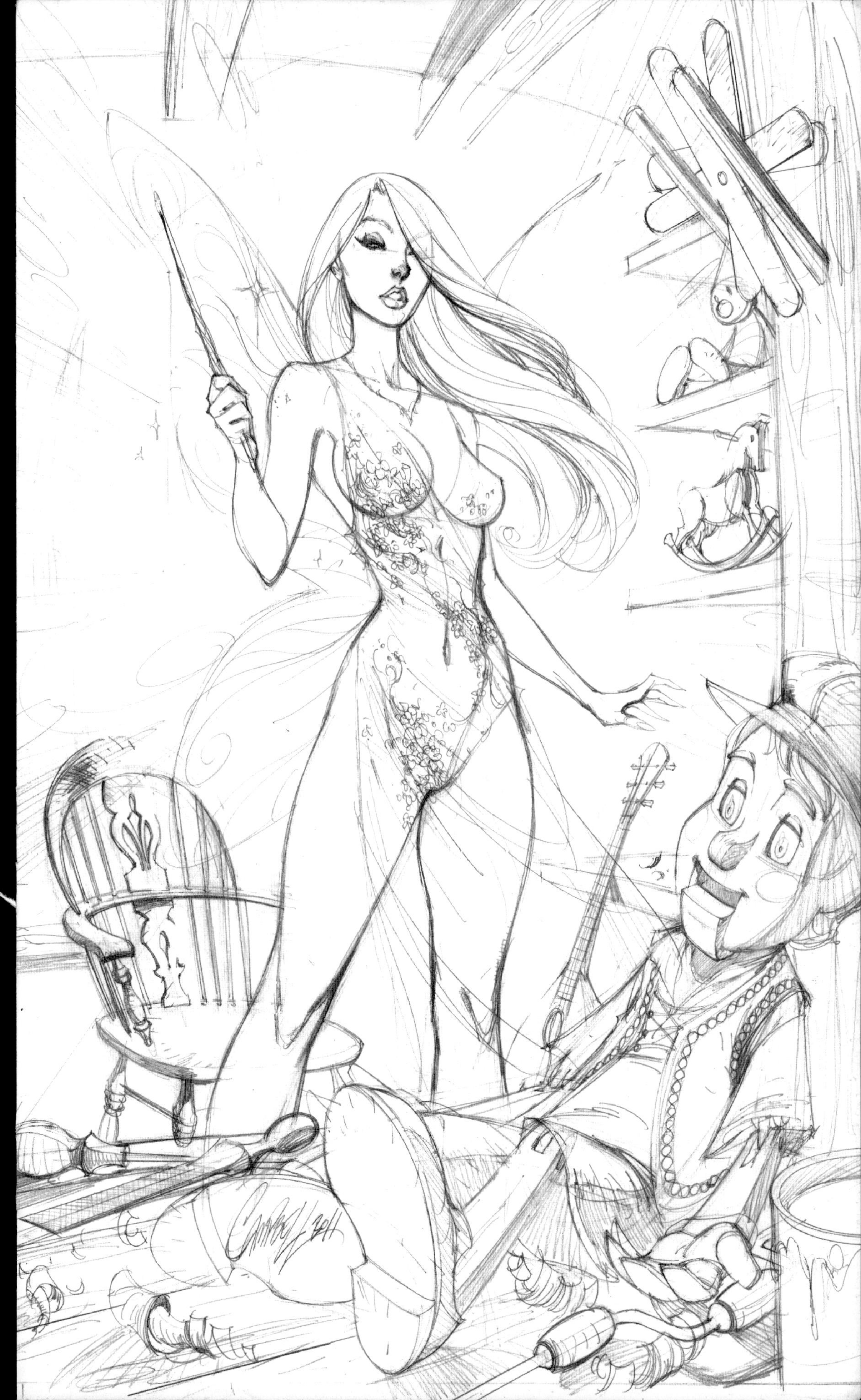

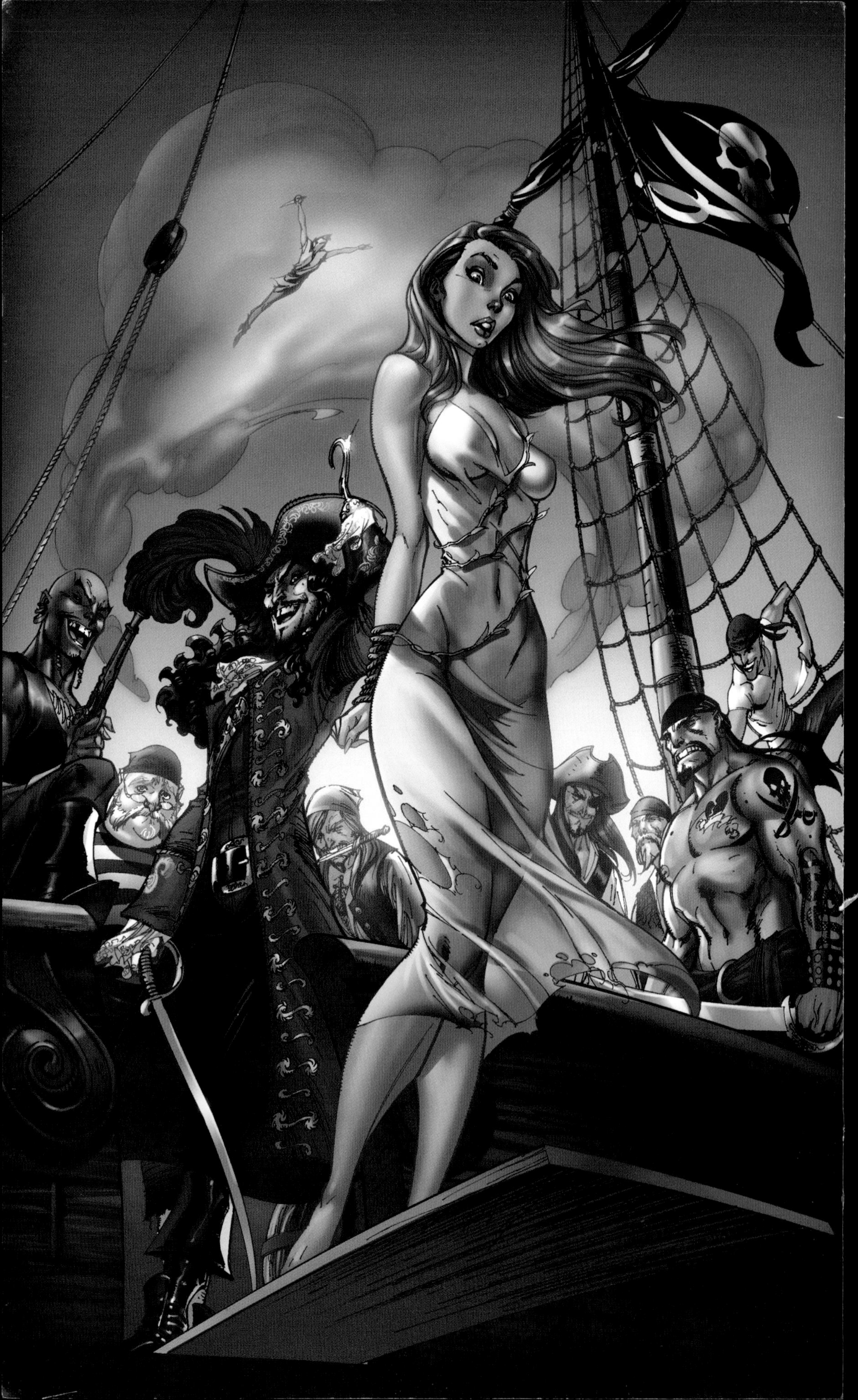

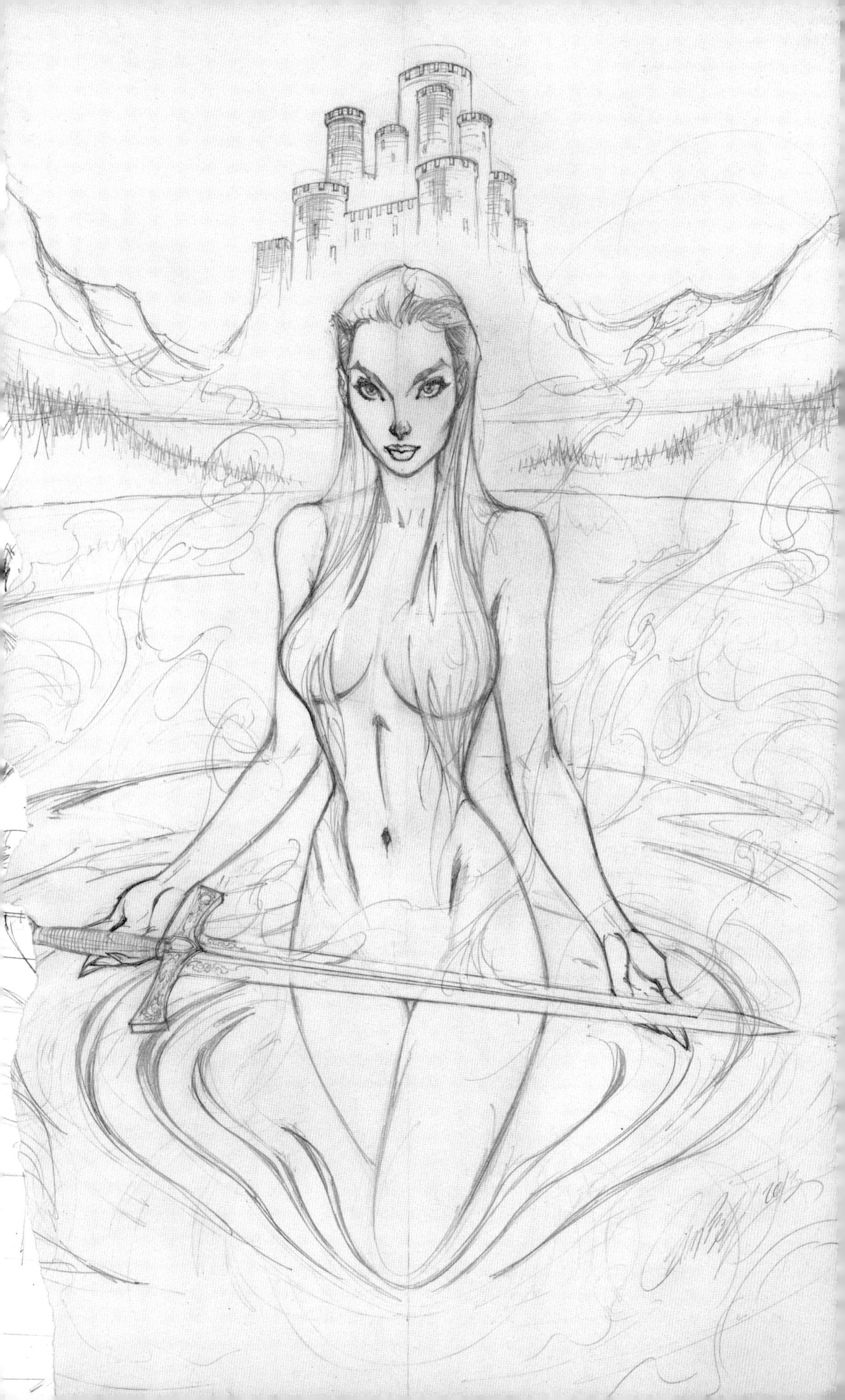

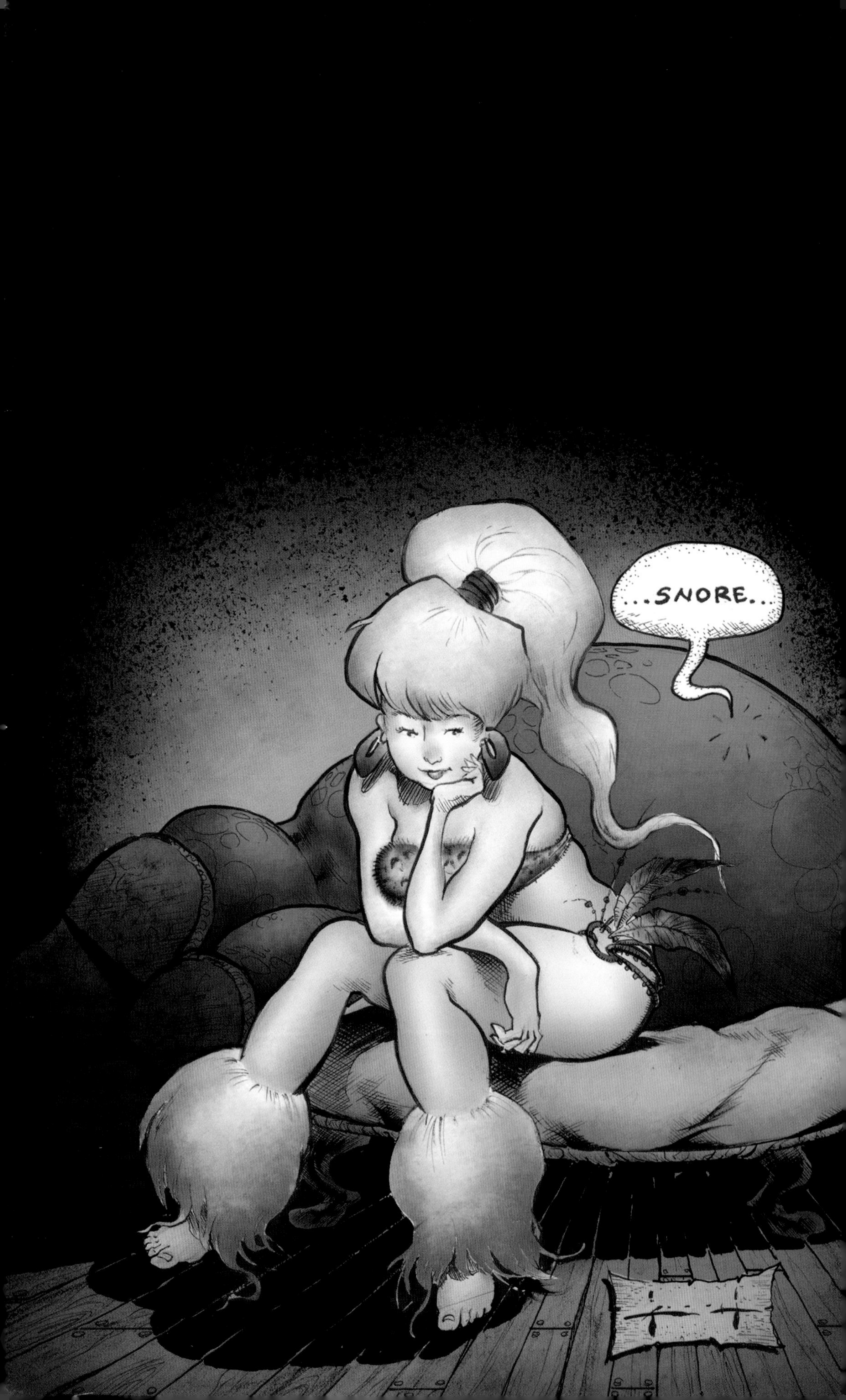
...SNORE...

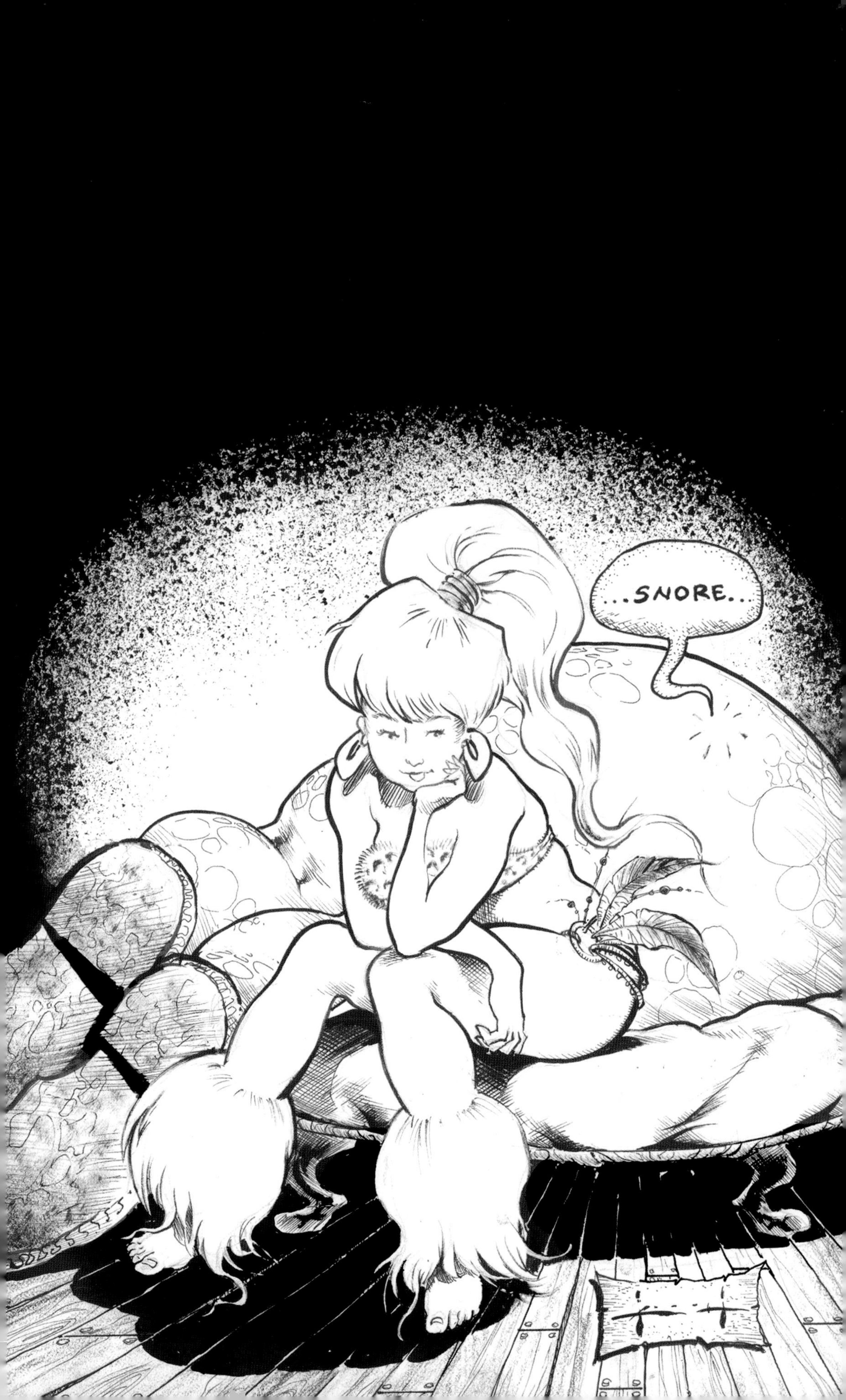
...SNORE...

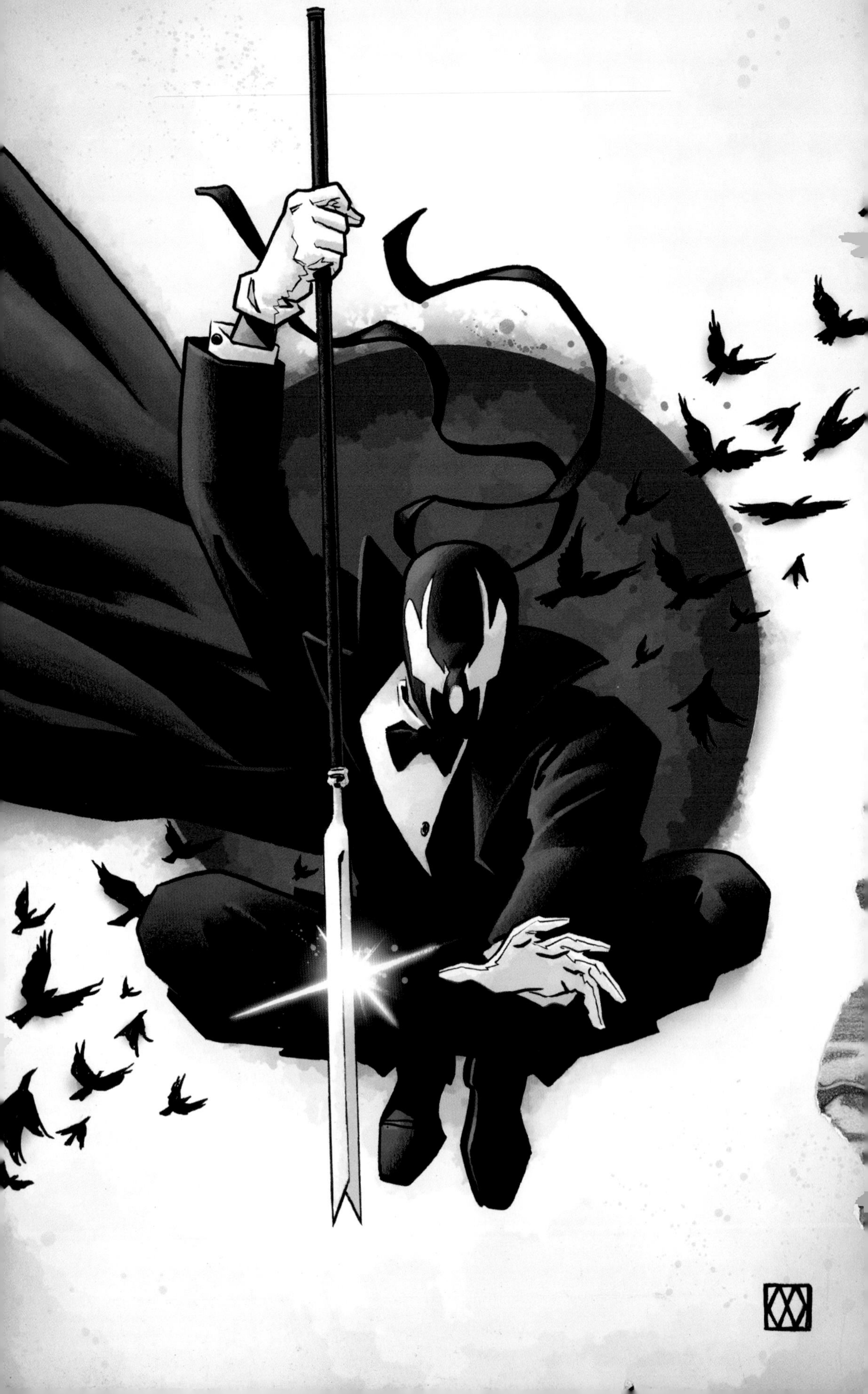

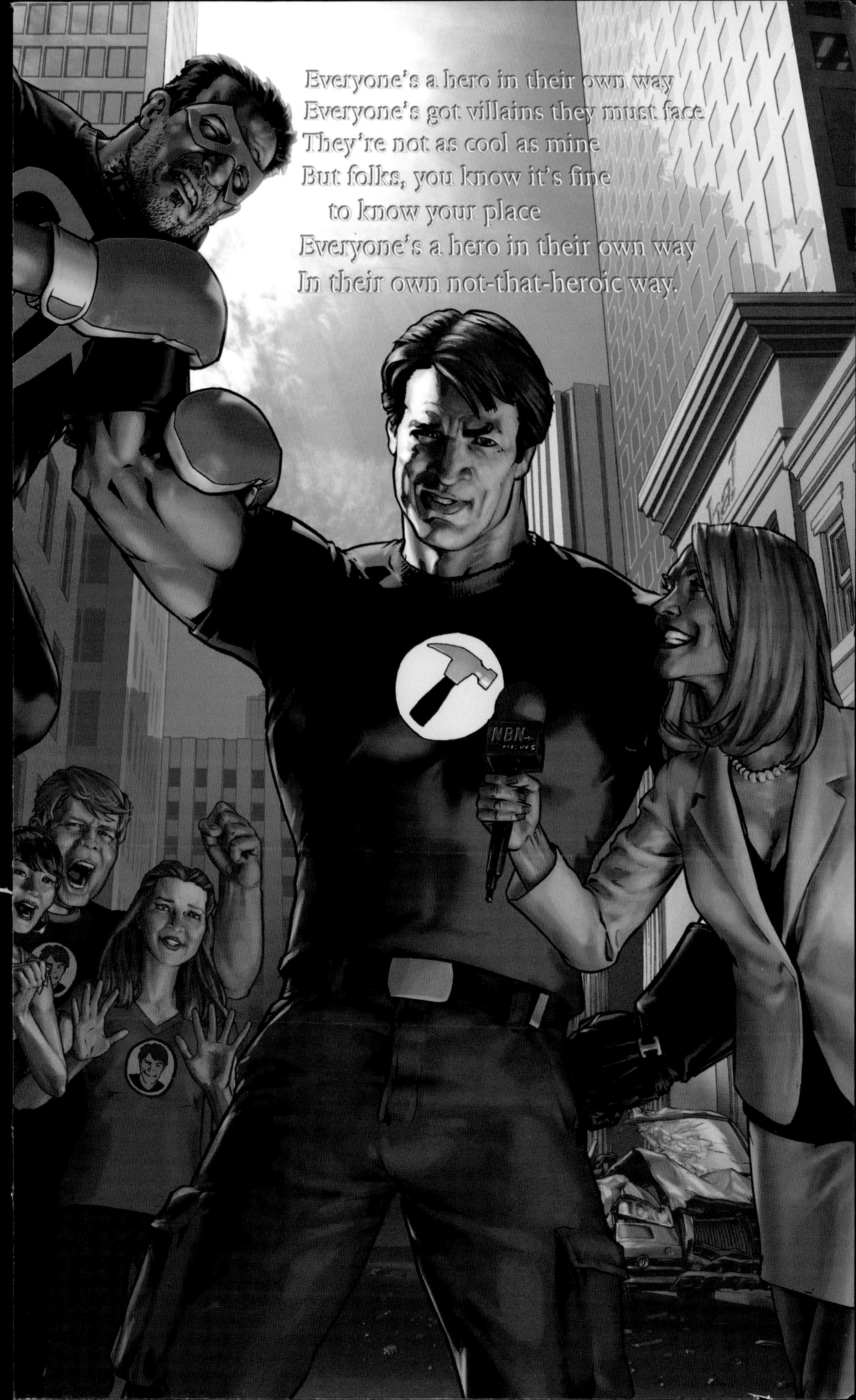
Everyone's a hero in their own way
Everyone's got villains they must face
They're not as cool as mine
But folks, you know it's fine
to know your place
Everyone's a hero in their own way
In their own not-that-heroic way.
NBN

THANKS, MIKE GRELL!

I need to say thanks to Mike Grell.

So hey, Mike—Thanks!

I thank him, largely, for one word: Dignity. Mike wrote a rather eloquent and very personal intro to this book and if you haven't read it yet, well… what's wrong with you? Who reads a book from the back on forward? I really hope you don't do this with murder mysteries.

Anyway, Mike relayed how Hero Initiative helped him when he was flat on his back with illness—a couple of times now—and kept the home fires burning for him. He relayed that he felt the situations were handled quickly, professionally, and with dignity. Quick and professional are easy. Dignity can and should be easy, too. But it's a stickier wicket. It's the one I worry about.

You see, I hear grown-ass men cry all the time. Flat-out cry. Tears, sobbing, that throaty trying-to-catch-your-breath, the whole nine. That's what happens when you help run a charity that helps comic book creators in medical or financial need. The needs can run deep, the circumstances behind them personal. Sometimes it takes a lot for someone to get to the point where they admit they need a way out; need some help.

But oddly, that's rarely when I hear someone cry.

I hear them cry *later*, when I call them back and say, "Hey, we went over your situation and your paperwork and all, and yeah—don't worry. A check's on the way to you. And we're paying off your landlord directly so you don't get evicted, and paying that electric bill to keep the power on, and we'll send you copies of those checks for your own records. Hang loose. In about 48 hours, everything will be up to snuff."

Often times, that's when the dam bursts. That's where I hear the crying. And I used to feel bad. It was awkward, uneasy. I felt like, I dunno, maybe I did something *wrong*, making someone's emotions move to this extreme. But one day, I had a minor revelation.

I realized that people would cry in this moment because for the first time in a long time, someone had heard a "yes," and they were so damnably used to hearing nothing but "no."

"No, I don't have any work for you."

"No, your style doesn't sell to a contemporary audience."

"No, we won't let you fall another month behind on rent. Pay by the 1st, or we start the eviction process and you can talk to the sheriff."

And then, finally, a "yes." And the emotions would pour out. In my earlier days in this job, that moment made me itchy. It was difficult to listen to. But after a little while, I came to recognize it for what it was: It was the dam breaking. It was relief. It was someone finally knowing, after God-only-knows-how-many weeks or months or years of dancing on the edge that everything was finally going to be all right. It was the mind, the body, or some intersection thereof not knowing what to do, so reason gets shut off. It was crying, but the tears were cleansing.

And I worried about dignity. Again, was this somehow something wrong?

Mike said the dignity "is more important than you might think." I agree. And I appreciate the hell out of him, and many others like him, telling us that we score high marks in that category. It completes the circle. Throwing a check at a landlord or buying a prosthetic leg are crucial deeds, yes. But making sure it's all done in a manner that makes people feel good about themselves brings it all on home.

Mike Grell has dignity. And he dignifies this organization with his words. And for that, I just have to say, "Thanks."

—Jim McLauchlin
President, Hero Initiative

(P.S. For the record, Mike didn't cry. He's a tough guy and all!)